Very heartfelt, impressive, sad yet up lifting! A Great story of survival!

-Lela Reed, Tampa Bay Buccaneers NFL mom

Wow! This is an inspiring book. It's straight to the point on how things really were and it's very honest. The book touched me and told me things about my mother that I never knew. My mother had a lot of issues that she covered up with alcohol - something that a lot of people do because they can't express their feelings. It's really, really a good movie...I mean book! I couldn't put it down. The book goes into depth, telling a story that kept unfolding. A story that unfolded as I read it and as I lived it. I experienced several emotions while reading, I got upset, then pissed, then sad, then happy. God is a forgiving God. I'm proud of my mother for having a relationship with Him and making the right choice.

-Salandra, Priscilla's Daughter

Growing up was hell! My mother was drunk all the time, so the streets raised us. The older we got the more distant we became with our mother. She never really got to know any of us, but we loved her any way and we loved her unconditionally. We survived all that hell and managed to come out of it pretty decent human beings. I thank God for remembering the Gibson family.

-Tyrone, Priscilla's son

Life with my mother as an alcoholic was very emotionally draining and tough. You never knew if she was going to have a bad day or a good day. Her day started with alcohol – everyday! Because of that my relationship with my mother was strained and distant. As a child regardless of what card life deals you, you always have to try to respect and acknowledge your parents. I never disrespected my mother during her illness, which caused a lot of pain. As a result of being a child of an alcoholic it caused me to make better choices in my life, especially never to drink. I went the opposite direction. I'm proud of my mother for taking the steps to recover from her addiction. I love her dearly.

-Shonte, Priscilla's Daughter

I have known my Mother-In-Law, Priscilla for almost 6 years and I know that all the words in this book are true. I was not there for all the 27 years, but 6 years of it I was there and the stories were too. Priscilla has come a long way. Even though the book is going to be out for the world to read, seeing it in person is beyond words – she really *was* drunk all day, everyday. When Priscilla started writing the book, I was there to see her write the first page. She didn't even know if it was going to be a book, she was just writing out her thoughts. I remember her asking me if I thought it would be a good book and I told her it would be a *wonderful* book. This is her victory over alcohol and life to her being restored; and God's victory of another one of His children being saved.

-William, Priscilla's Son-In-Law

DRUNK, FOR 27 YEARS

A Story of Victory - Her Choice to Live and Not Die.

Cynthia Banks

authorHOUSE®

AuthorHouse™
1663 Liberty Drive
Bloomington, IN 47403
www.authorhouse.com
Phone: 1-800-839-8640

First published by AuthorHouse 8/31/2009

ISBN: 978-1-4389-9315-7 (e)
ISBN: 978-1-4389-9313-3 (sc)
ISBN: 978-1-4389-9314-0 (hc)

Printed in the United States of America
Bloomington, Indiana

This book is printed on acid-free paper.

This book is a work of non-fiction based on the life of Priscilla Gibson-
Murray. Some names, characters, places, incidents and dialogues have been
changed to protect the identities of the people that were actually involved.

FOREWORD

"*Drunk for 27 years* is a very inspiring book. The writer tells a compelling and true story of a woman who began drinking at a very young age and continued into her adult years. Many factors manipulated the course of Priscilla's life, causing her to feel trapped in a lifestyle that she never chose for herself.

The book also reveals the unconditional love that her children had for their mother, who despite all they had experienced remained just the strength she needed to make it through.

This is the kind of story that anyone will be inspired by, no matter what their struggles may be. It's a must-read. May God bless Priscilla, the writer and the book."

Reverend John Reed

Founder of the Stop AIDS Leadership Project

Fort Worth, Texas

ACKNOWLEDGEMENTS

Melanie Colton is one of the greatest persons I know. She is not only my editor and the glue to my projects, but she is a real true friend. Ilene Maddox, just a reminder that you are my "bestest" friend for life.

Thanks to my staff at The Little Teapot Daycare Center for putting up with me. Thanks to my family for always supporting me; my kids, ShaVonne, Andrea and Cortney Banks, my mother, Sandy Gilbert (Cornell), my two sisters, Lawanda Gates (Stanley) and Sandra Walker (Larry); and my only brother, Michael Patterson, who's been battling Sickle Cell Disease for over 47 years and still has the victory; my nephews, Jared Patterson and Nicholas Gates, my step-daughter Teresa and grand kids, Kimora and Tim, Jr.

Special Thanks:

Photography:Torrence Williams -
www.torrence@torrencewilliamsphotography.com
Graphic Design:Aaron Perry -
www.perrydesigns.net
Make-up:Robbye Dobey -
www.robbyed@mindspring.com
Hair Stylist:J. Christopher Morgan @
J-Style Salon
Creative Input:ShaVonne Banks -
www.thebanksentertainment.com
Web Design:Lynette Green -
www.lgreen58@hotmail.com

Special, Special Thanks to Priscilla for being my "color purple".

Most of all, I thank God! God has brought me through many challenges. He has sustained me through my hard times and given me the victory. The Lord is my shield and my glory and the lifter up of my head - from Him comes my deliverance. Ps.3
Be Blessed,
Cynthia

PROLOGUE

"What is wrong with you?" he cried out with tears streaming down his face. "Why do you think I've been calling you Mommy Dearest ever since I was a little boy? It's because you drink just like that lady in the movie, and you act like her too! Why can't you stop drinking?"

"I don't know how to stop!" I said putting my head down on the table and crying. "I'm scared!"

"You're scared? Mama, you've scared us to death for years, wondering where you were, not knowing if you were dead or alive. What did you think could happen to you living in these streets?" Junior said before crying out with loud sobs.

"I'm going to stop drinking, I promise. I'm going to stop drinking! I don't want to be like my mother," I cried out loudly. I put my head down on the table and began to pray silently, '*God in Heaven, please hear my cry. I am an alcoholic and I have become just like my mother. If you deliver me from this alcoholic disease I promise I won't ever take another drink for the rest of my life. I want to live and not die*'

CHAPTER 1

"Mama! Don't kill her! *Please* don't kill Guinea," Marcus yelled frantically as his mother held his sister Priscilla's head under water in the bathtub. Marcus tugged and tugged at his mother's arms and clothes, but she just would not let his sister up. "I hate you," she yelled. "You make me sick! I wish you were never born!" She gripped my hair tighter and tighter to hold my head down in the water. I struggled to get loose, to get just a morsel of air, but my tiny body could not compete with the strength of my mother's grip. Soon, my body grew weak. I kicked less and less. I felt my life leaving my body.

Guinea is my nickname. It was the name given to me by my mother when I was born. I only weighed 2 ½ pounds at birth and my mother thought I looked like a guinea chicken so she nicknamed me Guinea, but my birth name is Priscilla Duncan.

I am the second oldest of four brothers and two sisters, born in Spalding County, Georgia on April 22, 1957. My parents were 23-year-old Jeremiah Duncan and 18-year-old Charles Etta Mae Thomas Duncan. My parents had married when my mother was 16 – after the birth of my older sister, Margaret.

When I was four, my father moved our family – my mother, my older sister, Margaret, and myself – to St. Louis, Missouri. He told us there were better factory jobs in St. Louis, and we would have a better life there. We moved into a two-story duplex off Clara Avenue.

When I was five years old, I was jumping on the bed and fell out the window of our second floor apartment. Fortunately, I didn't break any bones. My father was angrier than I had ever seen him. He beat my mother worse than I had ever seen him beat her before; I thought he was going to kill her. Because Mother drank a lot, he accused her of being drunk and not keeping an eye on me. My father beat her until she lay on the floor bleeding and unconscious. Later that night he moved out. We rarely saw him again. And ever since that day, my mother has hated me. She blamed me for his leaving.

From as early as I can remember, my father beat my mother. I've seen him punch her in the face, throw her down stairs and kick her on the floor. He would get mad at her, call her names, and tell her she was unfit to be a mother. "You're a sorry excuse for a woman!" he yelled.

Out of all my siblings, I seemed to endure the most of Mother's anger and abusive nature. The beatings started the day my daddy left, but the abuse began long before that. As an infant, mother burned me with an iron on my back, causing third degree burns. By the time I turned nine years old, my body was covered with so many scars that I could rarely wear shorts or short sleeve shirts or anything else that revealed too much of my body. I can't remember how I got most of my scars; I just know Mother did it.

Mother had been drinking all that day and acting strangely. I was getting undressed for my bath when she burst into the bathroom. She had a weird expression on her face and she startled me. The look on her face froze me in my tracks. Before I could say a word, she grabbed my hair and pushed my face into the bathwater. I was kicking and struggling to get loose, but she just kept pushing me down. Mother was so focused on what she was doing to me that she didn't even notice Marcus when he came into the bathroom to bring me a towel. Marcus saw her trying to drown me and started yelling at her and pulling at her clothes.

"Mama! Please, *please*!" Marcus continued to cry out. "I don't want my sister to die." Mother continued to hold me down in the tub of water. Marcus, small for his 5-year-old frame, tried desperately to rustle up enough strength to get me away from Mother. He grabbed my legs as they kicked in the air, trying to pull me from the water. At times, he lost his balance, but he didn't give up trying to save me.

"Guinea! Wake up! Wake up, Guinea," I heard Marcus screaming as he shook my body and slapped my face. "Please wake up!" he begged.

I opened my eyes to see Marcus leaning over me with tears streaming down his face. I coughed profusely until I eventually threw up on the bathroom floor. Mother was gone. "She didn't kill me?" I asked Marcus as he reached for the towel he had dropped on the floor to dry my face and to cover me. He rolled off some toilet paper and started cleaning my vomit off the floor. I leaned against the bathroom wall to catch my breath.

"Why didn't Mother kill me?" I asked Marcus in between coughs.

"I don't know, Guinea. She looked at me with this crazy look on her face and then she let you go. She went back in the living room."

I turned my face in the direction of the bathroom door. The apartment was very quiet. I smelled cigarette smoke. I wondered what Mother was doing. I began to cry. Marcus started to cry, too.

We finally got up off the floor and peeked out the bathroom door to see if we could see Mother. She had fallen asleep on the couch with the butt of her cigarette still between her lips. A bottle of gin lay spilled on the floor next to the couch. It must have fallen out of her hand when she fell asleep.

Marcus and I tiptoed to the bedroom that we all shared together and hid in the closet. I could not stop shaking and crying. Soon, Marcus fell asleep in my arms, but I tried to stay awake. I was too afraid to sleep, I thought Mother was going to come back and finish the job.

The next morning I woke up to Marcus crying. He had peed on himself. "I was scared to go to the bathroom," he said. I rubbed my eyes, surprised that I had fallen asleep, and climbed out of the closet to help clean up my brother.

"I'm sorry, Guinea," Marcus said in a whisper. "It's okay, Marcus, I'll help you." Marcus and I were very close. I always looked out for Marcus and Marcus always looked out for me. We built a bond early in our lives. I was not close with my other brothers; they always seemed to do their own thing. They were close with each other and enjoyed doing things together. My older sister, Margaret, was our mother's favorite – something she reminded me of everyday. She could do no wrong in Mother's eyes and I was always blamed for things she did. Everything was my fault. Marcus was the youngest boy. The other boys didn't want to be bothered with Marcus and Margaret didn't want to be bothered with me. So Marcus and I became close and we took care of each other.

The apartment we lived in was very small. It had two bedrooms, one bathroom, a small living room and a kitchen. Our bedroom was down the hall from the living room, across from Mother's bedroom. I peeked in Mother's room to see if she was in there. She was not. We crept down the hall towards the bathroom with Marcus clinging tightly to me. We did not see Mother anywhere in the apartment. We both took deep breaths and felt better that she was gone. She didn't return until four days later.

As kids, going to school was very tough because money was so scarce. We were teased everyday about wearing the same clothes or having raggedy clothes. I tried my best to wash our clothes or patch them, but all we had was what we had – which wasn't much. Many days we walked in the snowy winters of St. Louis to school with holes in the bottoms of our shoes or without a decent coat. Sometimes the neighbors would give us clothes, but most times my brothers would steal clothes or shoes off the neighborhood clotheslines just to have something to wear. Often times my brothers and I had to steal food from the local store just to eat because Mother preferred to drink than to feed us.

Months went by before I saw my father and when I did, it was only for a few moments. He never brought us anything and he never left us anything – like money.

By the time I was nine, I was pretty good at cleaning the house, shopping and taking care of my brothers and sisters. By this time, my mother had had two more children, bringing the total to seven, and I was taking care of all of them. Mother was hardly ever at home and when she was, she would be passed out on the couch or laid up in her room with some man. If she did leave the house, she would usually leave us about $15 in food stamps – if she remembered. Those times we most likely wouldn't see her for the next three to five days. One day, I overheard her talking to someone about selling our food stamps. I didn't understand why she would sell our food stamps when we barely had food to eat.

I woke up one morning to find that, *as usual,* Mother had left all kinds of beer and liquor bottles all over the house. As I started cleaning up, I picked up one of the liquor bottles and wondered what it tasted like. I took a sip and frowned at the taste. I turned the bottle around and read the label: vodka. I tasted another one: Wild Irish Rose. That didn't taste too bad. I finished off what little was left in the bottle and threw it in the trash. I felt funny so I sat down at the kitchen table. After a few minutes, I got up and looked in the refrigerator. There were a few slices of Spam, a half gallon of milk and a little bit of Wonder bread. I opened the cabinets. There were just a few canned goods and a little bit of corn flakes cereal left in the box. Unsure when Mother would come home, I made do with what we had, but planned to ask the neighbors for some food if she didn't come home soon.

Mother showed up late that night with a group of her friends. I was watching television in the living room with my brothers and younger sister. All Mother's seemingly intoxicated friends came in the apartment with some sort of drink in their hand or carrying brown paper bags full of beer or liquor.

"Get in your room!" Mother ordered.

We all got up and went to our room. We could hear music coming through the walls of the bedroom. Cigarette smoke and marijuana smoke seeped through the walls as well. I wondered how someone as tiny as Mother could drink as much as she did. She was only 4'2" and probably weighed about 110 pounds. She was a beautiful dark-skinned woman with a great figure. I guess that's why men were always attracted to her. I wondered what they were doing in the living room so I peeked my head out the door, and then eased down the hall to the bathroom, trying to see as much as I could see in the living room.

A man was sitting on the couch rolling a marijuana cigarette. He looked at me and smiled. I cracked a faint smile back, just as Mother came around the corner. She punched me in my nose and busted it.

"What is your fast ass doing out of your room and why you smilin' at my man? You flirtin' with my man?"

"No, Mother. I was just going to the bathroom."

"You lyin' and I'm gonna beat your ass." Mother dragged me into her room by my arm and beat me with an extension cord that she unplugged from the television. She ignored the fact that my nose was bleeding and I was getting blood everywhere. With every crack of the extension cord across my body, Mother yelled, "This will teach you not to flirt with my man ever again." I was ten years old.

CHAPTER 2

I sat on the floor packing boxes to move once again. Mother didn't pay the rent so we were being evicted...*again*. This was the fourth time this year and because we didn't have any money, we were moving in with one of her "friends." There was eight of us, including Mother, and we're moving into a two-bedroom apartment with one of her so-called friends who has four kids of her own. We'll be like sardines.

It was always the same thing with us. If we didn't have enough food to eat, it was the lights or gas being cut off; if that wasn't the case then we were being evicted. It was as if we lived in a movie that kept repeating over and over again - different times, but same station.

I didn't like any of my mother's friends; most of them gave me the creeps. I didn't like the way they looked at me or my sisters; and some of them were touchy-feely. Any time we told Mother about something one of her friends did she never believed us. She called us fast whores that liked to flirt and then she'd whip us. Once I realized Mother wasn't going to do anything about her perverted friends, I decided I wasn't going to tell her anything else and I made it a point to stay hidden as often as I could.

Whatever living conditions Mother put us in we learned to make do. We learned to do what we had to do to survive. All of us had gotten begging and stealing down to an art.

"I wonder how long we'll be in this place," I thought as I continued to pack.

Eventually we got moved and I tried to settle into our new living conditions. Mother slept on the couch and we shared a bedroom with her friend's kids. There were 12 of us in one bedroom and it was very challenging and crowded. We had three sets of bunk beds. Two kids slept on each bed, one at the head and the other at the foot. I slept in the closet. I loved the closet; it was a place I could go to for solitude. It was my private place where I could tune out the world and imagine I was somewhere else.

As usual, Mother left me to babysit *all* the kids - something she did *all* the time. My older sister, Margaret, never had to babysit. She could run the streets and do whatever she wanted and Mother never cared. I could never count on her to help with her own brothers and sisters; I knew she was never going to help with the other kids either. And where the heck was their mother? She was never at home to watch her own kids.

On the rare occasion that I got a chance to be a kid, I went outside to watch the neighborhood kids play in the water from the fire hydrant. My brothers and younger sister and the other kids were already out there having a good time running and splashing in the water. I leaned against the apartment building and watched. There were about 20 or so kids running and jumping in and out of the water that poured out of the hydrant. Sounds of laughter and joy filled the air. Everyone looked like they were having such a fun time. I didn't know what that was like because I hadn't learned how to have a fun time yet.

It was such a beautiful, hot day. The puddles of water on the ground looked like sheets of glass. A rainbow gleamed out of the fire hydrant spout as the water shot out. I smiled and I tried to count the beautiful colors I saw in the rainbow.

"What are you smiling at?" I heard a voice say. Startled by the sound of the voice and unaware that someone had walked up to me, I turned to look as the smile quickly left my face. There, standing beside me was a middle-aged, tall, dark-skinned man with a nappy afro. I looked up at him and rolled my eyes, and then I turned my attention back to the kids playing.

"What were you smiling at?" the man asked again.

"Nothing." I answered, turning my head quickly back in the direction of the kids playing.

"Why aren't you out there playing? It looks like fun."

"'Cause I don't want to," I answered softly.

"How old are you?" the man asked.

"11."

"You're 11 years old? You don't look like you're 11." I didn't make a comment.

"Did you hear that noise?" the man asked, looking behind him.

"What noise?" I asked, looking around and straining my ears to hear something.

"It sounds like it's coming from that old wooden shed over there behind the apartment building." The man pointed to a shed a few feet from where we were standing. "I bet a dog or cat got stuck inside," he said. "Let's go see. We can rescue it if it's stuck in there." I didn't know for sure if I heard anything, but I didn't want the animal to be stuck in the shed either.

"You hear it?" the man asked. "There it is again. Come on." I hesitated for a moment, and then I followed the man to the shed. The man opened the shed door and stepped inside, holding the door open for me to follow. He walked further inside and looked behind a dusty old shelf near the back of the shed.

"I don't hear anything...do you see it?" I asked curiously, as I stood at the door entrance. The shed had a musty smell and was very dusty. There were three windows, one on each wall, that let a moderate amount of light inside. Old tires, tools, and furniture covered with sheets were scattered throughout the shed. I coughed from the dust as I walked towards some boxes to see if the animal was behind them.

Suddenly, I heard the shed door close. Startled, I turned in the direction of the door. The man was standing in front of the door looking at me and unzipping his pants. My stomach suddenly knotted up and my heart started racing. I was terrified. The man lunged towards me, grabbing my arm. I screamed and tried to get loose from his grip, but he twisted my arm and threw me to the floor. He dropped his body on top of mine and covered my mouth with one hand as he pulled my pants off with the other. I struggled and struggled to free myself, but the man was just too heavy. Tears rolled down my face as the pain of the man forcing himself inside my body hurt so badly. With every thrust, I felt my breath leave my body until I was completely numb. When the man finished, he lifted himself off me and pulled his pants up. Without even looking at me or saying a word, he walked out the shed. I lay on the floor, in excruciating pain, too scared to move and sobbing hysterically. Blood was all around me on the floor. Everything had happened so fast.

I don't know if it was hours or minutes that I lay on that floor before I finally got up to go home. I reached for an old sheet that covered some furniture. I ripped it and used it to clean myself up. My legs felt like they had no circulation in them and I wasn't sure if I had enough strength to walk. Grabbing my pants that the man had thrown in a nearby corner, I slowly put them back on. Still crying, I made my way to the shed door, grabbing hold of anything for support as I walked. I peeked out the door to see if anyone was there. The neighborhood kids were still playing in the hydrant water. I looked around for the man. I didn't see him anywhere. I walked home as quickly as my sore and bruised legs would move, crying the entire way.

When I got home, I found Mother asleep on the floor in the living room. A half-empty glass of wine was nearby on the coffee table. Fortunately, my brothers and sister and all the other kids were still outside. Other than the sounds coming from the television, the apartment was quiet. Still in shock about what just happened, I went to the bathroom and ran some bath water. I stared in the mirror at myself as I undressed to get into the bath tub. My face was sore where the man had clamped his hand tightly around my mouth to silence my screams. I balled my clothes up and threw them in the bathroom trash can. As limited as my clothes supply was, I just didn't want them anymore. I climbed into the tub and sat crying silent tears as the warm water soothed my pain. After a long moment of deep thoughts and blank stares, I reached for my bath cloth and the Dial soap and tried to scrub the scent of the man off me.

When I finished my bath, I put on my pajamas and sat in the closet in my room. I couldn't stop crying or thinking about what happened. I was glad all the kids were still outside and Mother was still asleep. I really needed some quiet and alone time. As the ordeal kept flashing over and over in my mind, I promised myself that I wouldn't tell anybody about what happened to me. Who would believe me anyway? I cried until I fell asleep.

CHAPTER 3

Two years passed and the secret I kept hidden inside still burdened me. I tried not to think about it, but the memories continued to haunt me. I often stole liquor from Mother hoping it would help me to forget. I would mix any liquor with Kool-Aid or juice or whatever else I could find so she wouldn't find out. I just wanted to forget.

Later that year, we moved to a house near Hodiamont Tracks on the other side of St. Louis. Margaret had moved out a few months earlier with her boyfriend. Two of my brothers were in juvenile detention centers and I was at home as usual babysitting the rest of my siblings. After awhile, I started sneaking boys into the house. Mother was never there anyway, so I didn't worry much about getting caught. There were times, however, that I did get caught. Mother would beat me, but I kept doing it. She'd call me a slut or a whore and told me I was never going to amount to anything, but I didn't care. I had heard all that before and had become immune to her insults. And besides, she was wrong. The boys *loved* me. They seemed to be the only people that did, besides my brother Marcus. I loved the attention they gave me and I did anything to keep it.

Walking home from school one day, I ran into a boy name Randolph Jackson. Pooky was what he later told me he liked to be called. He was about 5'10" with dark chocolate black skin and pretty, curly jet-black hair. He was so fine. He was really popular at Soldan High School, too. I had seen him around our school but I never tried to talk to him. Every time I saw him, he was always with some girl. Besides, I was a freshman and he was two years older than me and a junior. I didn't think he knew me or noticed me, but he did.

"Ain't your name Priscilla?" he asked as he ran to catch up with me. I had just crossed over the railroad tracks and was nearing the turn to my street.

I stopped walking and turned around. Surprised at who it was, I asked "How did you know my name?"

"I know all the ladies' names, especially the fine ones." Randolph responded.

I looked down at myself. I was wearing some old hand-me-down clothes and dirty tennis shoes. My hair was nappy, although I did try to style it. I knew he had to be kidding if he was referring to me as fine, although I did have a nice figure.

"Whatever," I said trying not to blush.

"I'm Randolph, but I go by the nickname Pooky."

"I know", I said sarcastically.

"You do?"

"I've seen you around school" I continued.

"Really?" he said smiling. "Do you live around here?"

"Near Hodiamont Tracks, where do you live?" I asked.

"I live near Hodiamont Tracks, too, on Hodiamont Avenue.

"Really? I live on Wells Avenue."

"That's around the corner from my house," Pooky said with excitement. "Can I walk you home?"

I looked at him, surprised that he made that suggestion. "Okay."

On the way home, we talked about school and people in the neighborhood. We were both surprised that we had never seen each other walking home before since we lived so close to each other. Pooky asked why I didn't have any friends since he had always seen me by myself; after confessing that he had noticed me at school.

"I just never took the time to make any, I got too much stuff going on at home" I answered.

I really liked walking and talking with Pooky on that beautiful sunny afternoon. The sky was clear and the wind blew lightly; just enough to sway the trees and provide the perfect atmosphere. I found out that he liked sports, especially basketball and he wanted to go into the military after he graduated high school. Pooky was very confident about what his future plans were. I couldn't think of anything I wanted to do after high school. I wasn't even sure if I was going to graduate.

We finally arrived at my house. I felt sad, because I was enjoying my time with Pooky and I didn't want it to end.

"So, what are you going to do when you get in the house?" Pooky asked.

"I don't know. I guess see what my brothers and sisters are doing and watch TV."

"Do you have a phone? Can I call you?" Pooky asked.

"No, we don't have a phone," I murmured, feeling a little embarrassed.

"Oh, well. I'll come over in the morning to walk you to school." I smiled as I nodded my head in agreement. We said good-by to each other and Pooky headed off down the street. I walked in the house feeling very giddy.

That evening I took extra time to try to find something really nice to wear to school the next day. I washed my hair and tried to press it as best I could. I wanted to look nice when Pooky got here in the morning. I did my best to conceal my enthusiasm about Pooky from the rest of the family, but every time I thought about him I couldn't help but smile. I couldn't even sleep that night. The anticipation I was experiencing and all the butterflies fluttering around in my stomach kept me awake.

The next morning, just as he said, Pooky came to my house to walk me to school. I felt so special. I had gotten up extra early to get myself together. I put on a pair of blue bell bottom jeans that one of mothers' acquaintances had given me with a printed disco shirt. I had washed my old Safeway Grocery Store snickers with Purex bleach and let them dry in the window and they look a lot better. I parted my hair on the side and clamped it slightly with two white barrettes. I was excited and ready when Pooky got to the house. Today's walk to school was the best walk to school I had ever had.

After school, Pooky waited for me at my locker to walk me home. That did it! When I came around the corner from my English class and saw him standing at my locker. I knew I was special to him and he was definitely special to me. During our walk home Pooky asked if I wanted to come to his house to hang out for a while. I told him yes. So we walked to his house. He even held my hand.

Pooky was an only child and he lived alone with his mother,

Grace, who was not at home when we got there. He hadn't mentioned his father in any of our conversations, so I assumed his parents were divorced or his father had died. Pooky had a really nice house. The furniture was covered with plastic and it looked new. Every bit of furniture and décor was neatly spread throughout the house. There were pictures of Pooky at different stages of his life everywhere. I thought the house was beautiful, like a palace.

"My bedroom is in the basement," Pooky said. "Follow me."

I followed him through the kitchen and down the stairs. In his room, he had his own television on a stand and a couch. His bed was against the wall facing the couch and black and gold beads were hanging from the doorway. It was nice and cozy. "This is my room," he said proudly stretching out his arms.

"Do you want something to drink? Some water or some Kool-Aid?" he asked.

"Sure, I'll take some Kool-Aid."

Pooky ran upstairs to the kitchen. I stood in his room waiting for him to return and looking around at his stuff. He had posters of Julius Erving and Kareem Abdul-Jabbar everywhere. Pooky came back down the stairs in a short time with two glasses of grape Kool-Aid. "Sit down," he said pointing to the couch, "lets watch TV." I sat down on the couch as he walked over to the television and turned it on. *Lost in Space* was on, so we sat together watching the show. When the show went off, Pooky leaned over and kissed me on the lips. He startled me, but I kissed him back. We kept kissing and eventually moved over to his bed. We had sex.

From that day forward, I couldn't stay away from Pooky's house. Every day, after school and on weekends I was at his house. We had sex all the time. Sometimes we would skip school and stay home all day having sex while his mother was at work. I was in love.

I eventually met his mother; she was very nice to me. I suspected she knew what we were doing, but she never said anything about it. My mother, on the other hand, slapped me and cussed me out for being away from home so much and not being around to babysit. But, I was in love. I didn't care what she said or what she did to me, she wasn't going to stop me from seeing Pooky. I wanted to be with Pooky all the time. Pooky loved me.

Two months into our relationship, I showed up at Pooky's house unannounced on a Saturday afternoon. He was sitting in his living room on the couch talking with his friend, Mike. Ms. Grace wasn't at home. She was rarely ever had home. If she wasn't working, she was taking care of her ailing mother at her mother's house. I had come over to Pooky's house because I was mad at Mother. She had just hit my brother Lester on the hand with a baton and broke his thumb. Lester had reached for another piece of chicken after Mother had told him he couldn't have another piece so she picked up one of my sisters baton that was near the kitchen table and hit him on the hand as hard as she could. Lester screamed to high Heaven in pain and Mother acted like it didn't even faze her. Showing no remorse, she told him if his hand was broken she wasn't taking him to the hospital, because it was his fault that he didn't listen.

"Next time you'll leave stuff alone when I tell you to!" she yelled. Lester doubled over in pain. I got so mad at her. After we argued about what she did, I left. I couldn't take anymore of her stuff. I needed to see Pooky. Pooky always took my mind off my dysfunctional life.

Pooky let me in the house and introduced me to his friend Mike who was slouching in the arm chair in the living room. I didn't know Mike, although Pooky said he went to our school. I attempted to tell Pooky about what Mother had done, but he didn't appear to be interested. He disregarded what I was telling him and continued on with his conversation with Mike about last week's basketball game. I sat in the chair next to the couch and daydreamed as the two of them continued to talk as though I wasn't there. I wanted Pooky to tell his friend to leave so we could be alone, but he didn't. I even tried to make eye contact with him, but he wouldn't even look at me. As a matter of fact, he was acting really strange toward me, like he was annoyed with me. Whenever I tried to join in the conversation, he seemed to get irritated with me. He'd cut me off and give me dirty looks. I stopped trying to be included.

Pooky got up and went in the dining room. He opened the china cabinet and pulled out an unopened bottle of Manischewitz wine. He came back to the living room and sat the wine on the coffee table. "Let's have a drink," he suggested as he headed for the kitchen to get some glasses. Pooky poured three glasses of wine. We each took a glass to drink. "Let's go to the basement," Pooky suggested. "I don't want my Mama to walk in and see us drinking her wine." He picked up the bottle of wine and headed downstairs to his bedroom. Mike and I followed. Pooky sat the bottle of wine on his dresser and lit some incense. Then he walked over to his record player and put on a Marvin Gaye record. "Come on girl, let's dance," Pooky said as Marvin Gaye sang *"What's going on."*

Pulling me up off the couch by my arm, Pooky put his arms around me still holding his glass of wine started slow-grinding me. I joined in willingly, feeling special that he would show off in front of his friend. Mike sat on the couch drinking his glass of wine and watching us dance.

"Dance with Mike?" Pooky asked as he pushed himself away from me.

"Dance with Mike?" I frowned and said, "I don't want to dance with Mike!" laughing a little and not taking the situation serious.

"What?" Pooky said. He slapped me and I fell on the bed. "I told you to dance with Mike, so you better dance with him! " Realizing he was serious and feeling scared, I started to cry.

"Now get up and dance with Mike!"

Pooky pulled me up by my arm, twisting it around and handing me over to Mike like I was a Raggedy Ann doll. Mike stood up and came towards me, licking his lips like a hungry predator. He started trying to slow-grind dance with me. The closer he came to me, the more I kept backing up; and I couldn't stop crying which seemed to be irritating Pooky. I can't believe Pooky just slapped me and was making me dance with his disgusting friend.

"What's wrong with Pooky, and why is he acting like this?" I wondered.

Suddenly, I felt intense pain across my back. I fell to my knees. I looked up. Pooky had a clear plastic coat hanger in his hand. He started beating me with the coat hanger across my back, arms, face and legs. I screamed and begged him to stop hitting me. I felt like a child being scolded and punished by a parent.

"I told you to dance with Mike!" He yelled. "When I tell you to do something you better do it!"

Pooky kept on hitting me with the hanger. I begged him to stop as I tried to block the blows that hurt my hands very badly.

"Get up and get on the bed!" he shouted. "You gonna have sex with him now, since you wouldn't dance with him! Come on over here Mike and get you some of this!" Pooky pulled my pants off as I kicked and screamed. He raised the coat hanger over me and told me to stop screaming or he would hit me again. I stopped screaming. Mike eagerly walked over to me with his pants already off. He climbed on top of me. I lay still on the bed in silence with tears streaming down my face as he did his business. When Mike was finished, Pooky had a turn. After Pooky finished, Mike had a second turn. I lay on the bed quiet and motionless on my back. Tears rolled down my face and welled up in my ears. When I saw them both start to put their pants back on, I got up off the bed. I continued to cry with disbelief at what just happened. How could Pooky do this to me? He loves me. I put my pants on as I wiped tears from my eyes. Without saying a word, I walked up the stairs to go home.

"Thanks for coming over." I heard Pooky say as I reached the top of the stairs. Mike started laughing. I let myself out the front door and headed home. I walked home oblivious to my surroundings, completely engrossed in thoughts of what just happened and crying the entire way home.

It was a little after dark when I arrived home. The door was open so I walked right in. Mother looked up from the couch as I came through the front door. "Where your fast ass been?" she asked as she clutched a cigarette between her lips. I didn't answer. I went straight to my room and sat in the closet, crying.

CHAPTER 4

Getting out of bed seemed to be a challenge lately. I was so tired. I didn't know what was wrong with me. Maybe I had the flu or food poisoning because I couldn't keep any food down. Every morning I woke up I had to run to the bathroom to throw up. I couldn't even go to school; not that it mattered, I was failing in all my classes anyway. Two months had passed and I was still feeling sick. I had been so sick that I missed two of my menstrual cycles. The more I thought about how I was feeling the more I got scared. I must be dying, I thought. Maybe I have Tuberculosis, or Stomach Ulcers or Cancer. I wished I could talk to Mother about how I was feeling, but I couldn't. I couldn't even talk to her about my period when I first started having one when I was twelve. She refused to discuss anything related to my body or my menstrual cycle. "Ask somebody else, or figure it out for yourself!" I remembered her saying to me.

She did however buy me a box of Kotex and stressed to me with her fist in my face that I better not bring a baby up in her house. I ignored her comment, because I didn't know what she was referring to anyway.

I decided to go next door to talk to my neighbor Monica. Monica was always nice to us. She was in her late twenties and had three daughters of her own. She would come by and check on us occasionally to see how we were doing or if we needed something. She knew Mother left us alone at home a lot. I really liked her.

Monica worked during the day, so I waited until after 7:00 that night to go next door. I knocked on the door. Her eldest daughter, Faye answered. Monica's kids were around the same age has my younger siblings so they played together a lot. Faye yelled for her mother to come to the door. Monica came walking from the kitchen, wiping her hands on a kitchen towel as she approached the screen door.

"Hi Priscilla, is something wrong?"

I dropped my head and said in a somber voice, "Ms. Monica, I need to talk to you about something."

"Sure, baby, come on in."

Monica unlocked the screen door and let me in. I sat down on the couch. The smell of chicken cooking flowed through the air like air freshener. I looked around her living room, noticing how neat and clean it was, aside from a few toys on the floor. The furniture looked old, but everything was in its place. The assortment of photos throughout the room helped to comfort my mind. Monica threw the towel over her shoulder and sat down on the couch next to me.

"What's the matter?" She asked sounding very sincere.

I started to cry. "Ms. Monica, do you think a person could die if they've been sick with the flu for a long time?"

"They could, if it turned into pneumonia or if they didn't go see a doctor. Is that what's wrong with you, you're sick and you think you're going to die?" she asked curiously putting her hand on my shoulder.

"Yes. I've been sick to my stomach for a while now and I don't know what's wrong with me." Everything I eat makes me sick to my stomach. I keep throwing up.

Monica sat up in her seat. "Did you tell your mother that you were sick?"

"No, she wouldn't care anyway."

Monica took a deep breath. "Have you had your period?" I shook my head no.

"Have you been doing it with somebody?"

"Huh?" I said pretending like I didn't understand the question.

"Have you been having sex with somebody, Priscilla?" Monica asked again this time rephrasing the question. Feeling a little ashamed about answering, I nodded my head yes.

"Baby, it might not be the flu at all, you could be pregnant."

"Pregnant?" I really started crying. "I didn't think about that, I thought I was dying. I never thought I could be pregnant."

I began to panic and to cry harder. Monica used her kitchen

towel to wipe my tears. She gave me a comforting hug.

"Mama is going to kill me if I'm pregnant," I said with my face pressed into her shoulder. She already threaten me to not bring a baby up in her house. I never thought I could be pregnant!

"Well sweetheart, you're going to have to tell her if you are – she's going to find out anyway," Monica said. I leaned back on her couch and let out a long sigh.

"Go home and tell your mother. You're 14 years old; she'll need to take you to see a doctor."

"Okay, Ms. Monica, I'll go home and tell her, but I already know she's gonna be mad." I stood up and Monica walked me to the door. She opened the door to let me out.

"Come talk to me anytime and let me know what the doctor says," Monica said as I headed back to my house. I walked across the dirt patched yard to my house thinking how lucky her kids were to have such a nice and understanding mother. My mother was evil. I knew she was going to kill me, she already tried once. Monica stood in the doorway watching me until I made it inside my house. "Thank you, Ms. Monica," I yelled as I walked inside.

That night I decided not to tell Mother. I was scared and to upset over the possibility of being pregnant that I decided to wait until morning to tell her. Hopefully she will have slept off her high and maybe by then I'll have some courage. I didn't really believe that, but that's what I told myself.

The following morning I woke up kind of late. I climbed out of bed and made an attempt to walk into the living room where I heard the television playing. Mother was sitting on the couch watching Good Times and smoking a cigarette. I couldn't do it. I diverted to the kitchen without saying a word. I fiddled around in there acting like I was doing something, but really trying to get the nerve to tell mother about my predicament. Mother hadn't acknowledged me at all and I had been in the kitchen for over fifteen minutes. She continued to watch TV and smoke her cigarette. It was a school day and everyone else had gone off to school. Mother didn't even ask why I was at home and not at school. After several failed attempts to start the conversation, I finally I walked cautiously over to the couch where Mother was. "Mama, I need to tell you something." I said softly. Mother looked up at me with no expression on her face. She put her cigarette out in the ash tray.

"Did your trifling ass miss your period?"

"Yes," I said sadly.

"You pregnant ain't you!" she shouted.

Before I could say another word, Mother jumped up off the couch and slapped me across my face. I started crying and ran back to my room.

"I knew it had to be something wrong with you the way you been sleeping and laying around this damn house all the damn time!" she yelled down the hall.

I buried my face in my pillow and cried; regretting telling her and ever having her as a mother.

I stayed sleep in my room for what seem like hours until I heard a loud beating on the door.

"Get your stupid ass up so I can take you to the damn doctor." Mother shouted through the bedroom door.

I got up and got dressed and nervously waited for Mother in the living room until it was time to go.

Mother and I rode the bus to Comprehensive Clinic, a free clinic on Martin Luther King Drive. She fussed at me the entire bus ride. When we got to the doctor's office, she fussed at me there too. While we waited for my name to be called Mother created such uproar in the waiting room. She was loud and embarrassing.

Finally the nurse called me back to the exam room. After I peed in a cup and the exam was complete, the doctor confirmed that I was indeed pregnant, almost 12 weeks; Mother let everybody in the clinic know how she felt about it. She yelled that she was pissed off at me for being stupid and getting pregnant, and how she knew I was a slut. She didn't care who was listening. Mother was angrier than I had ever seen her before. She called me an ignorant dumb whore right in front of the doctor. He just walked out of the room without saying a word.

"Who's the daddy?" Mother asked hatefully as I was getting dressed.

"A boy named Pooky...I mean Randolph Jackson," I said through my sniffles and tears.

I was overloaded with emotions. I didn't want to be pregnant. I wasn't even talking to Pooky anymore.

"I hope you know you ain't having this baby!" Mother shouted.

"I told you, you ain't bringin' no damn baby up in *my* house! You gettin' an abortion!"

I looked at her and didn't say a word. I didn't want to be pregnant, but I also knew I wasn't going to kill my baby, either. Mother walked out of the clinic and slammed the door, yelling "bring your ignorant, foolish ass on here!"

I had to listen to her complain and call me every name in the book during the entire 45-minute bus ride back home. The ride back from the clinic was worse than the ride to the clinic. I tried to tune Mother out, but I couldn't. I wished her mouth would get dry and her tongue would stick to the roof of her mouth so she would shut up.

As soon as we got home, Mother made me go to my room. She had me take off my clothes, down to my underwear. When she entered my room she was holding a thick leather belt with holes in it. She walked up to me and slapped me so hard that I thought I got whiplash. After that, she beat me until she got tired.

By the end of the week, my body felt well enough to go out of the house. Mother had put so many welts and bruises on my face and body that I didn't want to go outside until they were almost healed. I hoped she didn't hurt my baby. I had decided that I was going to go over to Pooky's house to tell him I was pregnant. Even though Pooky did what he did, I still loved him and I still wanted to be with him although it had been a while since I had seen him or talked to him.

I put on a floral print sun dress and sandals, parted my hair in the center and braided it in two corn rolls and walked to Pooky's house.

Pooky wasn't home when I got there, but his mother, Grace was. Feeling that she would take the news far different then Mother did, I told her I was pregnant. She started to cry. Then she hugged me which totally surprised me. We sat and talked in the living room. I told her about my mother's reaction to the news.

"Can I ask you a question, Priscilla?"

"Yeh" I said nodding my head.

"Do you feel ready?"

"Ready like how? Like to be a mother?

"Yes," Grace answered.

"Well, ready or not, it's happening 'cause I'm not gonna kill my baby. It ain't like I planned it or something."

"You didn't use protection?" Ms. Grace asked. I blushed and felt embarrassed by the question. "I'm sorry to be so personal, but are you sure my son is the father?"

"Yes, I'm sure," I answered adamantly. "We didn't use protection because he said he didn't like how it felt. I *know* he's the daddy, Ms. Grace."

Ms. Grace shook her head and rubbed her eyes and forehead.

Just then, we heard the door rattling and keys jingling. I felt a hint of nervousness come over me. Pooky walked in the house. He looked at me and rolled his eyes.

"What you doing here?" he asked.

"Priscilla's pregnant," Ms. Grace blurted out.

"So why she here? I ain't the daddy," Pooky said with disrespect.

"Yes you are! I'm three months pregnant and you *are* the daddy," I screamed at him. Pooky looked at me with contempt and turned around and walked back out the door, slamming it.

"Yes it is *his* baby," I said as I started to cry.

"It'll be alright, I'll talk to him about this later," Ms. Grace said. "I know my son is not the type to turn his back on his child, like his own father did. I've raised him to take care of his responsibilities. I'll talk to him tonight," she assured me. Ms. Grace gave me another big hug.

"Thank you," I said, as I wiped my tears off my cheeks. I stood up and walked towards the door to leave. With tears in her eyes, Ms. Grace hugged me one more time just before she let me out the door. I walked home convinced that the baby would change things between me and Pooky and soon we would become a family. I still loved him and carrying his child made me love him even more.

When I got home, Mother was gone. I was glad. My two younger brothers were in the living room playing with cars and my sister Keisha was drawing at the kitchen table. I was glad they weren't getting into anything. Keisha never got into trouble, but my brothers, they were always in trouble. Stealing, fighting, cussing, you name it. If the school wasn't complaining, then the neighbors were. Mother was hardly ever around to handle a lot of the messes they got into, so I had to do it.

Mother stayed away from home for nearly a week. Luckily, we had food in the house that lasted. I never went back to school. I stayed home and tried to keep the house clean; and I cooked our meals. I wanted to do all I could to try to make Mother happy. Now that I was having my own baby, I tried to get in the mindset of a mother, so I secretly pretended I was taking care of my *own* family, not my sister and brothers.

A month passed and I hadn't heard anything from Pooky or his mother. I wondered why. Mother was being nice to me. She even bought me some prenatal vitamins. I wondered when she was going to take me back to the doctor since I was over four months pregnant. I thought a pregnant person was supposed to go to the doctor all the time, but Mother hadn't taken me back. I didn't even know when my baby was going to be born and my stomach was getting big.

I took my prenatal vitamins every day as Mother instructed; she made sure of that. Every morning and sometimes in the evenings, she reminded me to take them even though they made me sick to my stomach. Whenever I took them, my stomach would hurt so badly and within a short time, I'd have to throw up.

"It'll pass," Mother kept saying, "you'll get used to them."

But I never did. After a week, I stopped taking them, but I didn't tell Mother. I lied and told her I was still taking them.

It was uplifting to know that Mother finally accepted the baby and was helping me with my pregnancy. She had never been nice to me before, so this was a welcomed change that I liked. I did wonder why it was so important to her if I took my vitamins or not because she bugged me about them all the time. Her constant questioning me about the vitamins began to annoy me and to make me feel uncomfortable.

Late one night I couldn't sleep so I got up to get something to drink from the kitchen. Mother was outside on the steps with one of her friends, drinking and talking. I heard her say, "I don't want no damn baby in my house. I've been trying to make her have a miscarriage for two weeks now. I gave her dumb ass some Humphrey 11 pills that make you have an abortion, but she still hasn't miscarried. Priscilla's so damn stupid; she thinks they're prenatal vitamins."

My mouth flew open. "She's trying to kill my baby!" I whispered to myself. I started crying, then ran and got back in the bed. *I thought Mother cared about me and my baby and that's why she brought me the vitamins and was being so nice to me. Why is she so evil?* I mumbled to myself, *I'm glad I stopped taking those pills. I hate her! I hate her!*

It took me a while to fall asleep, but eventually I did. I was mad at myself for ever believing Mother could be nice to me. From that day forward, I vowed never to trust Mother again.

In the weeks to pass, I hardly said anything to Mother. I avoided her as much as possible. I was happy when she didn't come home for days and I wished she'd stay away longer. I was very angry at her. Whenever she offered me something to eat or drink, I turned it down. I didn't trust her to touch anything I had to eat or drink ever again. Some nights I went to bed hungry because I didn't want to eat anything she cooked.

"Have you been taking those vitamins?" she asked one morning I was sitting at the kitchen table eating a bowl of breakfast cereal. I didn't answer.

"Did you hear me?" she yelled.

"Yes!" I shouted back. I continued to eat my cereal.

"You lyin'! Let me see the bottle!" she demanded.

"I said I was taking them!" I shouted back.

Mother grabbed a wooden bat that we kept in the corner in case of an intruder. "If you don't get that bottle of vitamins, I am gonna beat you with this bat," she shouted as she raised the bat and pointed it at me. Knowing Mother was crazy enough to hit me with the bat, pregnant or not, I got up out of my seat and went to my room to retrieve the bottle. Mother met me half way back to the kitchen and snatched the bottle out of my hand. She opened it.

"I knew you were lyin'. You haven't taken hardly any of these pills!" She swung the bat and hit me on my thigh. I fell against the kitchen wall. She hit me again across my back as I tried to get my balance. I screamed out in pain.

"Mama please stop! Don't hit me no more!" I screamed. My

brother Marcus came running out the bedroom.

"Guinea!" He screamed.

The distraction by Marcus gave me an opportunity to run towards the front door. I opened the door and ran out, barely missing a swing at my head. All I had on was my night gown. I had no shoes, socks or jacket on and it was the dead of winter. The first thought in my mind was to run to Pooky's house. So I did.

With adrenalin racing through my body, it didn't take me long to run in the snow to Pooky's house. I was freezing and my feet were numb when I arrived at the house. I banged hard on Pooky's front door. Ms. Grace opened the door. "Oh, dear God," she said when she saw me standing there trembling and crying and holding my big stomach in pajamas with no socks or shoes on and without a jacket.

"Come in!" She said, grabbing my arm. Once in the house, she hugged me tight. I broke down crying in her arms. Ms. Grace hugged me so tight that the warmth of her body soothed my chills.

"Mama hates me! She tried to kill my baby! She tried to beat me with a baseball bat! Why does she hate me! Why!" I cried on Ms. Grace's shoulder. Ms. Grace cried with me.

"I don't know baby, I don't know" Ms. Grace said with compassion.

After our embrace, Ms. Grace took me in her room and gave me one of her night gowns to change into. She also gave me some socks and slippers to put on my frozen feet. Then we went in the kitchen and sat at the table to drink a cup of hot cocoa. I wondered where Pooky was, but I didn't ask. I told Ms. Grace what all transpired at home and how disappointed I was that I couldn't trust my own mother.

"Are *you* hurt? Do you need to go to the hospital?" she asked.

"No, I don't think so." I answered, but I really wasn't sure what I should do, Mother did hit me in my back with the bat and it was a little sore.

"Have you seen a doctor about the baby?"

"No. Mother hasn't taken me to the doctor since my first visit over two month ago," I answered. "I don't even know when my baby is going to be born." Ms. Grace reached out and squeezed my hand and said, "You can stay here with us until the baby is born."

I was glad to hear that because I didn't want to go back home and I had nowhere else to go. I agreed to stay.

I followed Ms. Grace to the guest room at the end of the hallway across from her bedroom. She made it clear that I would not be staying in Pooky's room. She also finally told me where he was. He had spent the night over one of his friend's house after a school game. The guest room was decorated in a very pretty pink and blue floral print. The curtains and the bedspread all matched. I had the entire queen-size bed all to myself. I loved the thought of that. I had never slept in the bed by myself before. When I finally went to sleep, I slept sound and good.

I must have been really tired, because I didn't wake up until just before noon. I walked into the kitchen. Pooky was sitting at the table talking with his mother. I could tell by the look on his face that he hated the idea of me living in his house. I had hoped that because I was having his child he would feel differently about me, and his attitude would change. I was determined to remain hopeful. The smell of fresh brewed coffee scented the air.

"Good morning" I said as I sat down to join Pooky and his mother at the table. "Hello," he grumbled as he got up and walked over to the kitchen cabinet. He opened the cabinet and pulled out a box of Coco Puffs cereal. Then he opened the refrigerator and took out the milk. After pouring milk on his cereal, he sat down at the opposite end of the table, near his mother.

"Good morning Priscilla," Ms. Grace said before offering me a small breakfast of eggs and toast. The morning sickness had passed and I was able to eat anything I wanted without feeling the repercussions of it later. Irritated at how comfortable I seemed to be in his house, Pooky took his bowl of cereal down in his room to finish. My eyes followed him as he got up and left. Ms. Grace poured me a glass of orange juice and didn't make a comment about Pooky's behavior. She leaned back down in her chair and started a new conversation. I felt it was important enough for her to know how I really felt about Pooky, so I told her how much I loved him and how I hoped that we could be a family.

"Priscilla, please don't think that just because you're having my son's baby that he's going to be with you, even if you love him," she said with sincerity.

"He'll play at being a father to the baby, but he's going to do what he wants to do."

"But I love him," I said. "When the baby comes he's going to love me and the baby, I feel it in my heart. He might be mad now, but I know Pooky's going to take care of us."

Ms. Grace just looked at me.

"Well, I'm happy to be a grandmother," she said as she got up to get more coffee.

"Ms. Grace, what kind of things am I gonna need when the baby is born? Won't I need a bassinet or something for the baby to sleep in?" I asked.

"Yes, and clothes and bottles and bibs and diapers and lots of other things," she answered, just as Pooky came back up the stairs from his room.

Ms. Grace and I continued to talk about the baby and what we would need; Pooky didn't say a word. He just slammed cabinet doors and made loud sighing noises. We both ignored him. We discussed me going to the doctor soon and my need to apply for welfare. Ms. Grace said she would take me to the welfare office sometime next week.

A few days later, Ms. Grace took me to apply for welfare. She had a car so it didn't take us long to get to downtown St. Louis to the welfare office. I was nervous. I hadn't ever been in the welfare office before. However, I did remember the welfare people coming to our house.

The case worker assigned to review my application explained to me that because I was a minor, I had to come back with my biological mother. She told me that my mother would have to sign an affidavit stating that I was a pregnant minor and that she would be responsible for me. It was the only way I could receive assistance. She said.

"After the affidavit is signed, you'll receive a welfare check in your Mother's name," the case worker continued. I lowered my head and clamped my hands around my eyes. Tears trickled down my face.

"I can forget that." I said sounding disappointed. "If Mother gets my check, I won't see any of it." Seeing my distress, the case worker said, "There is some good news. We can give you a Medicaid card.

That doesn't require your mother's consent. You can at least go to the doctor."

I nodded my head to let her know I understood. I was disappointed about the welfare check, but at least I could finally go to the doctor and find out when my baby was to be born. I thanked my case worker for her help. Ms. Grace, who had been sitting quietly the entire time, rubbed me on my back and told me not to worry, she said she would make sure the baby had everything it needed. We left and went home.

Eventually, Pooky's attitude changed and he started talking to me. When I first moved in, he avoided me as much as possible in the house, but eventually he realized that he had access to almost around the clock sex, so, he became nicer to me. He hadn't said anything to me in weeks and then one day when his mother wasn't home he came in my room. He started talking to me about how he couldn't wait to be a father and how much he really like me. He claimed to be mad because he thought I got pregnant on purpose.

"I know that you didn't try to trap me, so I'm not mad anymore and I want us to be together. We can be a family." He continued. He hugged me and rubbed my stomach. A little taken by his sudden change of attitude, I didn't give a rebuttal. I smiled and acted as though no hard times had passed between us.

"My son is going to be a basketball star, like his daddy!" Pooky continued, acting proud and sticking his chest out.

"How you know it's a boy?" I said feeling ecstatic that he was talking to me again.

"I just know." He said with certainty. Then he leaned over and kissed me. I had been waiting months to be kissed by him again. I felt a release of anxiety in my body. Our passionate kiss lead to a sexual encounter, something that Pooky wanted and something that I missed.

From that day forward, whenever Ms. Grace wasn't home, Pooky would always come in my bedroom. I did feel that he was sending me mixed signals, but I ignored it because I loved him. Sometimes he would act like he didn't care about me in front of people by being rude and inconsiderate and when we were alone he acted as though I was the only girl in the world for him. I was confused, but it didn't matter.

When the baby gets here, I knew we were going to get married.

I was so grateful that Ms. Grace let me live in her house. I missed my brother Marcus, but I didn't miss living in our cruddy old house with mean mama. Ms. Grace was nice and her house was so beautiful. I felt like I could stay there forever. During the day while Ms. Grace was at work and Pooky was at school, I made sure the house was dusted and clean when they got home. I wanted to show my appreciation for all their kindness. Occasionally I would cook something.

It took a few weeks, but I finally got my Medicaid card in the mail. Ms. Grace took me to the doctor. She had done some research on OB doctors, the ones that accepted Medicaid and felt she had found a competent one to deliver her first grandchild.

The doctor told me I was six months pregnant and my baby was due to be born in March. I felt relieved to finally know when my baby was going to be born that we both were doing okay despite all the drama surrounding my pregnancy. The doctor even gave me some *real* prenatal vitamins that I was not afraid to take. My stomach was getting really big and the baby was moving around a lot – it felt funny, like my stomach was growling or someone was tickling me. I couldn't wait to have the baby.

I hadn't seen my mother since the night I ran away. Ms. Grace had been gracious enough to go to my house to tell Mother where I was. I didn't know she had done that until one night while we were having dinner, we somehow got on the subject of my mother. Ms. Grace told me that when she went to see my mother, Mother told her she was glad I was somebody else's problem and not hers. It hurt my feelings to hear that and seeing that I cry over everything, I begin to cry. Ms. Grace apologized, and commented that she was unsure why she told me in the first place.

Mother never came to see me, not that I expected her to. Marcus heard Ms. Grace tell mother where I was so he came to visit me often. I was happy to see him because I had missed him a lot. I was worried about him too. Mother beat on him sometimes too, but Marcus was smart; he stayed in school as much as possible and as long as possible, and participated in as many activities as he could. The less he was home the better. The less contact he had with Mother the better.

After the New Year, Pooky was a lot nicer to me in public. We even went out a few times together and took walks in the neighborhood. He anticipated the arrival of the baby. We talk about the baby a lot; and things the baby needed. We even decided on the baby's name together. We chose Randolph III for a boy or Valencia for a girl. It made me happy planning things with Pooky.

I was ready to be a mother. I was going to give my baby lots of love - love that I never received from my mother. I planned to be a better mother then she ever was.

March seemed to come around very quickly. My stomach was huge and the baby had been pressing on my pelvic bone, causing a lot of discomfort. No matter what position I tried to lay in, I could not get comfortable. One Sunday afternoon, I had been having trouble resting because my back hurt so badly and I was extremely uncomfortable. Pooky and his mother had gone to visit his sick grandmother so I was at the house alone. Because I was in such pain I worried that something was wrong. Ms. Grace hadn't left me a number to call and I didn't know how to get in touch with her. The only thing I knew to do was to walk to my mother's house and hope she would help me. I hadn't seen her since the night I ran way, and that was months ago. I was desperate. I wished I knew how to get in touch with Ms. Grace and Pooky.

Fortunately, Mother was home. "What are *you* doing here?" she asked as I stood on the front porch wondering if she was going to let me in. Mother looked like she had aged twenty years since the last time I saw her. She looked tired and worn down. I told her I didn't feel good and that my back hurt really bad, more than usual and Ms. Grace and Pooky weren't home and I didn't know what to do.

"You're ass is probably in labor," she said coldly. I looked at her expecting her to tell me what to do. Mother pushed the screen door open and turned to lock the front door. Without saying another word to me, she stepped off the porch and got in her friend's car that was idling at the curb. They drove off. She left me standing dumbfounded on the porch.

Stunned at Mother's reaction and still unsure what to do, I walked next door to Monica's house, only to discover that she had moved. More and more scared and confused, in pain and still not knowing what was wrong or what I should do, I saw a man walking in my direction and asked him for bus fare to the hospital. The man reached in his blue jean pocket and counted out some change to me, without asking any questions. I waited at the bus stop with pain that hit me in three to five minute increments. Finally the bus came and I rode the twenty minute bus ride to the county hospital. Valencia Duncan was born later that night, on March 3. She weighed 5½ pounds, and according to the nurses, it was an easy vaginal delivery, because my labor only lasted 2½ hours. I went through the delivery scared and alone. I wondered if Pooky and Ms. Grace knew where I was.

The next morning I lay in my hospital bed thinking about life with my baby girl. I hoped she would love me as much as I loved her. I wanted to see her again, but the nurses hadn't brought her back to my room. I hadn't seen her since last night. Emotions I had never felt before begin to consume me – I felt anxious and overwhelmed. I hoped the feelings would go away.

"Priscilla Duncan," I heard a voice call out. Wiping morning sleep from my eyes, I turned over to see who had called my name. Two white women were standing in the doorway of my hospital room with identification badges clipped to their dresses. One held a notebook in her arms and the other was carrying a briefcase. The woman with the notebook approached me and stretched out her hand to shake my hand. She introduced herself as a social worker with the St. Louis Department of Human Services. The woman with the briefcase shook my hand and introduced herself as a representative of the St. Francis Adoption Agency of St. Louis Missouri. My eyes swayed from one ID badge to the other as I made an attempt to read them.

"Adoption agency?" I questioned. "Are you here to take my baby?" Tears welled up in my eyes.

"Priscilla, your mother came to our office yesterday and said that you were giving your baby up for adoption," the one with the briefcase said.

"We got a call this morning that you had delivered a baby girl so we came right over." The women sat her black leather brief case at the edge of my bed, opened it and pulled out some papers. "If you'll just sign here," she said pointing to a line on the paper, "then we can collect the baby and place her in a home that can better care for her. We have a family waiting now for her right now" he women continued with a smile on her face.

"I'm not giving my baby up for adoption! My mother lied! She lied! I didn't tell her I was giving my baby up for adoption!" I screamed. I started crying hysterically. I turned my back to the women and buried my face in my pillow. I sobbed very loudly.

One of the women walked to the other side of my bed. "You can't care for a baby at your age, you're a child yourself." "She's right Priscilla, It's in your best interest to sign the papers and let us take the baby." I heard the other woman say.

I didn't say a word. I just buried my face deeper and deeper in my pillow and continued sobbing. The women pleaded for some time for me to listen to them, but I wouldn't uncover my face or stop crying. Eventually, the women stopped talking. I heard footsteps and the opening and closing of the door. The women left my room. I never saw them again.

I stayed in the hospital a week. It was fun having people make such a fuss over me; a far change from being fussed at. Pooky and his mother figured out where I was and came to visit me the day after I delivered the baby. I didn't bother telling them about the women from the adoption agency that had come that very same morning. Ms. Grace couldn't stop talking about her new granddaughter. She held her the entire hospital visit. Pooky was disappointed that he missed the birth of his daughter *and* that he was wrong about the sex of the baby. It was a proud moment for me to see him emotional over baby, Valencia.

I found out from Ms. Grace that when they got home last Sunday, they wondered where I was. Worried, they asked my mother if she had seen me or knew where I was. Mother denied ever seeing me. They called around to the local hospitals until they found me. Unfortunately, I had already delivered. I was disappointed too that I went through the delivery by myself, but I was glad my baby was healthy.

The day I was to leave the hospital, I was scared and feeling depressed. I thought I knew how to take care of a baby, since I had taken care of my brothers and sister, but suddenly I felt unsure if I could care for my baby. I felt different. I was nervous and scared and overwhelmed and not ready to leave the hospital. I was worried I was going to make mistakes. Valencia was so tiny.

I asked one of the nurses to show me how to put the cloth diapers on my baby and how I was supposed to make baby formula because I didn't want to breastfeed. Breastfeeding wasn't even a consideration, because I thought it would make me feel weird.

The nurse showed me how to do all the things I was worried about doing wrong. She was very patient with me. She sent me home with encouraging words and told me she was convinced I would do just fine. "You're going to make a great mother," she said. *I hope so,* I mumbled to myself.

CHAPTER 5

Pooky was happy to be a daddy. His hidden skepticism about being the father, something that he thought I didn't know about, had disappeared. I knew from the very beginning that he questioned if he was the father or if Mike was the father after what they both did to me. But after seeing Valencia, he was fully convinced that he was her daddy since he thought she had his eyes.

"She looks just like me," he said smiling as he picked her up. He even nicknamed her after himself, calling her Pooky.

Valencia was a chubby little baby girl with her daddy's dark chocolate skin color and his black curly good hair. Pooky wasn't much on helping me with the baby, like changing diapers or bathing her, but he did occasionally hold her and feed her. Ms. Grace was a proud grandmother. She loved Valencia and helped me with everything I needed for the baby, just has she said she would. She even watched the baby so I could get some rest or to go to the store. Mother hadn't bothered to come to see the baby yet, but Marcus had been over a few times.

When Valencia was six weeks old, Pooky enlisted in the Army. I was completely surprised that he still wanted to join the Army since now we had a baby and our relationship had become much better. The same day he graduated high school, Pooky went to the Army recruiter's office downtown. I begged him not to leave us, but he was adamant about his decision to join the Military. I dreaded Pooky leaving for weeks. When the time arrived for him to finally leave, I was devastated. I couldn't stop crying. I had gotten so used to seeing him every day and being with him every day. Pooky promised to write often.

I looked forward to receiving letters from Pooky every week. He was going to be in boot camp for three months and I couldn't wait for him to get back so the baby and I could leave St. Louis and be with him wherever he was stationed. We would finally be a family and my dreams would come true. I would be with Pooky anywhere in the world.

Pooky sent us pictures of himself in his uniform. He looked so handsome. I counted the days of the three months he would be away. Every day I marked an X on the calendar – my excitement grew stronger and stronger with every day marked off the calendar.

"Boot camp is harder than I thought," Pooky confessed in one of his many letters "and I'm homesick too." "I miss my baby," he said in another letter.

I missed him a lot and I couldn't wait until he came home; and I was ready to go back with him.

By the second month, Pooky's letters stop coming as often. I worried about him and wondered if he was alright. Ms. Grace assured me that everything was fine and suggested that I not worry. I loved Pooky and I missed him, I couldn't help but worry.

The day Pooky was scheduled to arrive home; I took extra time and care to make sure that both Valencia and I looked extra special. Since I couldn't sleep the night before, I got up early and bathed the baby. I lotioned her real good and dressed her in a pastel pink and yellow dress with white ruffled socks and black patent leather shoes. I put baby oil in her hair and made little pony tails that I attached hair bows to. She looked so cute. I put on a beautiful yellow dress and matching sandals that Ms. Grace had bought me. Since I had been living with Ms. Grace, she had been buying me clothes and treating me as if I was her own daughter. It was nice to have brand new clothes instead of always wearing hand-me-downs.

Finally, I heard a car pull up. I jumped off the couch, grabbed the baby and ran to the door. Ms. Grace came out of her room with a big smile on her face and clapping her hands. We arrived at the front door at the same time. Both of our hands reached for the doorknob. We opened the door together, slightly pushing each other to try to be the first one out of the door. Pooky got out of a yellow cab in his Army uniform. He gave my goose bumps, because he looked *so* good. Then he walked around to the other side of the cab and opened the door. I thought he was getting his luggage, but out stepped a light-skinned woman with long black hair, dressed in an Army dress. My mouth flew opened, my stomach instantly knotted up and I suddenly felt sick. The smile on Ms. Grace's face faded away too. Unsure who this woman was, neither of us said a word. We watched Pooky at the cab, wishing he would hurry up and come tell us who this woman was. Holding hands with the woman, they finally made it up the walk way.

Pooky walked directly to his mother with a big smile on his face and hugged her.

"Mama, this is Amanda, my wife. We got married last week in the chapel on the base." He blurted out.

Ms. Grace, unsure what to say, stood speechless with a blank look on her face. Amanda walked up to her and gave her a hug. Without acknowledging me, Pooky grabbed Valencia out of my arms and said, "Amanda, this is my daughter, Valencia." Amanda gave me a brief awkward look and reached out to shake Valencia's tiny hand as Pooky held her in his arms. Amanda's demeanor let me know she was clearly unsure what to make of me or the situation, seeing that Pooky didn't even tell her I was the mother of his child and the girl he was supposed to marry.

I felt like I was going to pass out from the hurt, but I didn't say a word. I just turned around and ran into the house. It felt like Pooky had just yanked my heart out of my chest and run over it with a cement roller. Tears poured from my eyes. I went straight to my bedroom and immediately started packing my clothes and the baby's clothes. A few minutes later Pooky followed me inside.

"Priscilla, I never told you I was gonna marry you," he said as he stood watching me pack. I didn't say a word. I continued to pack, wiping away the tears that flooded my eyes.

Ms. Grace came into the room and saw me packing. "*Please* don't leave," she begged me. "Don't take my granddaughter away." She was crying also.

"How could you be so inconsiderate?" she yelled at Pooky as he stood in the room still holding Valencia with no remorse.

"Mama, I didn't tell Priscilla I was going to marry her. It ain't my fault that she assumed that I was. I love my baby, but I don't love

Priscilla! I'm in love with Amanda," he protested.

I looked at them both and continued packing as much as I could. I was broken hearted! I had continual flash backs in my mind of our intimate moments that we shared and how he kept telling me he wanted to be with me and we were going to be a family. He even said it in his letters, before he stopped writing them. I saved every one of his letters and would read them over and over again. How could I have misunderstood what he was saying to me? How could I have assumed wrong? Thoughts and unanswered questions poured through my head. I needed to get out of there before I lost my mind from the pain and misery.

I put my bag on my shoulder, grabbed Valencia out of Pooky's arms and headed for the front door. Amanda was sitting quietly on the couch, watching all the drama unfold. Ms. Grace continued crying and begged me again not to go – as Pooky stood and watched, not saying a word. I didn't say a word either. I was too hurt to stay any longer. I walked out the door carrying my baby in my arms and agony in my heart. I headed back to my mother's house, the only place I knew to go.

CHAPTER 6

I missed living at Ms.Grace's house. There was never any peace and quiet at Mother's house.

It was too much going on all the time; arguing, fighting, loud music, and lots of people. It was noisy too. When I first showed up at the house a few weeks ago, Mother gave me a hard time about wanting to move back in.

"I knew you would come running back sooner or later." Mother said. She also made hateful remarks about Ms. Grace, saying that Ms. Grace thought she was better than her; and she criticized me for thinking things were going to be so much better over at *Pooky's* house.

"They ain't no good and you stupid for thinking they was gonna treat you like you were somethin' special!" She never let me live it down for having to move back home and it was hard to ignore her on a regular basis. I was glad I chose not to tell her about Pooky getting married. She would have belittled me about that too. Nothing about her had changed in the months that I had been away, not that I expected it to.

All my brothers, except Marcus, were in the boy's home. My younger sister, Keisha, lived with her grandmother on her father's side. My older sister Margaret had recently moved back home after being beat up by her boyfriend. She was in the bed recovering from a recent abortion.

Almost every night, sleeping was impossible because of the loud music and all the company Mother had in the house. Poor baby Valencia was having a hard time sleeping too. Every time I'd finally get her laid down to sleep, loud music and loud voices seeped through the walls and would wake her up. She hated living here too.

Every morning when I got up, there was some strange person sleeping on the couch, on the floor in the living room or in Mother's bed. I learned to tune a lot of things out.

Still hurt about Pooky's marriage and depressed over having to live back at home, I started drinking again. I stole beers, wine coolers and other different bottles of liquor from Mother's stash inside the kitchen cabinet. She had so much liquor, she never missed what I took. I hid the bottles in my room. At times, I'd slide the doors back on my closet and sit in there, drinking and thinking about my miserable life.

I hadn't spoken to or seen Ms. Grace or Pooky since I had left and I needed money to take care of Valencia. Now that I was no longer living at Ms. Grace's house, my money source was cut off. I asked Mother to take me to the welfare office to apply for benefits. Mother was glad to take me, especially since she knew my check would come in her name. I believed that was the deciding factor as to why she let me move back in.

"You gonna carry your own damn weight around here with that damn baby! I told you I didn't want no baby in my house in the first damn place!" I remembered her saying the day she let me back in.

I got food stamps and a welfare check, all in Mothers' name. Only the Medicaid came in my name. As I predicted, I never saw a dime. We argued all the time about my welfare checks, because I needed money to take care of my baby and she wouldn't give me any.

"You ain't staying in my damn house for free!" she'd said often.

If I pressed her hard enough, she would give me money for diapers and baby food, but she would keep the rest. Thankfully, I applied for WIC or my baby wouldn't have had formula to drink.

I suspected Mother sold most of the food stamps. We had more liquor in the house then we had food. I hated her. She drove me to drink. And, the more I drank, the more I was able to stand up to her. So, I drank all the time. I would argue and cuss back at her and whenever she hit me, I'd hit her right back. We would fight like animals on the street. I was sick and tired of her.

Glad to get out of the house for any reason, I walked to the corner Laundromat to wash clothes. I had left the baby with Marcus to watch. He loved baby Valencia. As I stood sorting my loads of laundry a young man approached me.

"What's your name, pretty lady?" he asked.

"Priscilla. What's yours?" I said smiling because he was cute.

"James Gibson," he answered, looking me up and down. I felt him checking me out, but acted like I didn't notice. Since I had the baby, my shape was fuller. My breasts had increased two sizes and my butt stuck out more. I felt it was an improvement. James was nice looking. He was dressed in jeans and a button-down shirt. He looked to be around 19 or 20 years old.

"Do you live around here?" he asked.

"Yeah," I answered, "just around the corner on Burd Avenue."

James stayed in the Laundromat talking to me until I had washed and dried all three of my loads of clothes. I told him I was 15 years old and I had a baby at home, but he didn't seem to care, especially since I told him that her daddy wasn't around. James carried my laundry baskets as he walked me home. I was flattered by the attention he gave me; he was very nice.

After arriving at the house, I carried the baskets inside and brought out Valencia. James and I stayed out front and talked for a long time. Valencia seemed to like him. When she fell asleep, I took her inside and put her to bed, then came back outside to finish talking to James.

James and I became boyfriend and girlfriend about a week later and we were inseparable. I had gotten on birth control after I had my six week check up and I was glad that I had made that choice. James and I could not keep our hands off each other. Mother hated my relationship with James and she hated James. She hated the thought of anyone loving me and he did love me, because he told me so.

James was sweet to me. He'd write poems and sing songs to me all the time. He had a great voice and his poems would melt my heart. James' dream was to become a musician. He loved to play the drums and the piano. He had bought himself a drum set and his father had given him an old piano from his church. James had taught himself how to play the drums and the piano at an early age. Ellis Gibson, James' father, was the pastor of New Northside Baptist Church. He had been the Pastor for almost fifteen years. He let James play both instruments in his church. Every Sunday and Wednesday night Bible study, James was in church playing the drums or playing the piano. But now, according to James, he no longer had a desire to play for the church. He said his dreams were bigger. He wanted to be a professional musician. It was all he talked about.

James spent the night at our house all the time. Mother tried to complain about it, but I ignored her and did what I wanted to do. We'd stay up late at night drinking and talking about our future. He loved Valencia and she loved him. James didn't have any children of his own, so acted like he was Valencia's father. He even bought her diapers and baby food, and even an outfit or two. Far more than her biological father had bought. He hadn't done anything for Valencia since we left a while ago, he hadn't even seen her. But, I had started back talking to Ms. Grace again and she was helping me with the baby.

At the first of each month, Mother and I continued to argue about my check. I knew the welfare check was coming and she wanted to make sure I wasn't going to get it. A few days before the first of the month, Mother would pick a fight about something stupid and then put me out. She wanted to make sure I was never there when the mailman delivered the check. During these times, I would take the baby to Ms. Grace's house and then go stay with James at his house or anywhere we could find.

Once I figured out what Mother was doing, her trick didn't work anymore. I decided to meet the mailman down the street as he was delivering the mail. Mother was at home waiting for him. She almost had a heart attack when I held the check up to her after walking in the house. I threatened to tear the check up if she wasn't going to give me my money. She cussed me out and tried to fight me, but I didn't back down. Finally, she gave in and we both walked to the corner store to cash the check. After I got my money, James and I picked up Valencia from Ms. Grace's house, bought some hamburgers and went to the park. From that day forward, that's how I planned to get my money. I was going to meet the mailman down the street every month.

The next morning, the Department of Human Services showed up at our house early that morning. I was sitting at the kitchen table feeding Valencia. James was asleep in my room. Mother was dressed in slacks and a blouse and was sitting on the couch as though she was expecting company. She hadn't said a word to me as I sat in the kitchen feeding the baby. I guess she was still mad at me about the check incident yesterday. I looked around the house and noticed she had even cleaned up. She had to have gotten up pretty early to clean up this house. I wondered if it was our welfare inspection time. I turned my attention back to Valencia and continued feeding her. She was getting so big. She was even trying to pull up on things.

I heard a knock at the door. Mother jumped up off the couch and walked quickly to the door. Two ladies with their ID badges clipped on their outfits entered the house and sat down on the couch. They talked quietly with Mother. One of them pulled out some paperwork from one of the brief cases they were carrying. I saw Mother sign the papers. I tried to hear what they were discussing, but couldn't hear anything. Finally, everyone stood up and the two ladies walked over to me.

"Priscilla I'm Susie McGuiness, a social worker with the St. Louis County Detention Center and this is Mary Maddox also a social worker with the St. Louis County Detention Center, we're going to need you to hand the baby to your Mother and to come with us."

"Come with you for what? I'm not coming with you!"

"Yes you are!" Mary Maddox said, raising her voice.

"Your mother just signed papers to send you to the juvenile detention center for girls. She says you are a trouble maker and have behavioral problems. Please! Come with us." She demanded.

"Don't make us put you in restraints," Ms. McGuiness threatened, holding up a pair of handcuffs.

I started crying and screaming for James. I clutched my baby as one of the social workers tried to pry her out my arms, knocking the bowl of baby cereal to the floor.

"James! James!" I screamed. James came running out of the room wearing shorts and no shirt. "Mother's sending me to the girl's home!" I yelled. "These people want to take me to the girl's home!"

James didn't know what to make of what was happening; he didn't know what to do or say.

"Take my baby to Ms. Grace's house!" I cried out. James squeezed between the two ladies and grabbed the baby out of my arms just as the two women threatened to take her from me again. Mother stood watching with a smirk on her face as the two ladies grabbed me by my arms and forced me out of the house and into their car. They didn't even let me change out of my pajamas.

I was kicking and screaming all the way to the car. Marcus stood at the door watching and crying. James got dressed and gathered Valencia's things and took her to Ms. Grace's house.

CHAPTER 7

I was taken to the St. Louis County Detention Center for girls. Every day I cried and begged to go home, but they wouldn't let me. I missed my baby and I missed James. My counselor said I couldn't be released until my 16th birthday and that was six months away. The only good thing about being locked up was that once I was released, I could have a choice of where I wanted to live; and I could start getting my own welfare check. At 16 I was told I could be emancipated and that's exactly what I wanted to be.

I was unhappy every day. I never got used to the detention center. I hated all the arguing, fighting and stealing that went on. I was scared all the time. I tried my best to stay to myself and stay clear of the troublemakers. And there were a lot of troublemakers. The sleeping quarters held twelve girls per room and somebody was always fighting. There were group counseling sessions twice a day and daily individual counseling sessions. We were able to go to the gym and play in the recreation center at the end of the week if we didn't have any demerits. Demerits were given if we had a confrontation with someone, got caught stealing, weren't in our rooms by curfew, talked back to teachers or counselors, or for any other reason they could come up with. In group a lot of people got demerits for insubordination. During the week, we went to school and had devotion on Sundays. Saturdays were free days. Art and crafts classes were my favorites. I'd make things for my baby and cards for James. James came to visit every visitation day although the center was an hour's drive away. He brought Valencia with him. Sometimes he brought Marcus. He always remembered to bring me a poem that he had written for me or some special trinket that he had bought me. Visitation was every Sunday, Tuesday and Thursday for one hour. I looked forward to those visit, but that hour went by to quick. Marcus was doing well in school, as usual. He told me when he graduated high school he was going to go into the military. I had a sudden flash of Pooky, but I ignored it. James said he was still looking for a musician job, but wasn't having any luck so far. He said every now and then he would make a little money playing a gig at a party, but nothing big.

As it got close to my six-month release date, my counselor still felt I hadn't resolved my issues with my mother. I had met with him every Tuesday since I arrived and I was miserable. I didn't want to be there and I never wanted to open up and talk about anything. I just wanted to go home – to a new home, not my old home.

"Why do you feel you can't get along with your mother?" he would ask. He always asked that same question at every session. I was tired of him asking me that question. Mother had been the way she is for years, she wasn't going to change. I was so angry at her for sending me here that I didn't want to mention her name or think about her.

"I don't know," was my usual answer, always sounding annoyed whenever I answered.

One day, I finally answered his question. This particular day my heart was heavy. I started talking as soon as I entered his office. He looked surprised. He sat down in his chair and listened.

"Last night I dreamt about the time mother tried to kill me in the bathtub. I was only a little kid. Why would she do that? The dream started me thinking about a lot of other things that my mother had done to me. Aren't mothers supposed to love you? My mother doesn't love me. Why? Why does she hate me?" Tears rolled down my cheeks. "She has always hated me. I think it's because she blames me for my father leaving her, I don't know. She's done lots of terrible things to me. Things that are hard for me to forgive her for." I looked up at my counselor with tears welled up in my eyes. "I've tried everything to make her love me, she just won't. Now I don't care anymore and I want to be away from her. I shouldn't even be in here. I'm here because she was mad because I wouldn't give her my welfare check. That's just stupid!" I wiped the tears from my cheeks, and stopped talking. The counselor handed me a tissue and thanked me for finally opening up and sharing my true feelings. "Sharing is therapeutic. It's the beginning of the healing process." He said. He was right. So, I opened up more and more during my other visits. Once I stop being angry I was able to see more positive things in my future, like a life with James and Valencia.

The morning of my release, James was there to pick me up, this time without the baby. He had borrowed his daddy's 1972 Cutlass as he had done on every visitation day. We hugged and kissed before driving off. It was my 16th birthday and he welcomed me with a bouquet of flowers.

I was relieved to finally be leaving this dreadful place. I was definitely not going to miss it, but I was going to miss my counselor, Mr. Cornell. Mr. Cornell treated me with kindness like no one else had before, even though I was stubborn at first. He was nice and encouraging. After I had opened up to him about my feelings, he helped me to learn ways to heal my hurt; and he understood when I told him I just *couldn't* live with Mother any more.

Mr. Cornell found me a furnished one-bedroom apartment on the south side of St. Louis, just above his grandmother's garage. He also helped me to transfer my welfare out of my mothers' name and into my name so I could get my *own* checks and my *own* food stamps. When I told James about what Mr. Cornell had done, he was happy for me. He hated the way Mother gave me a hard time about my welfare check and the way she treated me. He told me that was the reason he helped me a lot financially, because she wouldn't. James drove me to pick up Valencia from Ms. Grace's house and then we went to see the apartment. I loved it and James did too He decided to move in with me.

After living together for two months, James asked me to marry him. I said yes. I loved James and we had a great relationship. That same day, we went to the courthouse to get married. I found out that being emancipated doesn't mean you can get married at sixteen. I had to get my mother's consent. This angered me because I thought that since I was 16 I didn't need my mother for anything else. The clerk explained that I had to have a marriage authorization form filled out because in this case I was a minor and it had to be signed by my mother before I could marry James. I hadn't seen Mother since the day she had me locked up. We waited a few days before deciding to go ask Mother to sign the form. I thought I wasn't mad at her any more, but the more I thought about having to see her, the angrier I got.

I was sure Mother knew I was out of the detention center, but when she saw me at the door, she acted like she was surprised. "Guinea!" Marcus interrupted, as he ran and hugged me when he saw me threw the screen door. I gave Marcus a big hug, noticing that he was much taller and that his voice was deeper. I small talked with him for a short time and then turned my attention to Mother. Marcus went over to the door and started playing with Valencia. She was walking now and was standing at the door with James.

I didn't feel like mincing words with Mother and I already had somewhat of an attitude, so I got straight to the point. I handed her the marriage authorization form and told her what I wanted her to do. She cussed and complained about my decision to marry James, giving me all the reasons she didn't like him, as though I cared. Then she started complaining about her food stamps being cut and her welfare check being cut and how it was all my fault.

"You got all my checks and food stamps for the entire six months that you had me put in that detention center! And you didn't do nothing for my baby!" I screamed at her. I could feel my ears get hot; I was getting so mad at her.

"I told you not to have that damn baby in the first place," Mother yelled.

"You better sign this paper right now," I screamed.

"I ain't signing that damn marriage paper," Mother yelled back at me.

Angry, I turned to James and said, "Come on, let's go!" We headed for the door.

Mother yelled out, "If you buy me a bottle of Madd Dogg 20-20 and a carton of Kool 100's, then I'll sign the damn paper."

"What?" I said, turning around to look at her with a frown on my face.

"You heard me," Mother said and repeated her demand.

James picked up Valencia and we walked out the door. Without discussing Mothers request, we went to the liquor store around the corner and bought Mother's liquor and cigarettes. Once we got back,

48

she was happy to sign the paper. I snatched the paper out of her hand and turned to leave. "Don't come back!" she yelled as we walked out the door.

"Don't worry, I won't!" I yelled back.

On June 24, 1973, James and I were married.

CHAPTER 8

I tried to make our apartment as cozy as possible. I found things throughout the neighborhood that people had discarded or went to secondhand stores to find items to put in the apartment. Our landlord, Mrs. Evans, was very nice to us. She told me her grandson, Mr. Cornell, had said nice things about me. She also gave me things for the apartment. I started getting child support from Pooky and I received my welfare check so I was able to make sure every month our rent was paid, as well as all the utilities. I used my food stamps wisely to make sure to have lots of food in the refrigerator all the time. I loved to cook, so I cooked all the time. I made sure James and Valencia had home cooked meals every day. Things were going great and I was happy. James couldn't seem to find a job anywhere, so he stayed home and worked on his music. I, on the other hand, found a job at a sandwich shop where the manager was willing to pay me under the table so I went to work during the day. Ms. Grace watched Valencia while I worked. James and I had all the things we needed and being in love was the icing on the cake.

One day, I came home from work with Valencia to find the gas shut off in the apartment and James not home. I didn't understand why it was cut off because I had given him the money to pay the bill last week. We didn't have a telephone in the apartment so, I went to the pay phone on the corner to call James' parents' house to see if he was over there. He wasn't there. I wondered where he was. It was winter and the apartment was cold, very cold. I didn't know what to do. I pulled the blankets off the bed to huddle in the closet with Valencia. As I pulled the blankets off the bed, I saw a bag of something fall from between the mattresses. I picked it up to look at it. It was a bag of pills, yellow jacks. I lifted up the mattress and found more drugs: Speed, Acid, PCP and Angel Dust. I had never seen these types of drugs before, but when I was at the detention center the counselors showed us pictures of different drugs and explained to us what they would do to our brains. I got scared and swore I would never touch any drugs. I didn't know if James was selling drugs or using drugs because I hadn't noticed any peculiar behavior in him. I put the bag back under the mattress along with the other bags of drugs and huddled with my baby in the closet until we fell asleep. It was a long cold night. Valencia slept good, but I couldn't get comfortable. I was cold and I was worried about James.

I took Valencia to Ms. Grace's house to stay until I got the gas back on. Every night the temperature dropped into the 20's. I couldn't pay the bill again until I got my check the following Friday, so I toughed it out until then. I went to work as usual, but every evening before coming home I went to a few of James' hang out spots to see if he was there, but he wasn't. I vowed never to trust James to pay the bills again and I meant it! I stayed in the apartment four days without heat and without James. I didn't know where he was.

James came home a week later, after the gas was turned back on. I was in the kitchen cooking when I heard keys rattling at the door, then it opened. James walked in the house looking exhausted and dirty. I stood looking at him with my hands on my hips. He immediately went into an explanation, never telling me where he had been for the last seven days.

"I spent the money and I knew you would be mad at me so I didn't come home," he explained.

"I froze in this house!" I yelled. "I had to take Valencia to Ms. Grace's house because it was too cold here for her! Why did you spend the money? Did you use the gas money to buy those drugs under the mattress?" James looked surprised that I knew about the drugs.

"No," he reluctantly answered. "I was on my way to pay the gas bill, but I stopped by BBJ's Jazz Club and found out that I didn't get the gig at the club that I expected. I got mad and flipped out.

Nothing is working out for me and I was feeling sorry for myself and so I bought some cocaine.

I'm sorry, I won't do it again, I promise," he said.

"It better not happen again, James, because I'm pregnant and we need all money we can get," I said bluntly.

James looked surprised. "You're pregnant? For real!" He ran to me and gave me an extra tight hug. "I'm going to be a real daddy now." He said with joy.

A few months later, James did the same thing again. I had promised myself that I wouldn't let James pay any more bills, but he convinced me otherwise. This time the electricity got cut off. Just as before, James left us in the apartment for over a week with no lights. I bought candles to use until I was able to get my check to pay the bill. James' binges were driving me crazy.

I wished I had someone to talk to about him. I decided to talk to his parents about his behavior. I met with James' mother and his grandmother and I hoped they could tell me what to do about him. But even they couldn't shed any light on why James was acting the way he was acting. Feeling the need for family closeness, I tried to develop more of a relationship with them. I spent more time at their houses and Valencia and I even went to church with them, but not as often.

James' mother and grandmother were very spiritual people; they went to church all the time; to every church meeting, every church event and anything else the church was having. Although James' father was the Pastor of his own church, his mother and grandmother attended a different church on the other side of town. I tried talking to James' father, but he didn't believe James had any problems. He told me just to let James be a man and not pressure him about anything he was doing. Because I didn't get any help from James' family, I didn't raise the issues with them again. They were however thrilled that I was carrying James' first child and couldn't wait until the baby is born.

One morning, James told me he would be at his grandmother's house for the day, so after work I went by there. I walked in the house and James and his grandmother were dancing around in the living room, in their underwear, chanting something in a strange language and waving incense. It looked like they were practicing some sort of voodoo. Strange voodoo-looking things were scattered around the dim room. They were so into what they were doing, they didn't even hear me come in the house. I watched for a second, but I got scared and left. Later that night when James came home he was high as a kite and talking crazy. I was lying on the couch watching television when he came in. He plopped himself down in the chair beside me and started babbling about all sorts of things. He told me when he was a little boy his grandmother got him addicted to valium and sleeping pills. James was raised by his grandmother, not his mother. His mother had him out of wedlock when she was a teenager and his grandmother felt his mother was too young to raise him properly so she took him. James' grandmother believed he was a hyperactive kid and the only way she could control him was to give him valium; and when he wouldn't go to sleep, she gave him sleeping pills. She started this when he was a toddler.

"I never knew she was giving me drugs until I got older." James proclaimed. "She always told me the pills were vitamins." James continued. I just listened. "My grandmother started practicing voodoo when I was in elementary school. She was fascinated by it. She claimed she could put a spell on anybody. My grandmother would mix a lot of ingredients together and try them on me. She would make me do some strange things and she would do strange things to me," he said as tears welled up in his eyes.

I continued to listen without making a comment. I didn't know what to say anyway. James finally stopped talking. He cried for a few more minutes and then got up out of the chair and walked to the front door.

"Where are you going?" I asked.

"I'll be back later," he said in a somber voice. I asked him not to leave, but he left anyway.

James stayed gone for three days. I stopped making a big deal about him leaving for days and his drug binges because nothing I said about the subject mattered to him. He still kept doing it.

I gave birth to our daughter, Sandra, on February 6, 1974. Fortunately, James was around for the birth of the baby and he stayed with me at the hospital. He was so excited about the birth of the baby that he fainted during the delivery. After he came to, James made so many promises to Sandra as he held her in his arms for the first time. He was proud that he had a part in bringing such a beautiful child into this world. He was also overjoyed at officially becoming a daddy.

I had hoped with the birth of Sandra that James would get it together and keep all his promises of being a good father that he made in the hospital. I was wrong. Despite his excitement about the baby, my life with James changed for the worse. We were arguing all the time. He was taking the rent money and stealing things out the house. He was getting high all the time and not bothering to look for a job. Every time we argued, he'd leave the apartment and I wouldn't see him for days, sometimes weeks. This became a welcomed act.

James' family changed too. Now that Sandra was born, they started treating the two girls differently. Most times, they only wanted Sandra to visit and not Valencia. It upset me because they were making a blatant discrimination between my daughters and I didn't like it. I decided that I wouldn't let Sandra go over any of their houses anymore if Valencia couldn't go. The family got mad and threaten to disown me from the family. My decision caused a lot of turmoil between James and me. He couldn't see my point of view and accused me of being controlling and difficult.

One night, James and I had one of our many arguments. Instead of leaving like he normally did, this time he decided when he left he was going to take Sandra with him. James grabbed Sandra off the couch and headed for the door. He had no blanket, bottles or diapers; and it was at night and chilly. I grabbed at the jacket he was wearing to try to keep him from leaving. He turned around and punched me in the eye. I grabbed my face and fell to the ground. James lifted his foot and stomped me on my back. As I lay crying on the floor, he walked out the house with my two-month-old baby. James had never hit me before. We cursed and yelled at each other, but we never fought. He punched me like he was punching a man on the street. My back had his shoe print on it for a few days and it was extremely sore.

Two months had passed and it felt like James and Sandra had disappeared off the face of the earth. I had searched frantically for them every place I could think of, but I could not find them. My life was hell. Poor Valencia wasn't getting very much attention either. I couldn't sleep and I couldn't think about anything except about where my baby girl was.

The following month, I didn't get my welfare check. I called the welfare office and found out that James had told them I was an unfit mother and he had to take his child away from me. He was getting a welfare check for Sandra, wherever he was. Despite not getting a check, I was relieved to have heard something about James. At least now I know my baby is alive. Now I need to find out where he is. I asked the welfare office to tell me where he lived, but their confidentiality policy prevented them from telling me, even after I explained the situation. I pleaded with them, but there was no changing their minds; not without a court order and I couldn't afford a lawyer.

That same month the welfare office investigated me for neglect. They came to my apartment and they came to my job. James knew I worked under the table and he was doing all he could to get me in trouble. My boss told them I didn't work there because he could have gotten in trouble too. Thank goodness he kept no records of my employment with him. I was glad because if the welfare office knew that I had a job, I would go to jail. Maybe that's what James wanted, I wondered. I wished I knew what was wrong with him and why he was acting this way. Once I really thought about it, he had been acting crazy months before he ever left. He had never hit me before either.

The welfare people questioned my landlord about my character and what sort of mother she thought I was. The landlord said she told them nice things about me. They interviewed me last. I was scared that they were going to take Valencia. I couldn't understand why James was doing this to me, his own wife. For a couple of months, I endured the investigation. I didn't receive a welfare check or food stamps while I waited on them to complete the investigation. I had to work extra hours just to pay my rent and bills until my welfare assistance was restored.

CHAPTER 9

Six months had gone by and I still hadn't seen James or my baby girl. I wondered how she was doing and I hoped wherever she was she was being taken care of. I continued to look, determined not to give up or to get weary. I asked anyone that knew us if they had seen James. I asked his parents and his grandmother all the time if they had heard from him or seen Sandra. None of them had seen or heard from either one. The stress led me to drink even more than my daily can of beer and glass of Hennessey. I was worried sick about my baby. I drank at work, on the way home and when I got home. I drank all the time to try to calm my nerves. I even picked up more hours at work trying to stay busy to keep my mind occupied.

Jason, a friend of James' came into the sandwich shop one afternoon. I hadn't seen him in over a year, but he remembered me.

"Aren't you James' girl?" he asked.

"I used to be," I answered rudely, though not really feeling like talking or answering questions. The stress was taking a toll on me, even though I was still trying to function as usual.

"How you doing? He asked sounding chipper, I just saw James the other day."

"What!" I shouted. "Where?"

Unsure why I suddenly became hysterical, Jason answered, "At his grandmother's house. He lives there with his baby daughter."

"I've got to go!" I yelled at my manager. Frantic, I grabbed my purse and ran out the door.

"I should have known his grandmother was lying. I'd asked her if she'd seen him at least a million times and she just kept lying to me," I screamed aloud as I headed for the bus stop. I anxiously waited for the bus to come; which seemed to be taking too long, I thought about all the things I was going to say when I got to his grandmother's house.

Unsure about what would happen when I got there, I decided to go by Mother's house to see if Marcus would go over there with me. I had sworn I would never set foot in my mothers' house again, but I didn't want to go to James' grandmother's house by myself either. My mother lived down the street and around the corner from James' grandmother's house. I hoped she still lived there. I hadn't been to her house since she told me not to come back after signing the marriage papers; and Mother did move around a lot. "Please let her still live here," I mumbled to myself as I knocked on the door. When Marcus answered the door, I was relieved. He was shocked to see me standing at the door. I was shocked to see him. He hugged me and told me he missed me. Fortunately, Mother wasn't home. He said he hadn't seen her for a few days. Marcus was handsome and looked so grown up. He was thirteen now and had muscles in his arms, like he had been working out and he had a little peach fuzz on his face. He had a short nappy afro and his voice sounded deeper than the last time we had talked.

"I missed you, Guinea," Marcus said hugging me again. "I haven't seen you in a long time. Why haven't you come to visit us?" I didn't answer.

"I need you to go somewhere with me, Marcus," I pleaded. "I can tell you everything on the way." Marcus agreed to go; he closed the door behind us and followed me up the street. On the way to James' grandmother's house, I filled Marcus in about James taking Sandra. Marcus was surprised to know I had another baby.

When we arrived at the house, I walked on the porch and banged loudly on the door. I had a stronger confidence since Marcus was with me. James' grandmother answered the door before asking who it was. When she saw it was me she looked very surprised.

"Ms. Bessie, where's Sandra!" I screamed in her face as I pushed my way past her and ran in her house. Marcus stayed outside on the porch.

I ran down the hallway looking for my baby and calling her name. I turned to go into the living room and was stopped in my tracks. At the end of the hallway near the living room was a closet that appeared to be some sort of coat or linen closet where the doors had been removed. Ms. Bessie had turned it into what looked like a voodoo shrine. I stared in disbelief; I could not believe what I was seeing. Inside the closet were bowls with chicken feet in them, a crucifix with rosary beads wrapped around it, feathers and a bowl with a lock of hair in it. Incense was burning around a picture of Sandra that was placed in the center of the shrine. My stomach knotted up and fear overcame me. I knew I had to get my baby and get out this devil-worshipping house. I heard sounds coming from the living room. I turned to look and saw a woman sitting on the couch in the living room holding my baby. She was humming something with her eyes closed.

"Give me my baby!" I demanded. I startled her because she didn't see or hear me walk into the room. I grabbed Sandra out of her arms and ran for the front door, passing Ms Bessie who was still standing in the hallway screaming for James.

"Where the hell do you think you're going?" I heard a voice say just before I made it to the front door. I turned around to see James standing on the stairs holding a crowbar.

"You ain't going nowhere with my baby," he shouted.

James lifted the crowbar and hit me across my forehead. I fell to the floor with Sandra still in my arms as blood poured down my face. Sandra started screaming.

"You better give me back my baby and get out of my grandmother's house!" he screamed as he tugged at my arms to free Sandra. I clamped her tightly in my arms.

"Marcus!" I shouted, "Help! Go home and get a knife! Hurry," I screamed.

Marcus ran home as fast as he could. I had no idea where Ms. Bessie or the woman in living room went.

"I ain't leaving without my baby!" I screamed.

"We'll see about that!" James said.

Still crouched on the floor cradling Sandra, James kicked me in my back. Sandra fell out of my arms. James grabbed my hair and pulled me up off the floor. Then he punched me in my face. I tried to fight him back, despite the blood flowing from my forehead and affecting my vision. By the time Marcus made it back with the knife,

James and had thrown me outside the house and onto the porch. Marcus ran up to me as I lay bleeding on the porch, in the fetal position. He stuck the knife in my hand. James pushed through the door and kicked me again, knocking me off the porch and into the yard. James was acting like a mad man. When James came off the porch to continue attacking me, Marcus ran past him, opened the door and picked Sandra up off the floor.

She was screaming and sitting in a pool of my blood. As soon as James turned his attention to what Marcus was doing, I stabbed him with the knife in his upper back. He fell forward, screaming and bleeding profusely from his wound. Marcus ran out of the house with Sandra. He helped me up and he and I ran back to Mothers' house.

We arrived at Mother's house exhausted and in a panic. Marcus took Sandra into his room to try to quiet her and I went into the bathroom to clean myself up and try to stop the bleeding from my forehead. I had bruises over my face and arms and my eyes were beginning to turn black. The gash on my forehead looked really deep and I couldn't stop the bleeding. I tried pressing towels on it, but my head was hurting very badly. Marcus knocked on the door and brought me a sandwich bag with ice in it. I sat down on the toilet lid crying and pressing the bag of ice wrapped in a towel on my forehead. My clothes were covered with blood.

I had been in the bathroom for a while, when I heard a loud knock at the front door. I jumped up off the toilet, scared and afraid to come out of the bathroom. I had no idea who it was at the front door. Suddenly the bathroom door burst open, startling me. I jumped, dropping the ice wrap on the floor. It was the police. Two armed police officers stood at the bathroom door.

"Are you Priscilla Gibson?" one officer asked.

"Yes," I said as I reached down to pick up my ice wrap.

"Did you stab James Gibson?" the officer asked.

"Yes, but I was defending myself. He stole my baby and he was beating me up," I said through tears.

Unfazed by what I was saying, or how I looked, the officer said, "You're under arrest for stabbing your husband James Gibson."

"But he was trying to kill me!" I screamed out, confused about what was happening.

The officer pulled out his handcuffs and cuffed me. After he cuffed me, the other officer turned me around and looked at my bloody clothes and at the gash on my forehead.

"Hmm," he said looking at his partner. Marcus stood watching with tears in his eyes and holding Sandra in his arms. I yelled to Marcus to take care of my baby as the officers led me out of the house and into the police car. I sat crying in the back seat with blood dripping in my eyes as we drove off. I wondered why I wasn't offered medical attention since it was clear that I had been beaten up and I had an open wound in my forehead; that was still bleeding. But, neither offered and I didn't ask questions. I was scared and I didn't say a word.

We arrived at the St. Louis County Jail, Precinct 11. The room was dirty and crowded. The officers took me over to a window with a female officer standing behind it. I was told to have a seat on the bench in front of the window. After a short wait, the female officer asked me to verify my name and address. She removed my handcuffs and she had me empty my pockets. Then she gave me some paper towels to clean myself up and offered me a cold compress. I was grateful because everyone else was ignoring me. Once I was cleaned up she put me in a holding cell with a lot of strange looking people, both male and female. I was scared to death because I had never been to jail before. I worried that I had killed James and that I was going to the gas chamber for murder. I cried softly to myself, very remorseful for hurting James; I just wanted my baby back.

The cell had three benches, one long bench against each wall, and all three were full of people. More people were sitting on the floor and leaning against the walls. After inconspicuously looking around, I moved to the back of the cell and stood in the corner. The conversations I heard around me were horrifying. There were prostitutes talking about johns they had been with and they were being very graphic; some people saying they didn't do what they were accused of; that it wasn't them that robbed that old lady or the liquor store. There were a few people that acted like they had mental issues, screaming and talking to themselves and slobbering down their chin. The conversation that scared me the most was from a man talking about how he had just raped someone. He was arrogant and cocky and talked explicitly about how he did it; and how it made him feel good to hear her scream and try to fight him. It was frightening and sickening.

People came and went all night in that cell; I was glad when the rapist left. No officer had come back to talk to me and it felt like I had been there for hours. I was scared I was going to be in jail for the rest of my life and I wasn't going to see either of my girls again. I was sure by now Valencia was wondering where I was. I thought I could get Sandra, and be able to get back to Ms. Grace's house to pick up Valencia before it got late. I had no idea I would be arrested for stabbing my husband. I stood alone in the corner, cold and worrying. I thought about Sandra. She had gotten so big. I hoped she remembered me. I wondered what they had done to my baby in that crazy house. My mind had so many thoughts running through it. I slid down on the floor in the corner and sat quietly. I didn't move or say anything to anyone.

Nearly eleven hours later an officer finally called my name. I walked to the cell door. "Priscilla Gibson, you're free to go."

"Huh?" I said as I approached the cell door.

"You're free to go miss; no charges are being filed against you. Go check out over there," he said, pointing to a desk at the other end of the room. Shocked to be leaving the jail, I walked to the desk where a clerk processed me out. I was given back my ID and the little bit of money I had in my pocket when I was arrested, then I walked out of the police station.

It was past midnight and the buses had stopped running, so I started walking the twelve blocks back to my mother's house. On the way, I stopped at a liquor store and bought a 6-pack of Colt 45. My head was still hurting and I hoped having a drink would make it feel better. I bleeding had finally stopped. I finished half my 6-pack by the time I made it to Mother's house. I sat outside on the step to finish another can of beer before going inside. It was after 3 a.m. and quiet and peaceful outside on the warm summer night. I sat drinking and listening to the crickets chirp and watching the lightening bugs fly around making the sky look as though it was sparkling.

CHAPTER 10

I didn't remember coming in the house last night. I was asleep on the couch when I felt a slap on my face. I woke up groggy and saw Mother standing over me.

"I thought I told you not to come back to my house," she said harshly. I didn't say a word. I rubbed the sleep out of my eyes and sat up. My body hurt badly and I had a bad headache.

"I see you got your ass beat," she commented with a smirk on her face. I got up off the couch and went into Marcus' room. It was early, so he was still asleep. Sandra lay beside him, asleep also. I picked her up and left the house without waking him up or saying anything to Mother. I rode the bus back home.

I rested at home for a couple of days before going back to work. My boss was nice enough to let me off after I told him what happened. I was worried about James. He stayed on my mind all the time. Despite everything, I still loved him and I needed to know how he was doing or if I had killed him. I went to a pay phone and called St. Mary's County Hospital on Clayton Road, where I thought they had probably taken him. I was wrong. I called the Homer G. Phillips Hospital and found out that's where he was. I asked for his room number and was told that James was in ICU. Worried, but relieved that I hadn't killed him, I decided to go to the hospital to visit him. Ms. Grace was kind enough to watch both girls that afternoon. I was embarrassed for her to see my face the way it was. She didn't ask what happened to me, she just gave me a comforting hug. I left her house and rode the bus to the hospital.

I arrived at the hospital, scared and nervous. All kinds of worries had been running through my mind as to whether he was paralyzed or worse. I felt so remorseful for stabbing him. I took the elevator up to ICU. When I got off the elevator, I followed the signs to the ICU ward and then asked a nurse where James Gibson was. She looked at me strangely, noticing the bruises on my face and my two black eyes. Without questioning me, she pointed to James through a glass window. James lay still in his bed with a lot of tubes coming from his body. I stood outside the glass looking at him and crying.

"He almost died," a nurse said as she noticed me staring at James through the glass.

"Another inch and the knife would have hit his heart," she continued. I didn't tell her I was his wife and the one responsible for him lying there fighting for his life. I stayed a while longer, silently praying for him, then I left.

A few days later, I came back to the hospital to visit James. I was happy to see him out of ICU and in his own room. I walked in his room to find him sitting in a wheelchair looking out the window.

"What you doing here?" he asked when he saw me walk through the door.

"I came to see how you were doing, this is my second time here," I responded.

James looked surprised that I had been here before.

"I told the police I didn't want to press charges against you. You owe me," he said, staring at me. I looked back at him without commenting.

"You know the best part of my hospital stay is the morphine," he said smiling. "That's some good stuff. All I got to say is I'm in pain and the nurses come shoot me with some. Ooh, I love it." I ignored his comment and sat down in the chair.

I stayed a while talking with James about what happened and why it happened. I wanted to get an understanding why he ran away with Sandra in the first place. He said he was mad because I wouldn't let Sandra go over to his grandmother's house anymore.

"My grandmother said she wanted to raise Sandra." He continued. That made me cringe. We discussed our relationship. By the time I left the hospital that evening, James and I had decided to get back together.

CHAPTER 11

James and I moved into an apartment in one of the hoods of East St. Louis. Living in this neighborhood was very tough, but it was all we could afford. There were a lot of robberies and shootings; and abandoned houses or buildings that housed people strung out on drugs or alcohol. Prostitutes and drug pushers were on every corner, and gang members were fighting and killing for turf rights. Every day we lived in this neighborhood was a challenge; there seemed to be some sort of drama every day. And if someone didn't get killed, we were wondering what was wrong.

James and I continued to have problems. He had become increasingly violent and abusive. I had to quit my job at the sandwich shop because we moved too far away. Fortunately, I found a job at a chicken factory picking feathers off chickens. James still hadn't found a job. He kept saying he would find one to help me with the bills, but he never did. The only job James had was staying home and getting high all day, every day. It was hard for me to work long hours, come home, take care of the girls and maintain the house and bills with an abusive junkie for a husband.

I took my lunch to work every day to save money, and every day I'd fill my thermos with Vodka. Vodka didn't have a smell or color so I didn't have to worry about getting caught. I made sure nobody suspected I was drinking while I was at work. I needed it; it helped me get through the day and relaxed my nerves by the time I got home to deal with James.

Every time payday rolled around, James had his hand stuck out. And every dime he took from me he put up his nose or shot up his veins. The more I worked, the poorer we got. We never had any money because every payday James would beat me up and take my check. He was driving me crazy. I drank everyday just to be able to deal with him. The more we fought, the more I drank.

Angelic Temple Apostolic Church was around the corner from our apartment. The girls and I would walk to church on Sundays and went to Bible study on Wednesdays. I would go to church whether I had been drinking or not. We really enjoyed church and anything was better than staying at home with James. I loved the Lord and wanted to learn more about Him. James hated for me to go to church. Whenever I got ready to go, he would say anything to ridicule me or to provoke a fight. He'd make fun of what I was wearing or tell me I was ugly. He would tell me that the Lord didn't care anything about me because if He did, I wouldn't be poor, black and ugly. If he was real high, he wouldn't let me go to church at all and if I tried to go anyway he would beat me up and choke me until I was almost unconscious. I couldn't understand how James had grown up in the church, and had a daddy who was a Preacher and have no desire to worship the Lord. He said he hated the Lord and he was never going to set foot inside another church again; he never explained to me why he was mad at God. My guess was that he prayed to become a famous musician and God didn't bless him to be one, so he was mad. I believed all the drugs James was taking was preventing him from becoming a musician. He couldn't stay focused, he was never on time for anything, and he couldn't remember things. I know the drugs were hurting his voice, because he was beginning to sound raspy. The only thing James ever wanted to be was a musician. That's all he ever talked about. He claimed he was looking for music gigs all the time, but he never found one.

"I think I would have a better chance of finding a job with a band, if we moved to California," he said to me one night just as I walked in the house from work. Before I could put my purse down and take off my jacket, he started telling me about the advantages of living in California.

"My Aunt Betty lives in Santa Barbara. She's my daddy's sister and my favorite aunt. I know she'll let us live with her and my uncle for a while until we get on our feet," he continued.

"I know we would have a better life and I'd be making a lot of money." I didn't comment, I just went right in the kitchen and started fixing dinner. I was tired and half listening.

Later that week James and I had another fight because he sold the television and the toaster. It was a week before payday and I had no money. James needed a fix and thought I was lying about not having any money so he decided to give me a black eye and bloody nose.

I was lying about not having any money, but I knew if I gave it to him, I wouldn't be able to pay the rent on the first. I couldn't let us get evicted, so I lied. After he beat me up he left the house, like he usually did. This time, I didn't hear from him for over three months. It wasn't until I received a letter from him that I found out he had left St. Louis right after our fight three months ago and moved to Santa Barbara with his aunt. He was living with his Aunt Barbara and his Uncle Matlock. I was surprised by the letter, but even more surprised that James actually moved to California. "Baby, I love you. I miss you and the girls," he wrote in his letter. "I want ya'll to come to California to be with me," he continued. James wrote things in his three-page letter that for a moment took me back to when we first met. Back to when he would write love letters and poems to me that would melt my heart. Words that made me fall in love with him. His words were so poetic, just like the lyrics in a love song. They reminded me how much I loved him, despite everything we had been through. I agreed to move to California. I know things are going to be better between us when I get there. I planned to ride the bus to California with the girls after I received my last paycheck from the chicken factory.

I told the landlord that I would be moving at the end of the month. It was no surprise that someone else was prepared to move in as soon as I moved out. In this neighborhood, the apartments rented fast because the rent was so cheap. The only downfall was the drugs, the murders and the robberies.

I got butterflies in my stomach at the thought of living in California. I pictured it as being very beautiful with lots of palm trees – far different from St. Louis. I packed what clothes I could carry and sold as much of our furniture as I could to people in the neighborhood. Anything left, I left in the apartment.

The day we left, I packed chicken sandwiches and drinks to help with the thirty-seven hour bus ride. The girls and I took a taxi to the

Greyhound bus station downtown. Four-year-old Valencia and three-year-old Sandra were able to help carry some of the lighter bags that we had. We had one bag with food in it, one with diapers, one with drinks and one bag with clothes in it. We were loaded down. Once we finally got settled into our seats, everything went smoothly. The ride was nice and comfortable. I didn't have any trouble with the girls crying or squirming in the seat. Valencia had her own seat, but I held Sandra in my lap. I couldn't afford three bus tickets. I had been up since 5 a.m. getting ready for our long journey so I was exhausted.

I relaxed in my seat and turned to look out the window. The mountains were very beautiful. I had never seen mountains before. The scenery was like something out of a Norman Rockwall painting. I continued to gaze out of the window at the beautiful autumn colors. The deserts were beautiful; they seemed to have a sense of serenity about them. The closer we got to California the more excited I got. I finally fell asleep.

James met us at the bus station with his Aunt Betty who drove her van to pick us up. I was exhausted from the long bus ride. It had been next to impossible to get a good night's sleep sitting upright, holding one child on my lap, while the other one leaned against my arm. My body was stiff and needed a good stretching.

I was happy to see James. I tried to hug him when I saw him, but he was too busy trying to take Sandra out of my arms. He introduced me to his Aunt Betty and I introduced Aunt Betty to Sandra and Valencia. Aunt Betty was a short heavyset woman with hazel eyes. She seemed to be a very kind person. She grabbed Valencia's hand and led her to the van, having friendly conversation with her along the way. James handed Sandra back to me and went to get our bags. After loading everything in Aunt Betty's van, we headed for her house.

As we pulled into Aunt Betty's driveway, I marveled at her beautifully, well-manicured yard, noting the difference from the dirt and patchy grass yards of our old neighborhood. The quietness of the neighborhood also struck me; a far change from the sirens and gunshot sounds that we were used to hearing. I think James was right, our lives would be better in California.

CHAPTER 12

Living with Aunt Betty and Uncle Matlock was *certainly* a change. James and I stayed in one of their upstairs bedrooms. The girls shared the bedroom next to ours. Aunt Betty loved the girls and she spent a lot of time with them and also with me. At times, I pretended she was my mother.

Aunt Betty had three kids of her own, two sons and one daughter. They had all grown up and moved away from home, starting their own families. Aunt Betty talked about her two granddaughters all the time. I got the impression that she didn't see them very often. I believed the kids and I helped fill the void she felt from missing her children and her grandchildren. I wondered why they didn't visit very often.

I loved Aunt Betty's cooking and she loved to cook. Every Sunday after church, we had Sunday dinner. Her specialty was neck bones with potatoes and cabbage and cornbread – the kind of cornbread that looked like pound cake. It was delicious and my favorite. Aunt Betty would spend time in the kitchen with me and the girls baking cookies and cakes. She taught me how to cook *real* soul food meals.

James' presence had become scarce around the house. I hardly ever saw him. When I first moved to California, James and I had been inseparable. Now most days, I didn't know where he was. Late one night when he finally came home, I asked him where he had been. James hit me on my jaw, threw me on the bed and almost choked the life out of me.

"Don't you ever ask me where I've been or anything about my business!" he whispered in my ear with his hand still around my neck. I guess he didn't want Aunt Betty or Uncle Matlock to hear him beating me up. Looking into his glassy, bloodshot eyes, I struggled to nod my head through the death grip that he had around my neck. Tears trickled down my face and rolled into my ears as he continued to cut off my air supply. Finally, he let me up. Then he walked out of the room. I sat up and cried softly because I didn't want Aunt Betty or Uncle Matlock to hear me. We had been here for two months and not had one fight; I hadn't even had a drink. I had believed things were going to be different, but James seemed to have picked up his old habits.

The following morning I asked Aunt Betty to take me to the welfare office to apply for welfare and food stamps. I had waited on James to get a job to take care of us, but he didn't and Aunt Betty was doing everything for us. I appreciated what she was doing, but I needed to have my own money to take care of my own kids. According to California law, welfare recipients received their checks twice a month and that was perfectly alright with me.

It felt good to have my own money coming in. Aunt Betty wasn't charging us rent to live with her, but I felt the need to give her something. She had been so kind to us and I didn't want her to feel as though we were taking advantage of her. I gave most of my food stamps to her and a portion of my welfare check. When James found out I was getting a check, I had to give some to him too. I secretly saved what I had left in a shoebox in the closet.

On an afternoon that Aunt Betty had gone to one of her church meetings and the girls were taking a nap, Uncle Matlock knocked on my bedroom door. I was lying across my bed looking at a magazine. I got up and opened the door. Uncle Matlock was standing in the doorway looking at me with a weird look on his face.

"I want to have sex with you," he blurted out, "right now before your Aunt gets back."

I jumped back, shocked at the boldness of Uncle Matlock.

"Are you crazy? I'm not having sex with you!" I shouted.

"Yes, you are!" he said with certainty. He unzipped his pants and exposed himself.

"I'm not leaving until you have sex with me or you ain't gonna live in my house!" Uncle Matlock let his pants drop down to his ankles, fully exposing himself.

I suddenly had an instant memory of the rape when I was eleven.

I started shaking and crying. "No!" I screamed. "Get away from me. I'm getting out of this house!" I grabbed my purse off the dresser and pushed my way past him to get my girls from their room. Uncle Matlock tried to grab my arm. I swatted his hand away.

"Leave me alone!" I yelled. I grabbed the stroller from my girls' closet and headed down the stairs with my kids. I was in such a panic that I lost my grip on the stroller and it tumbled down the stairs making a loud noise and scratching the wall along the way. In a frenzy, I dragged my girls down the stairs faster than they could walk. Uncle Matlock pulled his pants up and came running down the stairs after me. He grabbed my arm again and said, "If you tell Betty or James, I'll lie and say I put you out because you tried to come on to me! Who do you think they'll believe?" I looked at him with tears in my eyes and snatched my arm out of his grip. I pushed the stroller out the front door and quickly pushed it down the street.

I walked a few blocks with my girls until I came upon a park. I sat on the park bench and I let the girls play. It took me a minute to catch my breath once I sat down. They looked so innocent and carefree as they played on the merry-go-round. I sat trying to remember a time when I ever felt carefree. My life always seemed to have disaster in it. I sat crying and wondering what Aunt Betty would think. I guess she would believe Uncle Matlock because after all, he was her husband and they had been married for over 30 years. I wondered what James would say. I figured he would believe Uncle Matlock and beat me up.

I let the girls play a little longer then reluctantly decided to head back to the house. The streetlights had come on and night was nearing. I started getting scared. The anxiety of being unsure of what to expect when I got back to the house was taking a toll on me. I started getting bad feelings about what was going to happen when I got back. Fortunately, I had a few dollars in my purse, so I stopped at a nearby corner market. I bought the girls a soda and some chips and I bought a forty ounce bottle of beer. We walked and drank. I wished I had had enough money to buy some stronger liquor because my nerves were shattered. I didn't have enough time to grab my shoebox of money in the closet with Uncle Matlock bothering me. I started crying again.

James was home when I got there.

"Where you been?" he asked, as I walked through the front door. He had been sitting on the couch in the living room watching television. I started to cry as I headed for our room. James followed me upstairs.

"Where have you been?" he asked again grabbing my arm and turning me to face him.

Nervously, I answered, "I left the house because Uncle Matlock tried to make me have sex with him."

"What?" James shouted. "What did you do?" I looked at James strangely, annoyed at the question.

"I told him no and to leave me alone! Me and the girls left the house and went to the park."

"Aunt Betty!" James called out. "Aunt Betty come here!" he yelled angrily. I got scared and started shaking.

Aunt Betty came into the room in a panic, with a frantic look on her face.

"What is it?" she asked, nearly out of breath from running into the room. James told her what Uncle Matlock had done. I stood there crying unsure how she would react. To our surprise, Aunt Betty wasn't surprised.

"Your Uncle Matlock has a problem," she said, after taking a deep breath. "Obviously, when I shot him two years ago for messing with our granddaughter, he didn't get the message. Maybe I should have killed him." She said to me somberly, "I'm sorry, baby. Are you alright?"

James and I looked at each other with bewildered looks on our faces. We couldn't believe that this sweet lady that we had lived with for over six months knew her husband was a pedophile and sexual predator; had shot him and stayed married to him; but didn't feel the need to share this information with us.

"He babysat my kids!" James screamed. "We're leaving! Tonight! Get our stuff, Priscilla, so we can go!"

I started gathering as much stuff as we could carry and put it in trash bags that I had ran to the kitchen to get. I stuffed my shoe box with my money in it down in my purse. Aunt Betty pleaded with us not to go, but James was so mad that she couldn't change his mind.

"That's why none of your kids come to visit and you don't see your grandkids; because Uncle Matlock is a sick nasty bastard!" James said furiously.

Aunt Betty went into her bedroom and shut the door. James and I headed down the stairs with our bags and the girls. We didn't know where we were going; we just knew we had to leave. Uncle Matlock was sitting in his easy chair watching television, pretending to ignore us.

"I can't believe you tried to mess with my wife, you sick bastard!" James shouted as we headed out the door. Uncle Matlock stared at us without saying a word, a far cry from what he had threatened to say earlier.

James, the girls and I walked several blocks before finding the Sunny Sands Motel. Our arms were tired from carrying all those bags. The girls were tired of walking and were beginning to whine.

Surprisingly, James had enough money for the night's stay. Unfortunately, I had to tell him I had saved over $200 from my welfare checks. He looked at me hatefully. We used most of the money to pay for an extended stay at the motel.

"I knew you were a liar," he said as we walked to our room.

Room 135, on the ground floor, was our room. It was in the back of the building near the laundry room. The room looked like an efficiency apartment. It had a full size bed, a sitting area with a hide-a-way couch, a chair, a television, a small stove and a table that seated two. *Where was the refrigerator? I wondered.*

After we got settled in, James decided he was leaving. I was tempted to ask where he was going, but I remembered what happened the last time I asked. So, I didn't say a word. He took $20 from my purse and left. I put the girls to bed on the hide-away couch after I had given them a bath and then I climbed into bed. I didn't like being alone in the motel with the kids. I heard too many sounds outside the door that scared me.

Around 4 a.m. James came back to the motel. He staggered his way through the door smelling of marijuana and liquor. He climbed into bed, pulled my gown off and had sex with me. Then he fell asleep.

The next morning James got up and said he was going to buy us a refrigerator. The manager of the motel told us they didn't provide refrigerators because the neighborhood junkies kept breaking in the rooms and stealing them. I couldn't understand how someone could steal a large refrigerator without getting caught. The manager told James we could find an inexpensive refrigerator at the thrift store around the corner. James walked to the thrift store and bought a small refrigerator for $50. He had no one to help him get the refrigerator back to the motel, so he borrowed the store dolly and pushed it to the motel himself. I opened the motel door to watch for James to come back with the refrigerator. The breeze that came through the door felt good. I let the girls play on the sidewalk in front of our room while we waited. James turned the corner pushing the refrigerator. He was breathing hard and sweating profusely. By the time he made it to the motel door, James collapsed. "Daddy!" the girls screamed simultaneously. I screamed for help as he lay on the ground in excruciating pain. I ran back into the room to call an ambulance.

"Help! My husband fell out, he's in a lot of pain!" I yelled in the phone. "Please send an ambulance, hurry!" We all were crying as James lay in a fetal position on the ground, moaning. Me and the girls crowded around him, hoping to comfort him in some way.

The ambulance came within a few minutes. The paramedics loaded James in the ambulance without giving me any idea as to why he collapsed. "We'll be taking him to San Bernardino County Medical Center," is all they told me before they drove off. I was scared for James; I thought he was going to die.

The people standing around the motel room watching all the drama, finally dispersed back into their rooms after the ambulance left. The motel manager stayed to help me get the refrigerator the rest of the way into our room. He gave his regards to my husband and wished him well. He also offered to drive the girls and me to the hospital. I gratefully accepted his offer.

When we arrived at the hospital, the receptionist told me that James was in surgery. He had suffered a ruptured appendix. She took us to the waiting room, where we waited 4 hours before we were able to see him. After James was moved to his hospital room, the nurse came to get us. When we entered his room, he was asleep in his bed.

The nurse told me it might be awhile before he wakes up because the anesthesia had to wear off.

James didn't have a roommate, so I put the girls in the other bed and let them watch television. I sat in the chair next to James' bed and waited for him to wake up. I called Aunt Betty to tell her he was in the hospital. James woke up a little over an hour later. He said he was in a lot of pain. He buzzed the nurse to have them bring him some pain pills. That night the girls and I spent the night at the hospital.

The next morning the doctor came in and checked on James and said he needed to stay in the hospital for at least three more days. I took the girls back to the motel for a bath and a change clothes and then came back. We stayed with James every night at the hospital. I didn't want to stay at the motel by myself.

James complained so much about his pain that the doctor put him on a dose of pain pills every four hours.

"The pain pills are the best part of the hospital stay," he boasted. *I had heard that before, I thought to myself.* I was beginning to believe James enjoyed being in the hospital, at least here he didn't have to spend money for his drugs. The day of his release the doctor sent him home with a prescription for pain medicine with three refills.

CHAPTER 13

After three months in the motel, James moved us into our own apartment off East 109th Street in Watts near Imperial Courts; about sixty miles from Aunt Betty's house. Aunt Betty was so remorseful about what Uncle Matlock had done, so she gave us the money to move into our own place. She even helped us get furniture and let us use her van.

James' drug use had gotten worse. He had taken a lot of the electronic items in the house and sold them for drugs. He hardly came home unless it was the first or the fifteenth of the month when he knew my welfare check would be there. Because I had lied about saving money before, he never believed me when I said I didn't have any money. He beat me up and made me give him the money. Sometimes, I would endure the beatings; other times the beatings were so severe that I gave in and gave him the money. I was so tired of James, his drug habit and the beatings. I started drinking again. The stress of my toxic relationship with James really caused me to drink more. I had to drink something every day.

One night, James came home about midnight. My shoulders tensed up and my head started hurting. Whenever he came home, I became irritated and felt sick to my stomach. I was much happier when he wasn't around and when he stayed away for long periods of time. James appeared to be strung-out, as usual. I was asleep in the bed when he threw a cup of water up my nose and woke me up. I jumped out the bed unsure of what was happening. "Where's the money?" he demanded standing over me.

"What money? I don't have any money," I said scared and still trying to catch my breath from the water he threw up my nose.

James grabbed the collar of the yellow gown I was wearing and pulled me towards him. "I know you're lying. Now give me the money!" he demanded again. James let go of my gown and started searching around the room for money. He grabbed my purse and emptied it out on the bed, then he looked in the closets and in the dresser drawers. He looked like a crazed lunatic, searching everywhere like a mad man.

"I don't have any money! We don't even have food in the refrigerator or diapers for Sandra. I *don't have* any money," I kept insisting.

James slapped my face and ripped my gown. "Then you're gonna get dressed and get out there in the streets and make me some money!" I jumped out of the bed and ran into the kitchen. James followed me to the kitchen and punched me in the face. "You think I'm going to let you stab me again?" he yelled. Then, he hit me again and knocked me to the floor. James reached in the drawer and pulled out a knife. He sat on top of me as I lay on the floor holding my face. Starring down at me, he held the knife to my throat. In a soft, mocking voice he said, "Yolanda, next door, is a better lover than you. She's prettier and she's skinnier. You're fat and ugly and nobody will ever want you, not even me!" Then he pressed the knife into my skin and slit my throat from ear to ear. Blood poured from my throat. Then, James jumped up off me and ran out the front door. I could not believe what he had just done. The pain was incredible and blood was everywhere. I stumbled to the telephone and called Aunt Betty. Her 20-year-old granddaughter, Nicole, answered the telephone.

"This is Priscilla. Is Aunt Betty at home?"

"No, she's not here. What's wrong, you sound funny."

"James just cut my throat. Please help me. Can you please come take me to the hospital?" I begged as I held a towel to my throat. I was in a lot of pain and losing a lot of blood. I grabbed another dishtowel and pressed it against my throat. Blood had soaked the first towel and was dripping on everything.

It seemed like it took Nicole forever to get to my house. When she finally arrived and saw the blood soaked towels around my neck and the blood all over the furniture and the floor she panicked. Nicole helped me off the couch and out of the house and into her Volkswagen. She sped off to Martin Luther King Hospital, running red lights along the way with her car horn blaring. When we arrived at the emergency room entrance, Nicole jumped out of the car while it was still running and ran inside to find a doctor. Two nurses came running out, one pushing a wheel chair. They both helped me out of the car, into the wheel chair and inside the hospital. I was taken immediately into an exam room. The doctor removed the blood soaked towels and examined my neck. James had cut my throat within an inch of my jugular vein. The doctor put 19 stitches in my throat and said I was lucky to be alive.

The police were called to the hospital to investigate the incident. Afraid to press charges against James for fear that the next time he really would kill me, I told the police it was an accident.

"James and I fight all the time," I said, "but he wasn't really trying to kill me." I was amazed that they believed me and decided not to pursue any charges against James.

The hospital released me that same night. My throat was bandaged and I had instructions to come back in ten days to get the stitches out. Nicole and the girls were waiting for me in the emergency waiting room. Nicole apologized for being in such a panic and leaving the girls at the house. "After the nurses took you to the back, it dawned on me that we had left the girls asleep at home, so I went back to get them," she explained, "and they were still asleep in their beds." I assured her I wasn't upset. I was in too much pain to think about anything else. I was glad the doctor had given me a shot for the pain and hoped that it would kick in soon.

My throat hurt very badly and it was difficult for me to swallow. I lay on my blood-stained couch and tried to rest, but the replay of the fight with James kept playing in my head; and remembering the crazed look in his eyes before he cut my throat was something I didn't want to remember. Nicole stayed the night with me. I was glad, because I couldn't sleep at all and it was hard to get the girls back to sleep. Nicole played with the girls until they got tired and then she put them back to bed. Aunt Betty came by later to see how I was doing. She cleaned up the blood that was all over the kitchen and the living room. I took a few more of the pain pills; my pain seemed to be getting worse. *What was wrong with James? I wondered.* I was hurt that James was having an affair with Yolanda, my next door neighbor, right under my nose. She was supposed to be my friend. She was always over at our house, she babysat my kids on occasion, and we would sit and talk for hours. I would tell her all my business about James. I finally cried myself to sleep near dawn.

I went to the hospital to get my stitches out ten days later. The cut left a permanent scar on my neck. I certainly was not happy about that. For the rest of my life, people would know that my husband tried to kill me by slitting my throat. I hadn't seen James since the night of our fight. I wondered if he knew I was alive.

The following week when I got my welfare check, I moved back to St. Louis. I took what I could carry on the bus and left the rest in the house. I didn't even tell the landlord I was leaving.

When we finally arrived in St. Louis, the girls and I lived in a cheap motel for a few weeks. I went to visit Ms. Grace. She was glad to see her granddaughter and she agreed to watch both girls again when I found a job. I really appreciated that. Ms. Grace had been retired for some time now so she was always available to watch the kids for me. Fortunately, my old boss at the sandwich shop let me come back and he paid me under the table again, just like before. I quickly saved enough money to move out of the motel and into the Webbe Projects on Chouteau Avenue. Things seemed to be getting back on track. I found out through an old friend that Marcus had enlisted in the Army and was overseas. I was sad that I couldn't see him. I didn't know where my mother or my sisters were, but I did find out that my three other brothers were all in prison.

I finally called Aunt Betty from a pay phone near my house. I was sorry to hear that she had been diagnosed with ovarian cancer. She said she believed in God for her healing and she was going to do all she could to beat the cancer. We prayed together over the telephone. I gave her my new address and assured her I would keep in touch. After I hung up the pay phone, I walked to the liquor store and bought a bottle of wine and some beer. I sat at home drinking on the front steps of my apartment with a few of my neighbors.

I had been in my apartment for about two months when I got an unexpected knock at my door. I opened the door to find James standing on my doorstep.

"Priscilla!" he yelled with enthusiasm. He reached out his arms to hug me, but I didn't hug him back.

"How did you find me?" I asked with my hands on my hips, blocking the entrance into my apartment.

"You're my wife! I can find you anywhere," he said, sounding cocky. I figured he must have gotten my address from Aunt Betty.

I was so shocked to see him that I couldn't find any words to reply. My stomach knotted up just as it had done the last few times I saw him.

"Aren't you going to let your husband in?" he asked. I wasn't sure if I wanted to let him in or not, but before I could answer he pushed his way past me into the apartment.

"Daddy, Daddy!" Sandra called out when he walked through the door. She ran to him. James picked her up and gave her a big hug. I noticed he was dressed up and he looked really good, like he had gotten some rest and was off the drugs. He even had cut his afro down low and it was picked out very neatly. I still didn't know what to make of him showing up so I didn't comment on his appearance or anything.

"I missed you and the girls," he said as he walked over to hug Valencia, who was sitting on the couch watching cartoons. "If you take me back, I'll do better. I'll be a better husband."

"Uh huh," I said, as I closed the door.

"I promise," James continued. "Guess what? I joined the National Guard," he said smiling. *I knew something had to change for him to cut that big afro, I thought.* "I joined last month."

"Uh huh," I said.

I was glad James was finally doing something positive with his life, but it was just too late for us. I was sick and tired of him and I really didn't care what he was doing. Besides, he hadn't even said anything about slitting my throat, nor did he apologize. Irritated, I walked to the refrigerator and took out a can of beer. James sat on the couch talking and playing with the girls. I sat down at the kitchen table and started drinking my beer, wondering when he was going to leave.

James ended up spending the night, and the night after that, and the night after that. I didn't want him to be in the house with us, but I was too afraid to try to make him leave. Eventually, we fell into an unspoken agreement that we were back together. He never left my apartment. He never left for the National Guard, either, and we never discussed him cutting my throat.

CHAPTER 14

James stressed me out so much. His mere presence in the room upset me. *Why won't he leave, I wondered, why can't he just go away?* He soon fell back into his old habit of doing drugs. I found myself drinking a fifth of Hennessey a day, I was depressed.

For the past few days, I hadn't been feeling well. I had been bleeding for about three days. At first, I thought it was my period, but I started flowing so heavily I became unsure if it was my period or if something else was wrong. Another week went by and I was still bleeding. I was too weak to go to work. Then, one day, I blacked out at home. When I woke up, I was in the hospital. I had bled so much that my blood level was low which caused me to faint. James had called an ambulance when he found me on the living room floor. The doctor couldn't explain why I was bleeding, but he did tell me I was four months pregnant. I was totally shocked. I would have shared the news with James, but I hadn't seen him since the day I came to the hospital. He never came to visit; and I was worried about my girls.

The nurse inserted an IV in my arm because I was dehydrated, and told me I needed to stay in the hospital for a few days so that they could monitor me and make sure the baby was alright. I didn't really want to stay, but I didn't contest it. The nurse hooked me to a fetal monitor and told me to relax. I laid back in the bed listening to my baby's heartbeat and wondering where James and the girls were; and how they were doing. I had finally gotten a telephone in my apartment, but I couldn't call home because James spent the money on drugs and didn't pay the phone bill.

The following morning, the doctor did another gynecological exam and re-checked my lab work. "You didn't have enough fluids in your body and your blood count was low," he told me. "Your alcohol level was high, also," he continued. I just looked at him. "How much do you drink?" he asked.

"I drink a little, not much at all," I lied, looking away and not wanting to answer the question.

"Since you're pregnant, you shouldn't drink at all," the doctor stated.

I looked at him again. "I'm not going to drink while I'm pregnant," I said, offended that he felt the need to tell me this. I knew it would be difficult for me not to want to have a drink while I was pregnant, but I could do it. It wasn't like I was an alcoholic.

I left the hospital later that afternoon, and rode the bus back to my apartment. The bus let me off down the street from where I lived, so I walked the rest of the way. I lived in a lower class neighborhood where the people were friendly. More often than not, people were willing to lend a hand if they felt that you needed it.

As I approached my apartment, I could hear music and voices outside the door. I frowned and immediately got irritated. I opened the door to find a party going on in my apartment. James had about five to six people in my apartment, drinking, dancing and doing lines of coke on a mirror on top of my kitchen table. I said nothing to James, who was leaning back in the living room chair looking spaced out. I elbowed my way through the house looking for my girls. I saw a woman sitting on my couch with a necktie tied around her upper arm and a needle on the cushion beside her. Other people were dancing around the house to the music. Either they didn't notice me when I came into the apartment or they just didn't care.

I found the girls playing with dolls in the bedroom on the floor. They looked like they hadn't had a bath in days, and their hair was nappy and uncombed. They had on the same clothes they had worn the day I went to the hospital. I was relieved that they were alright, but I was mad at James. I stayed in the room for a while with the girls before I came out and made the people leave. James got upset, cussed me out and called me names, but I didn't care. He left with his friends.

I started cleaning up my apartment. Marijuana butts and cigarette butts filled all the ashtrays in the house. There were cigarette ashes all over the floor as well as burn holes in my furniture. Liquor bottles were scattered all around the house like decorative vases. I filled a garbage bag with empty beer cans, liquor bottles and trash.

After the house was clean, I gave the girls a bath and washed and combed their hair. Then I laid them down for a nap. I laid down on the couch to take a nap, also. I was very tired. The doctor had given me medication to stop the bleeding, but it made me sleepy and I still wasn't feeling very well. The girls and I napped until late that night; we woke up around ten o'clock. I got up and fixed them something to eat. James hadn't come home yet.

After four days of being at home, I felt well enough to go back to work at the sandwich shop. I called my boss at the shop to make sure it was okay to return to work the next day. After giving me the okay, I called Ms. Grace to let her know I was bringing the girls tomorrow. James still hadn't come home which was okay with me.

It was good getting back to work. I didn't realize how much I had missed it. A few of our regular customers wondered where I had been, since I rarely missed work. "I had a family emergency," I told them. I didn't tell them I was the emergency, a pregnant emergency.

"I hate when you're not here, I like the way you make my sandwich," one customer said. "You make better sandwiches than anyone else here," another said. I felt so appreciated. I had a knack for remembering my customer's names and remembering what my customers liked. They thought that was impressive, especially when they came in and I greeted them by their name. I always added a little extra meat, cheese, onions or whatever they liked to their sandwich. I would also put something extra in their bag, like a cookie or an extra pickle. It made them feel special and it kept them coming back to the sandwich shop. My boss loved me for my great customer service.

One of my favorite customers was Evangelist Johnson. She loved pastrami on rye with lettuce, lots of onions, black olives, vinegar and oil and no mayo. She hated mayonnaise. Evangelist Johnson was the church secretary at Angelic Temple, a nearby church that the girls and I had started attending a few months earlier. She befriended me one Sunday while the girls and I were at the church.

Evangelist Johnson was one of the intercessor prayer warriors at the church. The prayer warriors prayed for souls to be delivered, saints to be healed and demons to be banished. We must have looked like we needed prayer, because she prayed for the girls and me on our second visit to the church. We had just come into the church after walking in the rain to get there. That particular Sunday, I had another argument with James about something that I couldn't even recall. I stood shaking my wet umbrella at the church entrance door when Evangelist Johnson came over to see if I needed some assistance. She probably saw the frustrated look on my face or heard my girls crying because they were wet from the rain. "God bless you child, you look like you could use some help," she said.

"Yeah, you don't know the half of it," I said being facetious. She pulled a handkerchief from her pocket and dried the girls' faces. I was thankful for her help because I was already frustrated about the argument with James and how slow the girls were walking in the rain, not to mention I was late for church. The prayer comforted me.

After church, Evangelist Johnson gave me her telephone number and told me if I ever needed anything to call her. I called her all the time and we got to be really good friends. I told her things about my life and about James; I also told her I was pregnant. She prayed for me often over the telephone.

One day I knew I wasn't supposed to be drinking, but I did it anyway. I sat on the couch drinking a glass of Hennessey and Coke and feeling depressed about my life. Valencia sat on the floor watching television, while Sandra lay beside me on the couch, sick with a cold. She kept coughing so I got up to get her some cold medicine. I staggered my way to the bathroom, opened the medicine cabinet and grabbed some medicine. Holding on to the wall, I managed to make my way back to the living room. I sat Sandra on my lap and reached for the tablespoon on the coffee table that I had used to stir my drink. I filled the spoon twice with medicine and gave it to her. I kept Sandra on my lap, and went back to watching television and sipping on my drink. Within minutes, Sandra's body went limp. I shook her but she didn't move. I raised her arms and they fell limp. I put my ear to her chest, but I didn't hear her heart beat. I began to panic. I grabbed the bottle off the table to read the label. "Phenobarbital! Oh, my God! I grabbed the wrong medicine!" I screamed. I had given her two tablespoons of Phenobarbital, the medication that was prescribed for Valencia's seizures.

I called Evangelist Johnson. I was scared and shaking so much that I almost couldn't dial the phone. As soon as she answered, I hysterically screamed into the phone, "I need help, Sandra ain't breathing, and I think she's dead!"

"What happened?" Evangelist Johnson asked in a panicky voice.

"Sandra had a cold, I gave her some medicine and she passed out!" I continued. I didn't tell her I had been drinking and had given her the wrong medicine.

"Listen to me, Priscilla. Go into the kitchen and get some tomato soup."

"Tomato soup?"

"Yes, hurry, go get some tomato soup."

I ran to the kitchen to get the soup. With my hands shaking I managed to open the can. I ran back into the living room and picked up the telephone. "Okay, I got it, now what do I do?"

"Hold Sandra in your lap, and as I pray, you put the tomato soup in her mouth. Are you ready?"

"What?"

"Just do it!" she yelled.

"Okay, I'm ready," I said, holding the phone receiver with my shoulder and reaching on the table for the same spoon I had used before. Evangelist Johnson started praying loud. I spooned the tomato soup into Sandra's mouth as tears rolled down my cheek. I didn't understand what I was doing, but I followed instructions. I begged God to save my baby. "Nothing's happening, Sandra still didn't wake up! It's not working," I yelled through the phone.

"Have faith Priscilla, it'll work," she assured me. Sandra's mouth was so full of tomato soup that it was running down her chin. "Call Sandra's name three times slowly," Evangelist Johnson instructed me.

"Sandra!" I said in a whimpering voice as tears continued to well up in my eyes. "Sandra!"

Sandra!" I yelled. Sandra opened her eyes, but didn't move. "She's alive!" I yelled to Evangelist Johnson. "She opened her eyes!" I hugged Sandra and cried out to God, "Thank you God for saving my baby! Thank you Evangelist Johnson for saving my baby." I could hear

Evangelist Johnson rejoicing through the phone and thanking God also. "I'm taking her to the hospital!" I said to Evangelist Johnson. "I'll call you and let you know how she is doing."

I got off the telephone and dialed for a cab. Valencia had fallen asleep on the floor; she had slept through all the excitement. No one knew that when she was five weeks old Valencia started having seizures. I didn't know what was wrong with her. She would turn her head to the left and the right; raise her legs up to her stomach and bring her fists up to her face. Then her body would get completely stiff and her breathing would get heavy. It lasted anywhere between thirty seconds to two minutes, and then eventually her body would return back to normal. I was scared out of my mind, especially when her eyes rolled back into her head, and her body started twitching. I rushed her to the hospital. The doctor explained to me that she had had a seizure. He prescribed a teaspoon a day of Phenobarbital to control the seizures. He assured me she would grow out of it, but she hadn't yet; she just doesn't have them as often.

The cab company gave me a ten minute window. I grabbed my coat, put Valencia's coat on her, wrapped Sandra in a blanket and went outside to wait for the cab. Sandra was breathing, but she still had not said a word. "How could I be so stupid to have grabbed the wrong medicine? And I gave her two tablespoons of it too! Lord please let my baby be ok!"

At the hospital I told the doctor what happened; that I accidentally gave Sandra Phenobarbital, which was Valencia's medication instead of cough syrup. I didn't tell him I was drinking and grabbed the wrong bottle. He examined her. The doctor also questioned the tomato soup that covered her shirt and face. I told him about Evangelist Johnson and how she used the tomato soup to pray my child back to life. He raised his eyebrows and looked at me with a puzzled look on his face. I paced the floor, praying and begging God to save my baby. I said I was sorry, over and over again, and I couldn't stop crying.

"Your baby has her eyes open, but she has not moved or spoken a word since she arrived. It's possible that your child may have suffered some brain damage," he told me after the exam was complete.

"Brain damage? I rebuke that demon right now in the name of Jesus!" I blurted out. "My child won't have brain damage, I won't believe that!" I continued. I kept on pacing the floor swinging my arms. The doctor looked at me and said "I've done all I can for now. Bring her back every four months to have her brain activity tested. We'll have to monitor her very closely." I promised to bring her back to the hospital as he instructed. After signing the discharge papers, we left the hospital and headed home. Fortunately, I had enough money to take a cab back. During the ride home, I prayed and begged God to forgive me and swore I would never drink again.

CHAPTER 15

I preferred working over receiving welfare, so before my stomach got too big I found a second job at Baker's Shoe Store in downtown St. Louis. I found anybody I could in my apartment building to watch the girls while I worked. Ms. Grace still helped during the day at the sandwich shop, but at night I had to find another babysitter. James was too busy doing his own thing, and I couldn't count on him anyway to watch the girls.

I was seven months pregnant and my stomach was huge. In comparison to when I was pregnant with the girls, it looked double the size, like I was carrying twins. Each day it got more and more challenging to bend and stand for customers that were trying on shoes. After a while, the manager made me a cashier, which was so much easier on my back.

After a long exhausting day at both jobs, I went home because I didn't feel good. My side, back and feet hurt. I rode the bus home, catnapping along the way. I picked the girls up from my neighbor's apartment down the hall and went home, got in bed, and propped my feet up. It was tiring standing on my feet all day, and my feet were swollen.

That night, I woke up in the middle of the night in a pool of blood. My gown was soaked. Unsure of what was happening; I got out of bed and went to the bathroom. I checked my underwear and there was no blood in them. *Where is this blood coming from? I wondered.* I lifted my gown over my head to take it off and change into another one when suddenly I felt a sharp pain in my right side. I slumped over and immediately grabbed my side. Blood was coming from it. I began to panic, unsure of why I was bleeding from my side. Ironically, I thought about Jesus and how he bled from his side.

With my heart racing, clutching my blood-stained gown to my side, I called Evangelist Johnson.

"Evangelist Johnson, I'm bleeding from my side like Jesus," I screamed into the telephone. "What do I do? I can't get it to stop!"

"Let's pray," Evangelist Johnson said in a calm voice. She began to pray. "Priscilla, you got faith, you've always had faith. Pray for the bleeding to stop, believe that it will stop," she said with fire and force in her voice. I prayed in conjunction with her. Then I listened to her pray. Then she listened to me pray. Then we prayed together. Then we stopped.

"Check your side," Evangelist Johnson said. I pulled the blood soaked gown off my side to find that the bleeding had stopped. I cried out with tears in my eyes, "The bleeding stopped! I'm not bleeding anymore! You did it! You stopped the bleeding! Thank you God and thank you Evangelist Johnson." We talked for a little while longer before hanging up. I stood and went to the bathroom to clean myself up. I discovered that because my stomach was so big it had torn open an old wound that I had from one of my many fights with James. I cleaned the wound with peroxide and put a bandage on it. I changed into a clean gown and went back to bed, crying tears of joy until I fell asleep.

Two weeks later, I gave birth to a 7lb 14oz baby boy. I named him James Dewayne Gibson, Jr. James didn't even know I had the baby until a month after he was born. I hadn't seen him in over two months.

After all that time being away, James walked in the house one night, filthy and high as a kite. I was sitting on the couch feeding the baby. "Ah man, I didn't know you had the baby," he said as he staggered towards me. As he got closer, I could smell his bad breath and musty underarms. "I had a son?" he said.

"Yes, *I* had a son, two months ago," I said sarcastically.

James smiled at the baby and sat on the couch beside me. He leaned over and took James Jr. from my arms. I was nervous and afraid he might drop the baby. He held the baby in his lap and stared at him. "What's his name?"

"I named him after you, *James*, James Jr."

He looked at me then looked back at the baby. "Really? You

named him after me?" he acted like he was surprised that I named the baby after him. He seemed to be proud to have a son, especially a son that was named after him. I watched him for a short while as he smiled and played with the baby. James Jr. even smiled a few times as though he knew who James was. He had his father's light-skinned complexion, his eyes and his nose; he had my mouth, fingers and toes. James stayed at home for almost a full week before he left and we didn't see him again for a few weeks. This became his usual schedule.

I quit both my jobs to stay home to take care of my three kids; a very difficult decision. I felt like a single mother since I hardly saw James. If I needed diapers or food, I had to find someone to watch my kids or take all of them with me. It was exhausting taking care of three kids. James' drug habit had gotten worse. By now he was shooting heroine and snorting cocaine on a regular basis, and still drinking. His temper was twice as bad as before. When he was home, I walked on eggshells in the apartment, trying not to do anything to aggravate him or make him mad. But, anything would set him off. We fought twice as much as we had before. I called the police on him several times, but they never would arrest him. I would be standing there bleeding, with a busted lip or busted nose, a black eye, bruises on my face and arms, a knot on my head, clothes torn up or the house would be trashed and they still would not arrest him. After a while, I didn't see the point of calling the police anymore, so I didn't. They weren't going to help me anyway.

James came home on the first of the month, beat me up and took most of my check. He also took Junior's packages of diapers to sell. After he left, I laid on the floor crying hysterically and wondered where God was and why He hasn't come to rescue me from my awful life. I was tired of James. That same night I called Aunt Betty and asked if the kids and I could come back to live with her. I didn't care that Uncle Matlock was a pedophile; I needed to get away from James. I'd rather deal with Uncle Matlock, than to be beaten all the time.

Later that week, I received money in the mail from Aunt Betty to purchase our bus tickets back to California. The day after that I packed what clothes I could take. Using my food stamps, I bought a lot of food and drinks for our trip and made several sandwiches. I bought Junior enough Gerber baby food to last the trip. Later that day my kids and I left St. Louis for the second time.

I sipped on one of the four wine coolers that I had stashed in my purse as I gazed out the window at the beautiful California view that I remembered so well from before. The kids were all asleep, which was a relief for me. They had been fussy lately and my nerves were beginning to get frayed. I let my seat back as far as it would go and tried to relax. Ten-month-old Junior slept peacefully on my chest. Valencia and Sandra were cuddled together in the seat next to me.

I wondered what James would do when he came home to find us gone. I didn't even tell the landlord I was leaving, I just left. The rent was paid up until the end of the month, which was two weeks away. I thought about all my furniture and other things I had left behind. I felt sad that every time I tried to get established somewhere; I ended up having to move and leave everything behind. I was going to miss some of my neighbors and my boss at the sandwich shop. I was *really* going to miss Evangelist Johnson. She had prayed me through a lot of situations. I wished I could have said good-bye, but I was so stressed-out, that I just wanted to get away. I told myself I would call her when I got situated. I wondered if James would sell the furniture in the apartment for drugs. Thoughts of Uncle Matlock did slip into in my mind, I felt a nervous chill come over my body. I hoped he wouldn't bother me again, because I didn't have any place else to go. I worried if Aunt Betty was really doing okay, since she had been diagnosed with cancer. She didn't talk about it much during any of our conversations.

Junior stretched and woke up, bringing me out of my daydreaming zone. I hadn't realized how deep in thought I had been. I reached for his bottle in his diaper bag and fed him.

We arrived in California in the late afternoon. Aunt Betty was already there waiting to pick us up. I saw her standing at the end of the bus parking lot. She smiled and waved when she saw us getting off the bus. Aunt Betty looked different; she looked sick. She was frail and she had lost a lot of weight and I saw that she was wearing a wig. I hugged her, but didn't make a comment on how she looked.

Aunt Betty took the baby from my arms and led us to her van.

She was happy to finally get to see Junior. I noticed Aunt Betty still drove the same old burgundy Plymouth van as before. After getting the kids settled in the van, I went back to get the bags. I was tired and was beginning to feel sick to my stomach.

"I haven't been feeling very well lately, Aunt Betty. I've been really tired. I think I'm trying to come down with the summer flu or something," I said.

"Let me watch the kids while you take a nap when we get to the house," Aunt Betty volunteered. "You will be back in the same room as before."

"Are you sure you don't mind watching them?" I asked.

"Yes, I'm sure. The girls have gotten so big and I've missed them. It'll give us a chance to catch up, and for me to get to know my great-nephew," she said with a smile. Aunt Betty never mentioned Uncle Matlock and I didn't bring him up either.

I slept a long time. When I woke up, I still felt sick to my stomach. I ran to the bathroom and threw up. "Please don't let me be pregnant," I whispered as I leaned over the toilet and continued to be sick. I made my way back to my room, still feeling nauseous. The house was quiet, so I figured everyone was asleep. Aunt Betty always took good care of the girls so I didn't think this time would be any different. I looked in on the girls and found them fast asleep. Junior was asleep at the foot of their bed. I started crying. I couldn't stop thinking that I might be pregnant. "I just can't get away from James," I mumbled to myself. "My life is never going to change." I reached in my bag and grabbed my last wine cooler. It was warm, but I still drank it. A few minutes later I ran to the bathroom again to throw up, again.

Aunt Betty cooked breakfast the next morning. The smell of bacon cooking woke me up. I came downstairs and walked in the kitchen. The girls were already up and sitting at the kitchen table eating a bowl of oatmeal. Junior was sitting in one of the arm chairs at the table on a stack of telephone books, drinking his bottle. All the kids had been bathed and were dressed. I wondered where Uncle Matlock was, but I didn't ask. I hadn't seen him at all since I'd arrived yesterday. "Thank you for letting me sleep, Aunt Betty; I must have been really tired," I said.

"You're welcome, baby," Aunt Betty said with a smile. "I know it's hard taking care of three little ones." She turned to scramble some eggs she had just cracked in a skillet. The smell of the eggs made me nauseous.

"Speaking of three kids, there might be four," I sad in a low sad voice. "I've been throwing up all night and ever since I woke up this morning. I hope I'm coming down with the flu, but I don't know. I've been really tired too." I started to cry. "What if I'm pregnant again?"

Aunt Betty scraped the eggs out the skillet and onto a plate. She wiped her hands on her apron and came over to comfort me. Putting her hand on my shoulder and looking down at me, she said, "If you're pregnant, sweetie, then we'll just deal with it. It'll be alright." I hung my head and sobbed a little more as she patted me on the back.

Aunt Betty always had something positive to say. She never belittled me or made me feel bad about anything I did. I had told her so many stories about James and the unspeakable things he had done to me. She always offered encouraging words from the Bible that had been helpful in comforting her when she had an issue. Aunt Betty made me feel like a person and she was the only one that I felt cared about my feelings or thoughts, besides Ms. Grace. I loved Aunt Betty and I appreciated her for always being there for me when I needed her. I sure was glad that she didn't get mad at me about Uncle Matlock.

Later that morning, Aunt Betty took me to the Rx Drug Store to buy a home pregnancy test. Sure enough, I was pregnant. I cried every time I thought about it. "Why me Lord?" I kept asking God. "Why won't you help me?" I asked. "Don't you care about me and what I have been going through *all* my life?" God didn't answer.

CHAPTER 16

Determined not to let this fourth pregnancy get me down, I knew I needed to start looking for a job. I was hoping to find something before I started showing. The doctor told me I was almost four months pregnant and my baby would be born in December. I needed to find something really quick.

School was also about to start for Valencia and Sandra. Valencia would be in the first grade and Sandra was going to kindergarten. I hoped to be working while they were in school. Aunt Betty no longer worked. She was on disability because of her ovarian cancer, which was supposed to be in remission. She was more than willing to watch Junior for me when I found a job.

I kept procrastinating, until I finally realized that I didn't want a job. What I really wanted to do was stay home and take care of my kids. I was getting a welfare check, food stamps and Medicaid to go to the doctor. I didn't need to work.

Every morning, I'd get up and walk the girls to school and every afternoon I'd walk to their school and pick them up. Sometimes I would take Junior with me in the stroller, he liked that. While living at Aunt Betty's house I washed the dishes, dusted the furniture, and swept the floors or anything else I could do to keep the house clean, especially since my kids were the ones that usually messed things up. I wanted to make things easier for Aunt Betty. I also gave Aunt Betty most of my food stamps. I wanted her to know how much I appreciated her. I saved my welfare checks again so we could eventually move out into our own place.

I stayed in my room a lot. I wanted to stay out of Uncle Matlock's way. I avoided him and much as possible, which was easy because he was avoiding me. As a matter of fact, he hadn't said a word to me since I moved in. He and Aunt Betty argued a lot. He said he didn't want me living with them because he said I lied about him. "She's got to go or else," he would say. I didn't know what *or else* meant, so I did my best to save as much money as possible in order to be able to move out as soon as possible. I worried about Aunt Betty. She looked stressed and tired all the time. She was spending a lot of time in her room in bed.

The girls had open house at school one cool October night. They had been talking about it all week. I was excited about talking with their teacher and seeing what progress they had made. We ate dinner early so we could get to the school by 6:30. It was breezy outside so I had to make sure everyone had a light sweater, and Junior wore a hat to cover his ears since he was just getting over an ear infection. Aunt Betty didn't feel well enough to go, so the girls and Junior and I headed out for our walk to the school. The closer we got to the school the more excited the girls got.

I met with each one of the girls' teachers. I let the girls lead me around to show me different things in their classrooms. They proudly introduced their little brother and me to their new friends, and they made sure to point out their new baby brother in my stomach. I was glad that they liked their school and their teachers and had made lots of friends. Despite all the dysfunction in our lives and moving back and forth from St. Louis to California, California back to St. Louis, and then back to California again, and all the drama they had seen between James and me, they seemed to be happy and adjusting and learning well in school. I was proud of that and I thanked God for blessing them and prayed for happier times in the future. I finally felt like something good had come out of my life.

Valencia and Sandra led me to the school cafeteria where refreshments were being served. There was an assortment of cookies and a bowl of punch spread out on one of the lunch tables. Parents were seated at the tables with their children. I let the girls each get two cookies and a cup of punch. Junior even got a cookie, which he totally made a mess of. The girls were little chatter boxes; they talked about school and their friends and anything else that came into their heads. I was half listening as I looked around the cafeteria at all the parents with their children. Everyone looked so happy. I thought how nice it was to have a wonderful mother and father that liked taking care of their kids. I tried to remember a time when my mother ever came to my school for anything. I wished my life had been different. I snapped out of my daydream when Valencia patted me on the arm and asked if she could go to the bathroom. I let both girls go to the bathroom and I waited at the table with Junior.

After the girls returned to the table, it was time to head home. It was getting late and we had to walk. The girls said good-bye to their friends and we headed out the door. The night had gotten cooler and the sky was clear. The full moon looked like a beautiful orange ball in the night sky. We walked home quickly. I was uncomfortable being out at night walking with the kids, even though this neighborhood was far different from our neighborhood back in St. Louis.

We arrived at the house just in time because Sandra had to go to the bathroom again. As I stood on the porch knocking and waiting at the front door for someone to answer, I could hear voices talking in the living room. The voice sounded familiar, but I couldn't make it out. Finally the door opened, "Hey, baby, I'm back!"

"Oh, God," I said under my breath. It was James.

"Daddy, Daddy!" the girls yelled as they pushed past me and jumped in his arms. He bent down to hug them.

"You're pregnant?" he asked, looking up at me. My heart stopped and I got a sick nervous feeling in my stomach. I didn't answer. I pushed the stroller carrying Junior through the door and over to the couch. Aunt Betty was sitting on the couch and Uncle Matlock was sitting in his easy chair. Neither said anything. I was speechless.

James walked to the stroller and took Junior out. "Man, you've gotten so big," he observed. He hugged Junior and sat down on the couch, placing Junior on his lap. I was scared.

I remembered Sandra had to go to the bathroom. Shaking, I took her to the downstairs bathroom. Inside the bathroom, I tried to hold back my tears. I wasn't sure what was about to happen or who had told James I was here. A million and one emotions were going through my head. After we came out the bathroom, I made the excuse that I had to get the kids ready for bed. I took the kids upstairs and James followed.

As soon as we got upstairs in the bedroom, James shut the door and slapped me. I fell backwards onto the bed. "How the hell you gonna leave St. Louis with my kids and not tell me? And you're pregnant? Why didn't you tell me you were pregnant?" He was asking questions so fast that I couldn't answer them. I sat on the bed crying and scared. I hoped things wouldn't escalate. James let me give the kids a bath and put them in bed. He played with Junior until he fell asleep. Later that night he told me how he found me. "Uncle Matlock called my daddy's house where I was living after *you* got us evicted. He told me you were living here and he wanted you out of his house," James said sounding irritated. I didn't comment. That night I got little sleep because James complained most of the night.

James wasn't comfortable with us living in the house with Uncle Matlock. The next time I got my welfare check, we moved out. We moved into a small, furnished duplex in Watts. My life quickly went back to the way it had always been with James: full of drugs, violence and dysfunctional behaviors.

I tried to get the girls settled and comfortable in their new school, but they hated it. Every day when it was time to go to school, they started crying. Their teacher told me they cried sometimes during the day and were becoming withdrawn. They missed their old school, their teachers and their friends. They missed Aunt Betty. I hated my life with James. "Why did he have to come back?" I questioned God, "just when things were starting to look up for us."

The neighborhood we moved into was drug infested. Just like the neighborhood in St. Louis, there were drunks standing on the corners, and people hanging out all hours of the night and day. I hated having to walk my kids to school around the corner because we had to pass drug dealers working, step over winos laid out on the sidewalk and walk through all the trash and filth left on the streets from the habits of these people. Trash would be piled up in front of houses for days; dogs, cats and rats ran around like people and it seemed like everybody in the neighborhood smoked something. Walking through cigarette smoke or cigar smoke, made me sick to my stomach.

James had befriended several people in the neighborhood, most of whom came over every day. James would sit out on the back porch with his new friends and they would get high together. One friend, named Travis, would sometimes spend the night after a night long of drinking and doing drugs. He would pass out on the floor and James would leave him there asleep.

I tried to be as inconspicuous as possible by staying in the bedroom with the kids. I only came out to cook or to do things around the house. No matter how scarce I made myself, James' insecurities would come out and he'd accuse me of messing with one of his friends. How he thought that was possible with my big eight-month pregnant belly, I couldn't figure out. He didn't fight me while I was pregnant, but occasionally he would slap me in my face and call me names.

Travis and James became close friends. So close that Travis practically moved in with us. He was there nearly every day of the week. I liked him, but not in the way that James thought. James was very jealous of our friendship; Travis never made a pass at me. He was very helpful around the house. He would clean up and wash the dishes and help buy groceries. The kids really liked him. He babysat all the time. Travis was a really nice person. I told James I was going to name our baby Travis, if it was a boy, because I really liked that name.

Christmas was a fun time for the kids. I worried about Christmas presents, because we didn't have a lot of money to buy presents, thanks to James. The local mission gave us a food basket with a ham and the kids each got three wrapped presents. I thanked God for blessing us.

The doctor had given me a due date for my baby – New Year's Day, but for some reason I felt the baby was going to come early. My back had been hurting since Christmas Day. The baby hadn't let me sleep for the last few nights, it was moving around a lot in my stomach and pushing on my tail bone like it was anxious to come out. Since I was eight months pregnant, I had been dilated to two centimeters and was convinced the baby would come out any time.

On December 30, James and I had an argument about something stupid. He threw a glass across the room and shattered it everywhere then he went outside. He sat on the back porch drinking a beer and smoking a joint. I cleaned up the broken glass and sat down at the kitchen table. My back was hurting really bad. Suddenly my water broke. I yelled for James. He came in the house and I told him the baby was coming. I called a taxi. The taxi came and we all went to the hospital. James stayed in the waiting room with the other kids and I went up to labor and delivery in a wheelchair.

The nurse tried to make me as comfortable as possible, but the contractions were hurting very badly and coming quickly. She helped me into my hospital gown and helped me get into the bed. The baby was pushing hard on my pelvis. "The baby wants to come out," I said calmly to the nurse. "It doesn't want to be in my stomach anymore."

"That baby is going to have to wait for the doctor," the nurse said, "so I don't want you doing any pushing. I need to step out for a minute to call the doctor. You'll be fine, I'll be right back," she said as she walked out the hospital room and closed the door behind her.

I lay in the bed as still as I could. The baby really felt like it was pushing and pushing to come out. Then I had a strong contraction. "Jesus please help me," I called out. Within seconds another contraction came. "Jeeeesus!" I yelled. "Oh, please help me, Lord." I wondered what was taking the nurse so long. I tried to lie back in the bed and relax, but another contraction hit me. This one was stronger than the first two. I screamed for Jesus and pushed my baby out just as the nurse walked back in the room.

"Oh my God," the nurse yelled as she ran over to catch the baby. I had pushed my baby out and he was on the edge of the bed with one foot hanging off. "Why didn't you wait for us?" she asked, smiling.

"I told you he wanted to get out," I said trying to catch my breath while laughing.

"Well, I guess your son is just impatient," she said with a smile.

"I have a son?"

"Yes you do, a healthy-looking son. Let me clean him up and I'll hand him right to you." The nurse cleaned my baby and placed him on my chest. He was so cute with his chocolate skin and he looked just like me. The doctor finally came in.

"It's too late, Dr. Henry," I said. "My baby boy, Travis, didn't want to wait for you, so he delivered himself." We laughed together. Dr. Henry took Travis and looked him over to make sure he had all his fingers and toes. Travis weighed 7 pounds and 4 ounces. The nurse went to the waiting room to get James. He too was proud to have another son. He also liked the name Travis.

CHAPTER 17

After the birth of Travis, I told my doctor to tie my tubes before I left the hospital. I didn't want any more children, especially by James. I was sick and tired of James. My skin crawled every time he touched me. He always wanted to have sex and I didn't want him to touch me, because he couldn't be trusted. I was sick of all the sexually transmitted diseases he gave me. I always was scared that one day I would die of Syphilis, AIDS, Hepatitis or something, because he was always sleeping around and shooting up heroin. My attitude had gotten very bad. I had started cussing and arguing back at him. Anything he said got on my nerves and anything he did got on my nerves. Sometimes I would provoke an argument just so he would get mad and leave. And when he hit me, I fought him back. That shocked him. He didn't know what to make of that, because I had never defended myself before. I used to just run and hide from him in the closet, but I was fed up. I wanted to be away from him.

One day James came home mad about something and slapped me because I hadn't cooked dinner yet. I kicked him in his leg so hard that he doubled over and couldn't continue beating me up. The next morning he woke up complaining of chest pains. I called the ambulance. At the hospital it was discovered that when I kicked James in his leg, I had created a blood clot that traveled from his leg though his body and settled in his lungs. "Did you hit your leg on something?" the doctor asked James after noticing the large bruise on his left shin. James looked over at me. Scared at what he might say, I looked away. "Yeah, doc, I hit my leg on the coffee table," James lied. He stayed in the hospital for over a week, enjoying all the pain medicines that they gave him.

My happy times were when James was not at home. The kids and

I had fun and there was peace in the house. When James came home from the hospital, my headaches and stomachaches started up again. I'd look at him, and in my mind, I would think of a million and one ways I could kill him. From putting some crushed pills in his drink to bashing his head in while he was asleep. Or, maybe I could put rat poison in his food. I hoped he would overdose on the drugs he was taking and die. I imagined myself doing all sorts of horrible things to him when he was passed out on the floor or in bed. I couldn't bring myself to do any harm to him, as much as I was tempted, I just couldn't do it.

"What's the matter with you?" James often asked. I would ignore him. Over time, he finally got the message that I didn't want him anymore, that I was sick and tired of him, and I no longer wanted to be married to him. I told him if he touched me again, I would kill him. And I also told him that if he dropped dead I would not lose one night of sleep. James thought I was crazy.

One night James came home high as usual, demanding money and sex. I was not in the mood for any of his mess. I didn't have any money anyway and I sure didn't want to have sex with him. He pulled at my pants pockets, and reached his hand in my shirt to see if I had any money stashed in my bra.

"Where's your purse?" he asked.

"I don't have any money, James!" I insisted, as I pushed away from him. He cursed at me and called me a liar, than he threw an ashtray at me. I jumped out the way. The ashtray just missed my right shoulder. It shattered against the living room wall. I looked at James, rolled my eyes, sat down on the couch and took a sip of the Hennessey that I had been drinking.

"If you don't find some money in this house, I bet you're going outside the house to get me some money," he said pointing his finger at me. I just looked at him without saying a word. James' eyes were glassy and bloodshot red. He could barely stand up and he was slurring his words. James bent over to pick up a picture frame with Junior's picture in it and fell against the television. The television wobbled, but didn't fall off the stand. He threw Junior's picture. I took another sip of my drink and continued staring at him without saying a word.

"Don't you hear me talking to you?" he screamed. "I need some money and I want it right now! You are going to go out there in those streets and get me some money tonight or I am going to beat you to death!" he said shaking his fists at me. I still didn't say a word, I just continued to stare at him. James stared back at me. "So you think I'm playing with you?" he said angrily. I stood scared with my body wedged between the couch and the corner wall as he ran toward me with his fists balled up to hit me. He fell over the coffee table. I jumped back and tried to think what my next move would be. James would have to kill me if he thought I was going to go in the streets and hustle for him money for drugs. For years, he'd tried several times to get me to sell my body for money, but I wouldn't do it. The times he was desperate, he would beat me up real bad, but I still I wouldn't go. Tonight I was sick and tired of James and his mess. I wasn't sure how I was going to handle him; I just knew I wasn't going to let him beat me again.

James was closer to the telephone than I was. If I made a dash for the telephone to call the police, he would catch me before I reached it. I was far from the kitchen and I knew if I tried to make a dash in there to get a knife I wouldn't make it in there either. I looked around the living room for something I could use as a weapon as James fumbled around on the floor trying to get his balance.

I grabbed a small ceramic figurine that sat on the end table and clutched it in my hand. Scared and feeling like I didn't have a good enough weapon, I decided to try to make a run for the telephone. Sure enough, James caught me by my hair and threw me against the wall. Just as he reared his fist back to hit me, four-year-old Travis came around the corner from the bedroom.

"Daddy, don't hit my Mama!" he screamed over and over again while pulling at James' pants. James looked down at Travis. Travis kept pulling at his dad's pants and looking up at him and crying hysterically. "Daddy please don't hit Mama no more," he said in a sad, quivering voice as tears poured out of his eyes. James dropped his fist and stared at Travis as though he was in some kind of trance. While James' attention was on Travis, I slipped away from his grip and ran to the telephone and called the police.

"I called the police, James," I shouted breaking the stare that he had fixed on Travis. "They'll be here in a minute!" I said with the telephone still to my ear. James looked over at me and ran out the door, leaving it open. Travis ran over to the door and slammed it shut, then he ran over to me, wrapping his arms around my waist and crying. I hung up the telephone. I stood crying and hugging my son.

Finally, we released each other and Travis started picking up the broken picture frame and ashtray that had shattered in pieces on the floor. I straightened the television on the shelf and pushed the furniture back in place. I finished helping Travis pick up the rest of the glass that was scattered throughout the living room. I wondered what my other children were doing and why they didn't come out of the room. My girls were scared; they hated the fighting and the loud commotion that went along with it. After the fighting was over, I usually would find them hiding in the closet in their room, a custom I'm sure they got from me. After this fight, I found Junior asleep in his bed. How he could sleep through all this noise I don't know. He usually stayed in the room with the girls. He hated the fighting, too, and usually, they all would be huddled up in the closet together. Thanks to Travis's help, things didn't get any worse than they could have. "Mama, I heard something crash against the wall, so I came out to see what was wrong," Travis told me later.

Later that night as I lay on the couch watching television, I thought about the all fights James and I had had over the years. We were usually at home during most of our fights. If we had company over or were at someone else's house, I knew that James wouldn't fight me. Even when his friend Travis used to stay with us, James didn't hit me if he was around. But after James put Travis out for stealing some weed from him, James had been acting like a fool. I thought about all the mean and repulsive things James did me. He would hit me with whatever he could find within his reach and if he couldn't find anything, he would beat me with his fist like he was fighting a man. I realized that James was a coward. I took a deep breath and leaned back on the couch and thought, *I'm glad he's gone and I hope he never comes back.*

CHAPTER 18

I did my best to make a good life for my kids and me. I didn't work so I could stay home and take care of them. We hadn't seen James for months, but I found myself edgy and nervous every day since he left because I was unsure if and when he was going to come back. The uncertainty finally overcame me and I decided to move. I felt if we moved, James wouldn't know where we were and I could get some sleep at night.

It had been years since I had spoken with Aunt Betty, who, I believed, was the source of James always knowing where I was, other than when Uncle Matlock told him. I decided not to call her. I wanted to make a good life for us on my own.

All the kids were in school. Valencia was in the sixth grade and Sandra was in the fourth. They loved school and had become good students. It was a regular practice to get good reports from their teachers as to how well-mannered they were and how good they were doing. The girls never got in trouble at school or at home. At home, they helped keep the house clean and occasionally helped me cook.

My boys on the other hand, were mischievous. They were always in trouble at school and at home. Junior was in 1st grade and Travis was in kindergarten. The school called me all time to report that they had cussed out some teacher, pulled some girl's hair or were fighting with some boy. Almost every day it was something different.

At home, I'd have to whip them for stealing bikes in the neighborhood. They would steal bikes, bring them home and change the parts on each bike to make a new bike. We had all kinds of bike parts all over the house. I'd have to whip them for stealing the neighbors' clothes off their clotheslines. Both boys would steal the clothes then come in the house and say, "Look Mama, we got some new clothes," lying about where they got the clothes. They were so rambunctious that they would jump off the roof of the house and off abandoned buildings, landing on old mattresses they found in the neighborhood. The higher the building, the more fun they had. One day Junior and Travis found a puppy in a nearby field. They decided to put the put puppy in the washing machine to give it a bath. I heard a squealing noise coming from the kitchen and ran in just as the puppy was going through the spin cycle. I had to stop the washing machine to get the puppy out. They were always doing something crazy.

One day, after walking the kids to school, I went to the local check-cashing place to cash my welfare check. As I waited in line, I struck up a conversation with a middle-aged white woman who was waiting in line behind me to purchase money orders.

"Good morning," she said politely. "I'm Ann."

"I'm Priscilla," I answered back.

After a few minutes of conversation, Ann told me that she cared for four elderly invalids in her home and she needed some help feeding and bathing them and keeping her house clean.

"I can do that," I said.

"Really?" she responded, sounding surprised.

"Yeah, if I can come after I walk my kids to school and leave in time to pick them up from school, then I can work for you. I can clean your house and cook your food," I said, sounding eager and hoping she would accept.

"How wonderful," Ann said with a smile on her face. "That would be great and certainly take a load off my mind. I can even pay you cash. That way you can continue getting your welfare check," she continued noticing my check in my hand. *Wow, I thought, that made the job sound even a better.* We shook hands although we had not yet discussed a salary. "If you are available now, you can start today," she suggested. Not having anything to do except pay my rent, I agreed. I waited near the entrance door after I cashed my check and got my money order for my rent. Ann finished her business and we walked out of the building together. I followed her to her station wagon. It had wood paneling on the sides and was parked next to the building.

The drive to her home in Hemet took about an hour. I wondered why she was so far away from home, in Watts, getting money orders, but I didn't ask any questions. We talked along the way about the job and the people she cared for. I told her about my kids. I did try to calculate how many buses it would take to get all the way out here. I could ride the bus to Imperial Highway and Wilmington Avenue, then take the Metro Link to Paramount Blvd, then ride the bus to San Bernardino County, change buses in Riverside County, then ride the rest of the way to Hemet. It was a lot, but I felt I could do it.

Ann's house was a big, spacious two-story house, hidden behind a lot of trees in a neighborhood that was filled with similar looking houses. The first thing I noticed when we walked inside was the dust on the furniture and the odor in the house. The house smelled like urine and old trash, but I didn't' comment.

Ann gave me a tour of the house and introduced me to her patients who were all lying in their beds. The patients were Caucasian, two men and two women. They were elderly and all seemed to suffer from some form of mental retardation. The house had four bedrooms. One was Ann's bedroom, one was a guest room and the other two were shared by the patients; two in each room.

The television was on in each of the patients' rooms, but no one seemed to be paying it any attention. The patients were either curled in a ball in their bed, or lying on their back, staring into space. No one spoke a word. I could see urine stains on some of the bed sheets, which would explain the urine smell in the house. I didn't see anyone else in the house, so I figured Ann must leave her patients by themselves whenever she went out. We made our way to the kitchen. It had dirty dishes in the sink that looked like they had been there for a few days.

"I apologize for the mess, but my time is so limited. I have too many things to do, that's why I need some help," Ann explained as she opened a closet full of cleaning supplies.

"I'll take care of it, Ann," I said as I reached for supplies to start cleaning the kitchen.

The kitchen was the largest kitchen I had ever seen. I felt like I was in a palace. The kitchen had a side-by-side refrigerator, *a dishwasher*, a stove with *a microwave* and a trash compactor. I had never seen appliances like these before, especially a trash compactor and a microwave.

After I finished cleaning the kitchen, I started dinner. I found some ground meat in the freezer and decided to make a meatloaf after finding onions and bell peppers in the refrigerator and tomato sauce and crackers in the cabinet. I added mashed potatoes and green beans to complete the meal along with some homemade cornbread.

Time sped by and before I knew it, it was time for me to leave. I told Ann I had to leave to get home to get my kids. Fortunately, she offered to drive me home. "That meal was wonderful," she said during the drive back. "And the kitchen looked great."

"I'll clean the rest of the house tomorrow," I said. "By the way, how much does this job pay? And when will I be getting paid?"

"Well, today is Monday," Ann said taking a deep breath, "how about I pay you $150 a week and pay you at the end of the week on Friday?"

"Okay, that's fine," I said feeling like I hit the jackpot. With this money and my welfare check, I could do a lot for my kids now, I thought. I daydreamed about the Christmas presents I would buy my kids as I looked out the window during the ride home.

Working for Ann went well for a while. Even the subway and bus rides weren't that bad and I always made it home just in time to get the kids from school. Ann paid me every Friday as agreed. I helped her bathe her patients, and I kept the house clean and cooked all the meals. I would even cook enough food to store in containers in the refrigerator or freezer. The house smelled good and there was no dust anywhere. I liked my job.

After four months, Ann began to make excuses about paying me. At first, she started giving me a portion of my money. Then she complained that she didn't get her payment from the State of California for taking care of the patients so she couldn't pay me. Then her excuse was that her utility bills were too high or that she had to repair something in the house or any excuse she could come up with to keep from paying me. Because I liked the job, I accepted her excuses and continued to work. I kept believing that she would get things together and that she would pay me soon.

Then Ann's attitude changed. She was edgy, and soon became irrational and belligerent. She began to yell at her patients. I would come in to work and some of the patients would be soiled from the night before. The food that I cooked before I left would still be on the stove or in the refrigerator because she didn't feed them. The patients had unexplained bruises on their faces and arms. I tried not to question anything, but the few times I did she yelled at me. Then she started to treat me even more unfairly by complaining about how I cleaned or what I cooked or how I needed to do more. I had begun to get frustrated, but I continued to come to work for her because I was worried about the patients. Three weeks later, when Ann still had not paid me, I finally quit. I considered reporting her to the State in order to protect the patients, but I never did.

I quickly landed another job in housekeeping at the Hilton Hotel at the LAX airport. I was there two weeks before I was fired for continually being late for work. They were not understanding about me having to walk my kids to school and then catch the bus to get to work.

The Vagabond Motel on Figueroa Street in downtown LA was hiring. I applied for a job and was hired on the spot. I worked in housekeeping. Because I had to be at work early, I had to trust Valencia to walk everybody to school. I got off work early enough to be able to be at the school to pick everybody up in the afternoons. The job was great and things with the children were going well. Even the boys weren't getting in as much trouble.

Every Friday when I got paid, I'd treat the kids to some candy from the candy store and I would buy myself a bottle of liquor. I'd sit outside on my steps and drink and watch people in the neighborhood.

After six months at the Vagabond Motel, a friend of mine told me about a possible better job in housekeeping at the Best Western Hotel on Imperial Highway. I applied for the job and got it. I liked this job better because it was a little closer to my home and it had the same hours. I did, however, have to work some Saturdays, something I didn't like, because I had to leave Valencia home to watch everybody. This went well for a while until I got fired for having to leave work to get Junior out of trouble. A woman in my neighborhood came to my job to tell me that my boys had stolen her son's bicycle. She told me that the police had my boys and I owed her $80 for the bike. I asked my boss if I could leave and he told me no. I left anyway. When I got home, Valencia told me that the boys had gone outside after she told them they couldn't and that's when they took the bike. I called the police station to see if they had my boys. I was told that the boys were in custody and I had to come down to the station. The police station was about a 30-minute walk from the house, so I headed out walking, hoping the bus would pass so I could ride it. When I arrived at the police station, I saw Travis and Junior seated on a bench inside the station. They both ran up to me, each trying to give their own explanation of what had happened. The police sergeant at the desk next to where the boys had been seated motioned to me to come over. I listened to the sergeant explain to me about the stolen bicycle. He told me that Junior took the blame for taking the bike. I looked at both boys; neither said a word. The sergeant told me that because Junior stole the bike he had to spend three days in juvenile detention.

"He's only seven years old!" I started to cry and pleaded with him not to take my son. Junior started to cry. A female detective walked over and took Junior by the hand and led him down the hall as he kicked and screamed, yelling that he didn't want to go. Travis started to cry as he watched Junior being taken away and I cried harder. The sergeant gave me the information for the juvenile detention center that Junior would be in and told me I could pick him up on Wednesday. Travis and I left the police station and walked home.

On the walk home, Travis looked up at me with tears in his eyes. "Mama, Junior didn't steal the bike, I stole the bike," he confessed. "Junior didn't want me to get in trouble, so he took the blame. I'm sorry." I looked down at Travis as he wiped tears from his eyes. I didn't say a word. It didn't matter to me who stole the bike; I didn't want either of my boys to go to juvenile.

CHAPTER 19

A year and a half passed and we hadn't seen or heard from James. I knew he couldn't find me because I didn't talk to anyone in his family. After his grandmother helped him steal Sandra when she was a baby, I decided never to speak to his mother or his father ever again. I saw an obituary in the newspaper for Aunt Betty. I was very sad, but I didn't go to the funeral.

I decided to file for divorce. I had heard about a Do-It-Yourself divorce place in Santa Monica, from a lady that I worked with at Wadsworth Elementary School. After Junior came home from juvenile, I thought I needed to keep an eye on the boys a little better, so I applied for a job at the Los Angeles Independent School District. I was fortunate to get a job as a part-time teacher's aide at their elementary school. It was comforting to me to be able to be with my children all day and to see what they were doing. Six months into working at the school, the boys hadn't gotten into any trouble and their grades were improving.

I called the American Budget Divorce Service in Santa Monica and was told that for $99.00, the company would show me how to file for my own divorce. I didn't really like this policy, but if that's what I needed to do and all I could afford, then so be it. It took me three months to save $99.00. As soon as I saved the money, I rode the bus to Santa Monica and took the necessary steps to file the divorce papers. I felt like as long as I was still married to James he still had a hold on me. After ten long years of marriage, I wanted to be rid of him. Six months later, my divorce was final. That was one of the happiest days of my life.

Every morning I'd walk the kids to school and come back home until it was time to go back to work at noon. My part-time shift at the school didn't start until after lunch so I could go home, clean up or cook my dinner and then be back at work by noon. I loved my job. The kids and I would walk home together after school.

On my walk to the school, I passed a house that an older man lived in. Every day as I passed his house, like clockwork, he was on his porch with a cigarette in one hand and a glass of something in the other. He looked to be around 60 years old, tall and slender. Every day, it was the same thing.

"Hi friend, how you doing?" he would ask.

I walked to the elementary school twice a day and each time going and coming he was on that porch, dressed in that same blue shirt and those same brown pants, holding a cigarette and holding that glass of whatever he was drinking. I'd wave back at him after he spoke and continue on to the school. It wasn't long before the kids noticed him. They looked forward to him being on the porch every day and waving. The kids always waved back at him. They thought he was funny.

Finally, one morning on my walk back home from the school, the man came off his porch as I was getting closer to his house. I got nervous because he had never left his porch before. I saw him set his glass down on the porch railing and put his cigarette out on the bottom of his shoe. Then he walked up to me on the sidewalk.

"I've watched you and your kids pass my house every day for months and I've never introduced myself. My name is Charlie Murray; what's your name pretty lady?" he asked as he stuck out his hand for me to shake.

"My name is Priscilla Gibson," I said, blushing and thinking he really is old.

"Are those kids your kids I see you walking with?"

"Yes, all four: Valencia, Sandra, James and Travis," I said with a bit of an attitude.

"Okay, pretty lady, I didn't mean anything by it, I was just asking," he said in a defensive way. I laughed a little. "Can I interest you in coming inside and having a drink with me?" he asked politely.

"What are you drinking?" I asked.

"Old Fosters."

"Yeah, I'll come in and have a drink with you."

I followed the man inside his house. It was an old house that could have used a good cleaning. Most of his furniture was old, the floors were dirty and I saw a few roaches crawling on the wall. It also had an old smell to it. Compared to my house, though, this was like being in a hotel. My house was a dump. It was falling apart and had holes in the ceiling that leaked when it rained. I called my landlord a slumlord because he never would fix anything. But even though my house was raggedly, I kept it clean.

Mr. Murray fixed me a drink. He fixed himself another drink and lit a Moore's cigarette. We sat on the couch drinking and talking.

"How old are you?" he asked.

"29. How old are you?'"

"65," he answered. "Is that too old for you?" he asked. In my mind, I thought *Yeah, that is too old*, but I ignored the question and sipped on my drink. "You sure are pretty," he said. "I look forward to you walking past my house every day, that's why I'm always outside. I wait for you to walk your pretty self past my house four times every day. What a treat," he said, smiling. I blushed and gulped down my drink. Mr. Murray made me another one.

After two drinks, I was feeling a buzz. Mr. Murray came and sat next to me and we started kissing. Before long, we ended up in his bedroom. I stayed at Mr. Murray's house until it was time for me to go to work at noon. I took a bath and rinsed my mouth out with mouthwash. I went to work feeling like I had never felt before. It was mind-blowing to be with a man who thought I was beautiful and desirable.

After work, I went back to Mr. Murray's house and spent the night. We stayed up all night drinking, talking and having sex. After a while, I started spending a lot of time at Mr. Murray's house and the kids did too; they liked Mr. Murray. We began to spend more time at Mr. Murray's house than we did at our own house. Eventually, we moved in. Mr. Murray and I spent a lot of nights up talking and drinking, either outside on the porch or in the bed. It was nice to have someone to talk to.

Mr. Murray catered to my kids and me, and they adored him. I think he liked having us around as much as we liked having him around. He thought it was funny that even after we moved in together,

I still kept calling him Mr. Murray; but I couldn't help it – he was 36 years older than me. Eventually, he got used to it. He gave us anything we asked for. I had never had that before. Six months later, I married Mr. Murray in the Los Angeles County Court House.

CHAPTER 20

After my marriage to Mr. Murray, I quit my job as a teacher's aide at the elementary school. He didn't want me to work anymore. He thought I should stay home and keep the house clean and make sure the food was cooked and the clothes were washed. Mr. Murray stayed at home, too. He didn't work. Because of his high blood pressure, diabetes, emphysema and liver and kidney problems, he drew his social security and disability. He stayed home all day, every day. Just sitting on the porch drinking his Fosters and smoking his 2 pack a day Moore's cigarettes.

After about a year, it became difficult to be married to Mr. Murray. I was bored out of my mind and I felt like a servant. All I heard all day long was, "bring me this, bring me that, fix me this, and fix me that." Mr. Murray wanted something every minute. He wanted to know where I was every minute and what I was doing. I couldn't do anything without him and couldn't go anywhere without him. I felt the walls caving in on me, like I couldn't breathe. I was very stressed and I began to have migraine headaches and refused to have sex with Mr. Murray, which created a new set of problems. We argued all the time, I felt trapped. Every day I asked myself why I married him.

Mr. Murray sucked every bit of air out of the room so at times I felt as though I was going to pass out. He timed me when I walked the kids to and from school, which was the only place he allowed me to go by myself. He didn't allow me to go anywhere or do anything without him unless it was with the kids; and even that was monitored. He questioned and controlled my every move. If I took longer than he felt I should take in anything I did, he would yell at me, cuss me out and accuse me of doing something wrong. "I know you are messing around or thinking about another man," he often screamed, just after he slapped me. He was driving me crazy and it was taking a toll on me. I started drinking even more.

I played Curtis Mayfield's album on the record player as I pranced around the room with a feather duster in one hand and a glass of gin in the other. I was supposed to be dusting the furniture, but I was getting into the groove of the music that was sounding so good. This was my fourth glass of gin and I was feeling a buzz. *"Freddie's dead... that's what I said,"* Curtis sang in my ear as I dusted the bookshelf and popped my fingers to the beat. *"Freddie's dead...that's what I said,* "Curtis sang again.

"Freddie ain't dead, Priscilla."

I stopped dancing and I looked around to see who was talking to me. I saw Mr. Murray outside the window in the driveway working on his truck....my kids were at school. My heart started beating fast. I sat my drink down on the table.

"Freddie's not dead, Priscilla," I heard the voice say again.

Startled by the voice, I dropped my feather duster. Feeling terrified, I looked around the room hoping to see someone, but no one was there. I turned the record player off.

"Don't be scared, Priscilla, I love you. I'm your friend," the voice said. I sat down on the couch.

"Who are you?" I asked, looking around the room hoping to see someone.

"I'm your friend, Freddie, and I'm not dead. I'm alive and well."

I didn't see anyone in the living room, but I could hear a voice talking to me as though someone was right in front of me.

"Finish your drink," Freddie said. "As a matter of fact, drink the whole bottle. I'll come back and visit you later." I turned the gin bottle up to my mouth and drank as much as my stomach could hold before passing out on the couch. That day I was too drunk to get the kids from school, so Mr. Murray went to pick them up.

Later that night I woke up in the bed. I couldn't remember going to bed, so I assumed that Mr. Murray put me there. As I looked over at him sleeping beside me, I noticed the alarm clock beside my bed said 3 am. I desperately had to pee, so I got up to go to the bathroom and found that I was completely naked. Mr. Murray had taken all my clothes off; I reached for my robe that was thrown across a chair in the corner. I still felt a buzz from the liquor, so it was a bit of a challenge making it to the bathroom down the hall. I managed to make it to the bathroom only stubbing my toe twice and falling against the wall once.

Freddie was waiting for me in the bathroom. "I love you, Priscilla," Freddie said as soon as I walked into the bathroom.

"You do?" I asked as I closed the door and sat down on the toilet.

"Yes, I do. I'm the only one that loves you," Freddie continued. "I'm your best friend. No one knows you better than I do and no one loves you more than I do. I'm the only friend that you have." I sat listening. It felt good to hear someone say I love you. Mr. Murray had said that to me once, before we were married, but not since then. "Go get the rest of that bottle of Old Fosters that Mr. Murray keeps under the kitchen cabinet and bring it back to the bathroom, let's sit and talk some more," Freddie suggested. "Don't worry about what that old bastard Mr. Murray's going to say, he doesn't care about you anyway and he sure don't love you. As a matter of fact you don't love him, you never did. You only married him because you thought he had money and so he could help you with your kids. That's the only reason."

I sat listening, wondering how Freddie knew all my business. "I'm the only one that loves you," he said again. "I'm your best friend and nobody's ever going to love you more than me," Freddie kept repeating.

"I never had a best friend before, Freddie."

"I know Priscilla, that's why I'm here. I'll take care of you. I'll love you. I'll be there for you from now on," Freddie continued. It felt so good to hear those words from someone. I had been longing to hear them all my life, since I was a little girl. I walked out of the bathroom and into the kitchen. I opened the cabinet under the sink and pulled out a half a bottle of Old Fosters. I went back into the bathroom and ran some hot bath water and climbed in. I lay back in the tub, drinking the Old Foster's straight from the bottle and talking to Freddie.

CHAPTER 21

Summer came rather quickly and I was glad. Freddie told me to find a job when the kids got out of school for the summer and to ignore Mr. Murray if he got mad about it. I did. I found a job at the M & T's Donut Shop a few blocks from the house. Mr. Murray complained, cussed, pushed, shoved and slapped me, but I didn't care. I felt strong with Freddie around. I fought him back and eventually Mr. Murray gave in. I was drinking everyday now. Freddie told me I needed to have a drink when I got up and before I went to bed and several times throughout the day. So I did. He said by doing this I would be strong and feel like a different person.

I liked working at the donut shop. The ladies at my job loved to party and loved to drink too. And that was just fine with me. They invited me to a club after work on a Friday. I hadn't been to a club before so I was excited all week and couldn't wait until we got there. Freddie told me not to tell Mr. Murray I was going, so I hid a dress in my purse to change into after work.

My co-workers and I went to the Tip-Top Club, on the south side. It was a small hole-in-the-wall bar where everyone looked like they were having a good time. I was hooked. I had not seen anything like this before. People were dancing with someone or by themselves; others were drinking at the bar or sitting at tables surrounded by lots of people. Everyone was partying and having a good time. Fine men were everywhere. Freddie had me drinking and dancing with as many men as I could. They were all over me and I was loving it. I loved the attention. That night I got so drunk I didn't even go home. I went home with this fine younger man that I met.

The next day, Mr. Murray called the donut shop looking for me. To his surprise, I answered the telephone. The man I spent the night with dropped me off at work that morning. I had a hangover, but I made it to work. Mr. Murray was very mad at me. He cussed me out over the phone, before he hung up in my face.

I was nervous about going home after work, but I went home anyway. As soon as I walked into the house, Mr. Murray slapped me and threw me on the couch. The kids, who were sitting on the floor watching television, turned to see what was happening.

"Where were you and why didn't you come home last night?" he asked.

"I went to a club with my friends and I didn't want to come home," I answered.

"You gonna quit that job, and you ain't going to the club again with those whores!" he barked at me.

"You don't tell me what to do and I'll go to the club if I want to!" I yelled back at him, pushing him away from me. I got up off the couch and went into the bedroom and slammed the door. I caught a glimpse of the kids staring at me as I ran into the bedroom, they looked scared. Mr. Murray followed me, but I locked the bedroom door before he could get in. He beat on the door, but I ignored him. I got in the bed and went to sleep. Later that night I came out of the room. Mr. Murray was on the couch sleeping and the kids had gone to bed. I sat at the kitchen table and poured a glass of Old Foster's. I sat and drank and had a conversation with Freddie.

When Monday came, I went to work. Mr. Murray and I had argued all weekend long and I was sick of hearing his mouth. I finally told him I was going out whenever I wanted and he couldn't stop me. He didn't know what to make of my new attitude. He just stared at me with a look of frustration and walked out of the room.

Going to work was a welcomed change from being at home. As soon as I got to work, I pulled a bottle of Hennessey from my purse and poured some into a Styrofoam cup with a lid and a straw. I stashed the bottle in a box in the storage closet. I wanted to make sure I always had something to drink while at work, just in case I needed it. Drinking made me feel strong just as Freddie said it would and I did feel like a different person.

Later that day, Mr. Murray called me at work. "Since you like to go out so much, I'm going to start going to the club with you and your friends," he stated. I didn't like that idea, but I didn't argue about it.

I met the girls at the club almost every night after I got off work. Mr. Murray joined me a lot at first, but I got out of hand at the club and that made him mad. I was drinking and dancing with different men, letting them buy me drinks and dancing by myself. I had fun and I acted like Mr. Murray was not my husband. It didn't take long for Mr. Murray to realize that he couldn't control me. Although opposed to how I was behaving, I finally broke him down. He agreed to stayed home and take care of my kids and I could drink and party as much as I wanted, whenever I wanted.

Eventually I became dependent, mentally and physically, on liquor. I worked, held a good job and drank heavily every day. I was the classic, functioning, and in-denial alcoholic during the day. At night, when I hit the bar or the club, my drinking got worse. I became a drunken party animal. I was bold and aggressive and I didn't take no for an answer. I changed into a woman who was the total opposite of who I really was. My after work cocktail hour turned into all day long and all night long and the weekends started sooner and sooner. After a while, I stopped coming home. I'd call just to hear the voice of one of my kids who answered the telephone, but most times I didn't call at all for days. I didn't worry about my kids because I knew Mr. Murray was taking care of them.

I lay in bed, naked, sweating and shivering, cold and coming off a blackout. Who was this man I was with and where was I? I had no memory of what happened to me from the time the first drink entered my mouth last night.

"Freddie what happened?" I whispered under my breath, but he didn't answer. I tried to piece together in my mind the night before or the day or two before that, for that matter. I realized that these blackouts had progressed from occasional to inevitable. They scared me, but not too much because I knew Freddie was with me everywhere I went and I knew he wouldn't let me get into harm's way.

The man, a tall, slender, middle-aged bald guy, was getting dressed. "Don't leave, stay with me," I pleaded without asking his name.

"I gotta go," he replied.

"Why do you have to leave?"

The man didn't answer; he just continued to get dressed. I crawled across the bed towards him and tugged at his belt. I kissed him and did things to him to entice him to change his mind about leaving. He let me do what I wanted to do to him and when I finished, he still left.

I didn't want to go home so I kind of moved into the apartment of my co-worker, Shelly. Most times, I'd spend the night with the guy I met the night before until I finally found a steady man named Jonathon. Jonathon was tall, high yellow and ten years younger than me. We met at the club and immediately there was an attraction. We drank and danced all night long. I fell in love with him that night, right on the dance floor.

Jonathon and I were inseparable; we spent all our time together. I told him I had kids and a husband at home that I didn't love and he didn't care. We went drinking and dancing all the time. Soon, he moved in with me at Shelly's house. I spoiled this man. I gave Jonathon anything he wanted because I was in love with him. Jonathon didn't work, but I still worked at the donut shop. I spent all my paycheck on him. Occasionally, I'd have Jonathon drive me to my house to see my kids, but I didn't go very often. When I did go, Mr. Murray would be furious at seeing me with another man – but I didn't care.

Mr. Murray's health was beginning to fail. During the three years I had been with Jonathon, Mr. Murray had three heart attacks and was in and out of the hospital several times for his diabetes. I stayed at the house with my kids during the times he was in the hospital. Sometimes, Jonathon would stay with me.

Mr. Murray had been in the hospital for two weeks, suffering with emphysema and diabetes. I stayed at the house with the kids. The Friday he was released from the hospital, his niece Michelle drove him home. Two weeks in the hospital and I only went to see him once. I didn't have time to visit him.

"My uncle is getting old and weak, Priscilla. He needs your help. He needs you to help take care of him. You are his wife!" Michelle said as she walked in the house with Mr. Murray.

"I'm not staying home to take care of him. He better go back to the hospital or get a nurse or something! I'm leaving." I started to walk out the door. Disappointed at what I said, Mr. Murray, as frail as his body was, ran towards me with his fists raised in the air and tried to hit me. I stood in the yard cussing and screaming at him and Michelle, who was cussing me back.

"I've been your husband for five years, I took care of your kids while you went whoring around in the streets and getting drunk! This is how you treat me? This is how you repay me?" He chased me around the front yard trying to hit me. Michelle grabbed him and tried to calm him down after she noticed him panting and breathing hard. Mr. Murray was extremely upset. My kids and the neighbors heard the commotion and came running outside to see what was going on.

"Get your things, Uncle Murray, you're coming to live with me," Michelle declared.

"Good!" I said, "'Cause I ain't taking care of his old butt!"

"Get back in the house!" I shouted at my kids who were standing on the porch watching with tears in their eyes. "I'll be back later!" With sad confused looks on their faces Valencia, Sandra, Junior and Travis all turned around and walked back in the house, closing the door behind them. I started walking down the street to the bus stop. Mr. Murray was still yelling obscenities at me as I left. Later that day, Mr. Murray moved out of his house and into Michelle's apartment in Compton.

I came back home Sunday afternoon. The kids were in the living room watching television. In my short assessment of the house, they seem to do okay by themselves. The house wasn't in too much disarray. Valencia, who was 12, made sure everybody ate. She did all the cooking. Sandra, who was 10, took care of the cleaning in the house - she was the little Mama. Sandra made sure everything was straightened up in the house and everybody did what they were supposed to do. My boys, Junior, age eight, and Travis, age seven, were still the mischievous destructive ones. Valencia always had to get on to them for something, but they never listened to her. They did however listen to Sandra. I'd come home and Valencia would tell me something they did and I'd have to whip them. They were always getting a whipping about something; getting in trouble at school, for stealing something, fighting or cussing teachers out. I whipped their butts, but it didn't do any good. As soon as they went back to school they'd get in trouble again for something else, pulling some girls hair or talking back to the principal. I was sick of the principal always at my house telling me how bad my boys were. I was sick of going to their school to get them out of trouble. I finally got tired enough that I let them do whatever they wanted to do.

I continued to be with Jonathon. I let him move in with us in Mr. Murray's house. My kids hated Jonathon living with us; they hated him. They hated his weed smoke that always reeked in the house like some sort of bad air freshener. They hated the fact that he laid around all day without a job, while I went out and worked. They hated the way I catered to him and not to them. The only time he said anything to them was to make them go get something for him or to boss them around.

"You ain't my daddy!" the kids would tell Jonathon. "You don't tell me what to do!"

"You better control your kids, 'fore I go off on one of them," Jonathon told me angrily. I yelled at my kids and told them they better learn to be nice to Jonathon because he was my man and they weren't going to run him off. The girls spent most of their time in their room and the boys spent most of their time outside. It made things easier in the house and Jonathon was happier.

Jonathon and I continued to hang out at the bars and clubs. Sometimes we would stay at home and get drunk or go to the park and drink with friends. It had been months since I heard anything from Mr. Murray, not that I expected him to call. But, for whatever reason, I sometimes wondered how he was doing. I thought about calling him, but I never did.

One Saturday night I was at the park with Jonathon and a few other people getting very drunk. I fell asleep on the park bench. I dreamed about a wedding. In the wedding, the groom was dressed in a blue pinstriped suit and a white ruffled shirt. I jumped up screaming, "Somebody's going to die, somebody's going to die!" I startled Jonathon and the people in the park who began to laugh at me and my erratic behavior.

"What's wrong with your crazy self?" Jonathon asked. I began to cry and to look around for a pay phone. I saw one next to the store on the corner. I ran to the phone booth and called Mr. Murray.

I visualized Mr. Murray smiling when he answered the telephone and realized it was me on the other end. He sounded so happy to hear from me and he had no problem expressing his feelings to me.

"I was calling to see how you are doing," I said, slurring my words.

"It's so good to hear your voice, I miss you. I love you, Bay," (a nickname he often called me).

I didn't respond. I was so drunk, I could hardly stand up in the phone booth that kept spinning around.

"When am I going to see you?" he asked. "Will you come see me?" he asked sadly.

"Yeah, Mr. Murray, I'll come see you tonight," I answered.

"Really! I miss you so much," Mr. Murray said with excitement, sounding like he was crying tears of joy. "What time are you coming?"

"I'll be there around 7 tonight," I paused for a moment to try and catch my breath. "Mr. Murray, did you pay the insurance policy?" I asked.

"Yeah, Bay, I paid it. I paid it last week," he answered. "I can't wait to see you Bay."

"Okay, Mr. Murray, I'll see you tonight." I hung up the phone and staggered my way back to the park. I got so drunk that night, I forgot to go see Mr. Murray.

Sunday afternoon, a week later, I remembered that I forgot to go visit Mr. Murray. Sitting in a chair in the living room, I called his niece's house. Michelle answered the telephone. "Can I speak to Mr. Murray?" I asked as soon as she answered the telephone.

"Can you speak to Mr. Murray?" Michelle mocked. "You drunk heifer! No you can't speak to my uncle, because he's dead!" she yelled.

"What! He's dead?" I screamed into the telephone.

"Yeah, he's dead! He had a heart attack! And don't pretend you care!" My heart dropped down in my stomach. I couldn't speak. "He died last Saturday night and we have been looking for your stupid, sorry self since last week. Because you are his worthless, ungrateful, good-for-nothing wife, the morgue won't release his body to the funeral home until *you* sign the release." Michelle was shouting angrily and using harsher profanity than I had heard from her before.

Ignoring her verbal abuse, I asked through my tears, "Where is Mr. Murray's body?"

"At University Memorial, in the morgue," Michelle said sarcastically.

"I'm going down there!" I said just before I hung up on her.

"Mr. Murray's dead! I should have gone to see him," I screamed at the top of my lungs as I burst into tears.

Jonathon came running out of the bedroom. "What's the matter with you, Priscilla! What the hell you screaming about?" he asked sounding irritated.

"My husband is dead," I said, looking up at him with tears in my eyes. "I need you to drive me to University Memorial Hospital. I need to sign a paper at the morgue to release his body to the funeral home."

"I'll take you later before it gets dark, but right now I'm gonna finish this joint," he said holding it up at me. He walked back into the bedroom and shut the door. I poured myself a glass of Jim Beam whiskey and I sat at the table drinking and crying. The house was quiet because all the kids were outside playing. Freddie visited for a while. We sat at the table talking and reminiscing about Mr. Murray. He told me not to feel bad about the way I treated Mr. Murray or for not visiting him before he died.

I finally got to the morgue around 6:30 that night, sloppy drunk and barely able to walk without the assistance of the wall. I cried uncontrollably as I tried to find my way to the morgue. People in the hospital stared at me as I staggered noisily down the hall, got in the elevator and walked to the morgue. Jonathon, who drove me there, stayed in the car to finish off a beer and a bag of weed he had started on before we left the house.

Ignoring my behavior, the medical examiner inquired as to whom I was there to see and asked for my identification. I fiddled around in my purse until I found my ID.

"I'm sorry your father passed away, Ms. Murray," the examiner said sounding sympathetic.

"He wasn't my father, he was my husband!" I said with a bit of an attitude as I wiped tears off my cheeks.

"I apologize, Miss," he said looking down at my identification again. "You look so young."

"Yeah, I hear that a lot," I told the examiner. The medical examiner led me to drawer number 59. As I followed him, my body began to quiver. I wasn't sure if I was shaking because it was cold in the morgue or if I was shaking because I was nervous about seeing Mr. Murray dead. I took a deep breath as the examiner pulled out the drawer. I clamped my hands around my mouth and stared at Mr. Murray's lifeless body lying cold and stiff on the slab, looking as though he was asleep. I screamed out loud and began crying hysterically. The medical examiner let me cry for a few moments then began to push the drawer closed.

"Wait?" I asked. The examiner stopped pushing the drawer. I bent down and kissed Mr. Murray on his forehead. "Thank you for taking care of my kids," I whispered in his ear. I stepped back and let the medical examiner close the drawer. He then led me to a desk that had the papers on it that I needed to sign to release Mr. Murray's body. I tearfully signed everything and left.

A few days later, the morning of Mr. Murray's funeral, I sat on a bar stool with Jonathon getting drunk in a bar on East 119th Street. We had been there since 5 am. The funeral was at 11:00 that Saturday morning at the Harrison-Ross Funeral Home and it was already 10:45. Both of us were very drunk. I finally told Jonathon we had to get my kids and go to the funeral. We drove the six blocks back to the house. I walked in the house and the kids were in the living room watching Fat Albert. "Get up and get dressed kids, we're going to a funeral," I announced.

"Who died?" Sandra asked.

"Mr. Murray died and we're going to his funeral," I blurted out as I plopped down on the couch.

"Mr. Murray died?" Travis said sadly as tears welled up in his eyes.

"Yes! He died! Now get your butts in your room and get dressed so we can go to his funeral!" I shouted with no concern at all for their feelings . The kids walked slowly to their room; all of them crying.

Jonathon, the kids and I arrived at the funeral home more than a half-hour late. Jonathon and I were so drunk we could hardly walk. I staggered my way to the front row of the chapel with Jonathon and my kids following me. Stares from the audience cut like a knife as their eyes followed me. I disrupted the ceremony by staggering up to the front of the chapel with my boyfriend and children, aiming for the front bench. Then I lost my balance and almost fell. Mr. Murray was lying in his white casket in a blue pinstriped suit and a ruffled white shirt, just like the groom wore in my wedding dream. Jonathon slouched on the bench, folded his arms across his chest, closed his eyes and fell asleep. My kids started to cry when they saw Mr. Murray lying in the casket. I couldn't take my eyes off Mr. Murray.

A few seconds later, I screamed aloud startling my kids and the other guests and waking up Jonathon. I jumped up and ran out of the chapel to find the bathroom. "Where is the bathroom?" I screamed, "Where is the bathroom?" A mortuary attendant directed me to a nearby restroom. I stayed in there for about 15 minutes. When I came out, Michelle was standing there staring at me.

"You drunk bitch! I can't believe you had the nerve to come to my uncle's funeral late, with your boyfriend and you are sloppy drunk," she screamed in my face. She lunged towards me to hit me, but someone grabbed her and stopped her. "Get out!" she yelled.

I staggered up to the front of the chapel and got my kids. I shoved Jonathon to wake him up. "Come on, let's go," I said somberly as tears ran down my face. As we turned to walk out, Travis turned back around and walked over to Mr. Murray's coffin. He stared at him for a moment and then touched his hand. "Bye, Mr. Murray," he said sadly. We proceeded to walk out of the chapel amidst disgusted stares and insulting comments.

CHAPTER 22

1988 was a difficult year for me. Michelle took Mr. Murray's house from us so we moved into a two-bedroom apartment on Rosecrans Avenue. It turned out that Michelle had power attorney over Mr. Murray's affairs, so she couldn't wait to put me out of his house. Fortunately, I was able to draw his Social Security, which gave me a monthly income and Medicare benefits.

Eventually, Jonathon left me for a younger, skinner woman. That sent me into a deep depression and into an even deeper alcoholic addiction. I cried every day. I didn't want to get out of bed at times. I'd stay in my bedroom, drinking and sleeping, and sleeping and drinking. I didn't want to eat and I let the kids fend for themselves. I didn't care where they were, what they did or where they went. All I cared about was Jonathon. I wanted Jonathon to come back to me.

"You ain't that cute no more! Fix yourself up," he'd say. "You done got fat! I don't want no fat woman. Lose some weight!"

I tried to fix myself up. I even dyed my hair blond for a different look. I tried to lose weight. I used diet pills and starved myself, but nothing ever worked. Then one day Jonathon didn't come home. I never saw him again. I looked for him everywhere. Sometime later the bartender at one of the bars we hung out at told me Jonathon had come in the bar with a young, skinny woman that he introduced as his *new* old lady. That really caused my depression to deepen.

I drank more, hoping it would take the pain away. Most times my kids would ignore me and my behavior, but there were times my kids would find me passed out on the floor in the living room, in the bathroom or in my bedroom. They would pick me up and help me to my bed. They'd find me passed out in a pool of vomit, a pool of urine or excrement, and clean me up and put me in my bed. I didn't care about anything anymore, I just wanted to die.

My nerves bothered me all the time. At times, I felt I was having a nervous breakdown. I began to pick at the skin on the shins of my legs. I picked and picked until my legs bled. Only Freddie understood the level of pain I was feeling. He kept his promise, never to leave me. Freddie stayed with me and talked to me all the time.

"Mama, you got to stop drinking. You need help," my kids would say.

"You can't keep living like this - we can't keep living like this," Travis said.

"Drinking is a bad habit, Mama, but you must like it because you keep doing it! It's making you sick!" Junior yelled.

"Don't you want to learn how to stop?" Sandra asked.

"We're tired of seeing you drunk all the time and finding bottles of liquor all over the house hidden in places where you thought we would never find them," Valencia said.

I sat up in bed, listening to them and started to cry. Finally, the guilt trip worked. They convinced me to go to the doctor and to get help for my alcoholism.

I found a doctor in Los Angeles and went to see him the following week. Dr. Thomas prescribed the antidepressant Lithium for my nerves and something to help me sleep. He also told me the reason I picked at my legs was because I had developed a nervous condition due to my drinking. "Your legs look like you have third degree burns and if you don't stop picking at them, you will get them infected and cause permanent nerve damage," the doctor observed. "You have got to stop drinking," he continued, "or you *are* going to die. I'm going to send you to an alcoholic rehabilitation center." I started to cry.

I went to the rehab center the following day. My kids were happy that I had finally made an attempt to deal with what they called 'my addiction.' As I packed my clothes in a small tote bag, I could see the excitement on the faces of my children. Valencia, my 16-year-old was seven months pregnant with my first grandchild, and Sandra, my 14-year-old was three months pregnant with my second grandchild. If I had a problem with alcoholism, I wanted to be cured of it by the birth of my first grandchild.

"I want you to be there with me when the baby comes," Sandra said.

"Me too," Valencia seconded.

"We want you to be sober so you can help us push when we go into labor." We all laughed together.

I showed up around 10 am that morning. As soon as I walked in the building I was greeted with a hug by someone I assumed to be one of the counselors, since she had a badge around her neck. "You made the right choice," she softly whispered in my ear as she hugged me. I cracked a faint smile but felt very uncomfortable. *I really don't want to be here, I thought, I can stop drinking any time I want to.*

"My kids wanted me to come, so I'm here," I said nonchalantly to the lady.

"Hmm," she said as she walked me over to the registration desk.

After the counselor checked my belongings for what she called 'unneeded substances', I was considered officially checked in and shown to my room. The counselor stayed with me and helped me to get settled in my room, which consisted of two twin beds, a dresser with no mirror and a closet.

"The bathroom is down the hall," she informed me. "It's shared with the other twenty ladies on the floor."

I didn't say a word. I think I was still annoyed about her searching my suitcase and taking my bottle of Robitussin cough medicine. I was led to a group discussion in the main conference room. Everyone was expected to attend this group meeting. I sat in a chair on the third row at the end and folded my arms across my chest and pretended to listen. A lady was standing at the front of the group talking about her addiction. I began to feel anxiety about being here. "I never thought I would steal from my own mother," the lady continued, "but no one ever told me that the microwave in her kitchen wasn't mine – or the toaster or the can opener. I took it all and I pawned it all. My mother would let me back in the house and I'd steal something else. Every time I was there, I stole something. Then one day, my mother didn't let me back in. We haven't spoken in over three years." She wiped tears from her eyes and sat down.

I don't want to be here, I thought. I don't have a drinking problem and I'm not worried about being sober at the birth of my grandchildren, I can stop drinking when I feel like it. The only reason I'm here is to appease my kids, I'm not an alcoholic like they think I am and I just don't want to be here.

"Thank you, Sarah, for opening up and sharing with us. Today is sharing day," another counselor with a badge around her neck said. I assumed she was the leader of this group session. "Do we have another person that would like to share?" I watched as she looked around the room waiting for a volunteer to stand up. Several of the people in the audience looked around also, anticipating the next story. A man stood up.

"I couldn't stop drinking. The liquor dominated me. It took more of me and gave me nothing back. My alcoholism took away my relationship with my wife." He paused for a moment and let out a sigh. "As a matter of fact, it destroyed it, but I was loyal to my addiction. I was so loyal to liquor that nothing stood in between me and my next drink. Not the need to hold down a job. Not the need to be a father to my children. And not the need to be a husband. My whole day consisted of one thing, the need for a drink." He clutched his hands over his mouth in a moment of shame and sat down in his seat. He began to cry. I yawned and squirmed a little in my seat.

Why couldn't these people just stop drinking? I wondered. It's so easy to do, you just stop. I can. I continued to twist and turn in my seat. *I'm already getting bored, I thought. I wonder if I can go to my room and go to bed. I don't really want to hear none of these stories.*

"My family tried to help me," a young woman that appeared to be in her early twenties began to share as she stood up. "They even tried to take me out of the environment and move me to a better neighborhood. My family figured if they did all this, it would stop me from drinking, but what they didn't realize is that there is a liquor store in every city. There's a corner store! There's a grocery store! There's a mini-mart or a gas station, in every city!" she shouted as tears rolled down her cheeks. "If I wanted liquor, no matter where they tried to move me, I would find it…'cause it's everywhere."

I don't want to hear this, I thought. I'm going to my room. I stood up to leave. A few eyes in the room turned in my direction.

"Did you want to share?" the counselor asked.

Stunned at the misunderstanding that I was about to share a

story, I quickly responded, "No, I was going to go to my room; I think I'm not feeling very well," I lied.

"The session is almost over, do you think you could give us a few minutes longer, maybe 5-10 minutes?" she asked sincerely. Too embarrassed to say no, I nodded my head and sat back down in my seat.

"I was scared of all the pain that was waiting for me in the straight life," the counselor volunteered. "I knew all about that kind of pain. I knew everything about it. The pain of my alcoholic addiction, I wasn't scared of that." I looked up, surprised that the rehab counselor had a story. "I wasn't scared of that at all," she continued, "because when I was out there, my brain was telling me, *YEAH!* This was pain, but it was pain I understood. It was pain I knew. That's what we have to understand in these meetings. To stop drinking is the easy part, that's a piece of cake. The hard part comes after. Thank you for coming to group, are there any questions?" The group began to applaud. I stood up and headed for my room.

The following morning I left the rehab center. "I don't feel like the other people. I don't think I'm an alcoholic so I don't want to stay," I told my roommate. "I might drink too much at times, but I feel like I have my drinking under control." My roommate just stared at me without saying a word. "Some of these people might need all this counseling and stuff, but I don't." I grabbed my bag and walked out of the room. The counselors saw me heading for the door with my bag. One of them waved and said, "See you next time."

I caught the bus to East Century Boulevard because I knew there was a liquor store on the corner. I got off the bus, bought me a bottle of Madd Dogg 20-20 at the store and went to Ted Watkins County Park. I stayed there all day drinking, and slept in the park that night on a bench. I didn't want to go home and have my kids find out that I left the rehab center.

CHAPTER 23

The park was the place to hang out. It generated energy for me and it was directly across the street from the liquor store. I started hanging out in the park back when I was messing around with Jonathon. *Damn, I miss him so much, I thought to myself.* The park was the information center of the neighborhood. If you wanted to know who got the good drugs, who got killed and why, this was the place to get your information. I enjoyed hanging out in the park with the same people every day. We would stay there drinking and talking for hours, sometimes all night. I hoped one day I would run into Jonathon, but that never happened. The park had people in it that were just trying to make it and others that were too high to know or care if they made it. It was a place of death, either the slow death of an addiction or the sudden death of a gunshot. A few times I was accosted and assaulted in the park, but I loved it anyway and I kept coming back. It became my first home and the place where my kids lived was my second home.

I was always in the park, or at Jenny's or Sarah's house, or wherever there was a place with liquor. Once, after hanging around for three days, I finally decided it was time to go to my own house. I walked in the house and the boys were lying on the living room floor watching television.

"Mommy Dearest!" Travis shouted as he ran and gave me a hug. Every since he had watched that movie, he'd been calling me that name.

"Hey, Mama," Junior said barely turning his head around to look at me. He continued watching *Underdog* on television.

"Where's the girls?" I asked.

"They're in their room," Travis answered.

Evidently, the girls must have heard our conversation because they came flying out of their room. Both girls looked at me with shocked looks on their faces. Then they turned and looked at each other.

"Mama! Where have you been?" Valencia asked. "Didn't you go to the rehab center?"

"I don't need no damn rehab center! Those people at that place are crazy! I didn't want to stay so I left!" I yelled back.

Junior turned around and looked up at us. "You left?" Sandra asked sadly. "Why didn't you stay to get some help?"

"'Cause I don't need no help. I don't drink that much anyway. When I get ready to stop drinking, I'll stop, and right now I ain't ready to stop!"

"You can't stop, Mama! And you *do* drink too much!" Junior yelled. "And you're dirty and you stink!" He ran out of the house.

"You make me sick! Valencia shouted. "All you ever gonna be is a drunk! When I have my baby, I'm moving out this house and far away from you!" She ran crying to her room, Sandra followed with tears in her eyes. Travis stood crying in the living room in disbelief. I went into my room and shut the door. I took off my clothes, climbed into bed, took two sleeping pills and chased them down with some Hennessey that I got out of my purse. Then, I fell asleep. I slept until late the next afternoon.

When I woke up, I took a shower and headed right back to the park. I didn't even talk to the kids before I left. I just yelled I was leaving and left. A new face was at the park, and it was love at first sight. His name was Darren. Darren was tall, dark and very handsome. Our eyes met and locked immediately. We spent the day in the park drinking and talking. He was digging me and I was digging him. Later that night we went back to my house. My self-esteem was very low since my weight was now up to 250 pounds. The thought of having a man want me was what I needed to complete me and to make me feel good. I asked him to move in with me a few days later.

Valencia gave birth to my first grandson, Isaiah. She did just as she said she would: she moved out. She married Isaiah's father and moved in with his parents. I didn't want her to move. I was sad that

I missed the birth of Isaiah. Isaiah was born with Autism and had seizures just like Valencia had when she was a baby. A few months later, Sandra gave birth to my second grandchild, a healthy baby girl. I missed that birth, too.

In the beginning, Darren and I got along great. He loved to drink and I loved to drink. Every month when I got my Social Security check, I made sure to stock up on liquor. I wanted to make sure he was happy and stayed happy. When he wasn't happy, I would have a bad day. It wasn't long after Darren moved in that his evil side surfaced. It started out with him calling me names and then escalated to him choking and beating me. On a regular basis, I had a busted lip or bruises on my face and body. I tried to hide them with make-up but my kids knew and so did everyone else. Anything and everything set Darren off.

Darren didn't work so I found myself using most of my check to keep him happy, which meant neglecting other important household needs, like utilities. The water, electricity or gas was always being cut off. The last time the lights got cut off, Darren beat me up and moved out. I never saw him again.

After Darren left, I longed for the comfort of a man so I started back clubbing. I partied wildly. I had a drink in one hand and grabbed men on the dance floor with the other hand. I met men and made out with them on the dance floor. Some men forced me to have sex with them and others I slept with because I thought they would stay with me. For years, I partied with a lot of men and had several short term relationships. We'd be drinking and having a good time and I'd be thinking the relationship was going great. Then before I knew it I was being beat up, slapped or choked because we were out of money and I couldn't buy my current boyfriend any more liquor or drugs.

When my boyfriends left me, I'd get so drunk that sometimes I pass out wherever I was standing. I scared my kids so bad that sometimes they thought I was dead. "I'm sorry, please forgive me," I'd say to my kids. I always begged for their forgiveness. I felt I would die without my kids.

At age 16, Sandra, pregnant with her second child married her children's father and moved far away. I fell deep into a depression because I didn't want her to leave, especially since Valencia had left over a year ago and I hadn't seen her in months. I was scared to take care of the boys by myself.

With the girls gone, it meant that I had to do more at home – chores that I had forgotten. It had been a while since I had done the grocery shopping, or washed clothes or cleaned the house, so I had trouble adjusting. One day while the boys were outside playing, I walked to the corner store to buy groceries. Using my food stamps, I paid for my two bags of groceries and headed out of the store, back to the apartment. I had almost reached home when a blue Malibu pulled up beside me. The driver smiled and reached over and rolled down the passenger side window. I stopped to see what he wanted. I noticed how cute and young he looked. His beautiful hazel eyes sparkled in the sunlight as he leaned across the passenger seat to talk to me.

"Can I give you a ride?" he asked.

"No thank you, I'm almost home," I replied. He motioned for me to give him a minute to talk. I waited on the sidewalk until he got out his car.

"I'm Bobby," he said.

"I'm Priscilla."

"Let me help you?" he offered, taking one of my grocery bags. "Can I walk you the rest of the way home?" he asked. I agreed to let him walk me the rest of the way to my apartment. When we arrived, he waited outside while I took the groceries in the house. After putting away the groceries, I went back outside and we sat on the steps talking and drinking White Lightning and beer until just before dawn. I was mesmerized by his looks, with his high yellow skin and his goat-tee. I learned he was a paramedic for Los Angeles County and was almost 20 years younger than I was.

The following two days, Bobby came over after work and we sat on the steps talking and drinking. The third day, he spent the night. A few weeks later, he moved in.

Bobby and I had a great relationship despite our age difference. My kids liked him and he eventually introduced me to his parents. Introducing me to his parents made me feel he really did care about me. Bobby's parents were very sweet people, they had been married for thirty years and he was an only child. They were very nice to my boys.

After six months of living together in my apartment, the landlord decided he wanted to raise my rent since Bobby lived with me so we decided to move. We found a cheaper apartment on 101st Street in Watts. At the end of the month, Bobby and I and my roommate George started packing and preparing to move. George was one of my drinking buddies who I let live with me when he had no place to go. George was a scrawny black man that looked older than he actually was and because of years of drinking, suffered from poor health. George was at a low point in his life when we met. He had recently been released from jail, after his fifth DWI, and his family no longer wanted to be bothered with him. Bobby understood that George and I were just friends, and had no romantic link to each other, so they got along very well. While carrying one of the packed boxes, Bobby lost his balance. He tripped and fell, hitting his head on the edge of the coffee table. Everything in the box spilled out on the floor and Bobby lay on the floor semi-conscious. Scared out of my mind, I called the ambulance. The paramedics arrived quickly and checked him out.

"We need to transport you immediately to the hospital. That's a nasty bump on your head and you could be bleeding internally," the paramedic said to Bobby.

"No, I don't want to go to the hospital. I have a headache, but I'll be alright," Bobby said.

"Please sir, you really need to go to the hospital to get checked out. You could have a concussion. These types of injuries could kill you within 24 hours to a week if not treated."

Bobby insisted on not going to the hospital so the paramedics left. He tried to go back to moving boxes but couldn't do it. Bobby's head was pounding like a drum every time he tilted it or bent down to pick up a box. He sat down on the couch. By a stroke of luck, Bobby's father stopped by to see how the move was going. I told him what happened to Bobby and he suggested we go to the hospital. Bobby's father drove and I rode with them, feeling so nervous that I thought I was going to throw up. Bobby was in the emergency room less than twenty minutes before coming out.

"Let's go," Bobby said. "The doctor said it's just a minor bump and

I'll be fine." I was puzzled that he came out so quickly, but relieved he had been checked out. We went home and Bobby went straight to bed. While he slept, I continued to pack. The next day we finished moving into our new apartment. Bobby still wasn't feeling good. His feet and legs had begun to swell making it difficult for him to walk or to wear his shoes. I offered to take him back to the hospital, but again he refused to go.

"All I want to do is go to the barbershop and get a haircut and shave, will you drive me there?" he asked. I drove Bobby to the barbershop and dropped him off, helping him into and out of the car and into the barbershop. While waiting for him to get his haircut I went to the Family Dollar Store to purchase a few items. In addition to household items, I found Bobby a pair of canvas shoes. I cut the backs of the shoes out to make it easier for Bobby to slip them on and off. Before we left the barbershop, I put the shoes on his feet.

By the time we made it home Bobby's legs and feet had swelled even more. I was so worried, but I didn't make a comment about them. As I helped him into the house, he said, "I'm hungry. Will you fix me something to eat?" I sat him on the couch and went into the kitchen to make him some soup. I gave him a glass of punch to drink. Bobby sat at the table a long while eating and resting his eyes in between spoonfuls of soup. "I think I'll go to bed now, will you help me to the bed?" Bobby asked. We had been in the new apartment a few days, and most of the boxes had been put away. The bedroom was the first place I got in order, because I knew Bobby didn't feel good and would want to rest. I wished he would go back to the hospital, but he was so sure he would feel better soon. I thought he was getting worse. He leaned on me as I helped him to bed. He lay on his back in the bed and I covered him up. I kissed him on his forehead and turned the lights out. I went back into the kitchen to clean up.

It was getting late and I was still up straightening the house. I was so into unpacking boxes and putting things away that I had lost track of time. The boys had been gone with George all day and had just come home. I put them to bed and then went in to check on Bobby. I felt his head and it was cold. My body trembled. I couldn't take my eyes off him as tears rolled down my cheeks. Bobby was dead. He lay there in bed looking so handsome. He had such beautiful skin and his haircut and mustache were shaped so perfectly. He looked asleep. I tucked the covers under his body to make him more comfortable and sat on the bed beside him crying softly. I couldn't believe he was gone. I don't know how long I had been sitting there crying, but I finally mustered up enough energy to call an ambulance.

"My boyfriend is dead," I told the operator. "He hit his head a few days ago. A little while ago he went to bed and now he's dead. He died in his sleep," I said though quiet somber tears. "We'll send someone as soon as we can," the operator informed me. I hung up the telephone and continued to sit beside Bobby on the bed and cry.

I decided not to wake the kids or George until the paramedics arrived. I paced the floor for hours waiting for the ambulance to come. I picked up a stuffed bear that Bobby had given me for my birthday and held it tightly in my arms, waiting for the ambulance to show up. The paramedics and medical examiner finally arrived six hours after my call. Rigor mortis had begun to set in Bobby's body. I knew we lived in Watts, near Nickerson Gardens a known bad neighborhood because of the gangs, drugs and weekly killings, but I couldn't understand why it would take over six hours to come to my house for my dead boyfriend. It was nearing dawn when they finally arrived.

I woke George and told him about Bobby. "Please keep my kids in their room," I asked George. "I don't want them to see any of this and don't tell them Bobby is dead."

After Bobby's body was removed, I rode the bus to Riverside to tell his parents. I didn't know their telephone number, but I felt I could remember their house despite the fact I had only been there once. I walked the block after getting off the bus, searching for the big Jacaranda tree and the two red flower pots that I remembered seeing in front of their house. I went to the wrong house the first time, but the second time I arrived at the right one. For a few moments, I stared up at the beautiful flowers on the Jacaranda tree as tears rolled down my face. The warmth from the sun warmed my face and helped my tears to dry. Bobby's mother answered the door. Telling Bobby's parents he was dead was one of the most painful things I ever had to do. After the hugs and tears, I collected myself enough to tell them where the medical examiner was keeping his body. I left Bobby's parents' house still shaken. Bobby's father had offered to drive me home, but I refused because I wanted to be alone. On the way back to the bus stop, I drank a half pint of Hennessey that I had in my purse. It didn't ease my pain.

The day before the funeral, I sat in my living room talking with Bobby's father. He told me when the emergency room doctor was about to examine Bobby and he told him he needed to draw blood and insert an IV, Bobby got scared and left the hospital without getting checked out. He was afraid of needles. "I never understood how my son could be a paramedic and give a shot or insert an IV into others, but be afraid of needles himself. I should have made him stay at the hospital. My son would be alive today if I had done that," he said sadly. I sat crying in the chair.

CHAPTER 24

After Bobby's death, life had gotten extremely hard for the boys and me. We decided to move again to a new place and George came along with us. It wasn't long however, before George was arrested for disorderly conduct and public intoxication and sent back to jail. Now I didn't have Bobby, I didn't have George, and I hadn't spoken to my girls since they had moved over a year ago. The boys and I had moved three times in two years and were now living in a motel. Although I hadn't spoken to Valencia, the boys kept in touch with her and were telling her how bad things were. One day, Valencia and her mother-in-law, Maebelle, showed up at the motel.

"Why don't you let me care for the boys until you get on your feet?" Maebelle asked sincerely.

I looked at her with contempt. "You think I can't take care of my boys?" I asked as I took a sip of my drink.

"That's not what I'm saying, Priscilla. I'm just suggesting that I raise them with the help of their sister until you get things together," she continued.

I looked at Valencia. "Do you think I'm not fit to take care of the boys?"

"Mama, you know you can't take care of the boys right now. Look at you. You can barely take care of yourself," she said as she looked around the motel room that was in total disarray and only had two double beds and a television. "Mama, Junior is eleven years old and just got out of juvenile for vandalizing property and Travis is doing terrible in school. Mrs. Maebelle and I will get them in school and make sure they are taken care of. I can help them because I'll be living there also," Valencia pressed. I was too drunk and too tired to argue. I knew Valencia and Maebelle were right. I couldn't take care of Travis and Junior. I started to cry.

"Okay, you can take them," I said, "just until I get on my feet." A smile lit up the boys' faces, making me feel embarrassed. It was like they were happy to leave me.

It *was* a welcome relief not to have to take care of anyone but myself. I moved out of the motel and into a shelter home with a man named Oliver that I had met at a bar a few nights earlier. We rented a room on the second floor of the South Central Shelter. There were 75 other tenants and only two bathrooms in the entire building. My kids didn't know where I was because I hadn't called to check on the boys.

Five months later, I called Maebelle to check on the boys. She told me that Valencia was pregnant again and had moved to Houston with her husband and son a month ago. "Their marriage is in trouble," Maebelle offered. "They moved to Houston to try to save it. Valencia said she couldn't save her marriage with the boys around, so she left them here with me."

"She did what! I'm coming to get my boys!" I insisted.

"Please don't, Priscilla. Your boys are so happy. They can stay here. There's no need to come and get them," she pleaded. "Just keep getting yourself together. They are doing so well in school."

"No! I'm coming to get my boys now! The only reason I let them stay with you in the first place was because they were going to be living with their sister, but if she moved away, then I'm coming to get my boys." I hung up the telephone.

One week later I showed up at Maebelle's house to collect my boys. As soon as the boys saw me they burst into tears. They begged me to let them stay, but I wouldn't. "I found us a two bedroom apartment on Avalon Boulevard with my new boyfriend Oliver," I told them with excitement.

"Mommy Dearest, we don't want to live with you and your boyfriend Oliver!" Travis said. "Please can we stay with Mrs. Maebelle?" Both boys begged at the same time with uncontrollable sobs while clinging to Maebelle. Maebelle hugged the boys and began crying herself. I resented the fact that the boys obviously preferred to stay with Mrs. Maebelle than to go with me, so I got mad and told the boys to get in Oliver's car. They resisted, but Maebelle convinced them that things were going to be better than before. She told them that I loved them very much – and that she also loved them very much and they could come visit any time they wanted. I was already tipsy and my nerves were beginning to get disturbed. Maebelle gathered as much of their belongings as possible and Oliver loaded them into the trunk of his car. We drove off and never saw Maebelle again.

Oliver and I argued all the time. The boys hated it. They hated living with Oliver and me. Every day one of the boys was getting in trouble about something. Travis at least came home and tried to go to school. Junior hardly ever came home or went to school. We had to go looking for him all the time in the neighborhood. If he did go to school, he got suspended for misbehaving. He carried so much anger that he would tear up a room, cuss anybody out and fight anybody that got in his way. I got so tired of whipping him that I finally said forget it and left him alone.

I had begun to get tired of Oliver and tired of all the problems we were having at home. As an escape, Freddie told me to have an affair with his best friend Aaron. So I did. Although Aaron had a cocaine habit, I welcomed anything that would take me away from the stresses Oliver and the boys were creating in my life.

Oliver had found a job at the scrap yard and I didn't work. Shortly after Oliver left for work every morning, Aaron would arrive at my house. Oliver and Aaron had been best friends for over twenty years. They were such opposites. Oliver was slightly taller than I was, with a medium build and was very conservative. Aaron was tall, around six feet, with a slender build and he was a party animal. We had a good time together for nearly a year until Oliver got off work early one day and saw Aaron leaving the apartment. Aaron didn't see Oliver, who watched him leave the apartment building, walk to the liquor store, purchase some whiskey and then return to the apartment. Oliver confronted Aaron just before he entered the apartment building. "Hey man, what are you doing going and coming from my apartment building when I'm not at home?"

"I've been with your woman!" Aaron boldly said. "I've been sleeping with her for months," he continued without remorse or shame.

"You're lying!" Oliver shouted as he got up in Aaron's face.

"No I'm not, ask Priscilla," Aaron offered. Oliver pushed Aaron out the way and ran into the building and up to our apartment. Aaron followed. Oliver used his key to open the front door. "Priscilla!" he shouted as he walked into the apartment.

I came out of the bedroom with my robe on. "What!" I shouted back noticing the angry expression on Oliver's face.

"I caught Aaron leaving the apartment. He told me that ya'll have been sleeping together for months while I'm at work. Is it true?"

I looked at Aaron standing in the doorway. "Yeah, it's true," I said with a cocky attitude.

"Aaron is my best friend!" he shouted.

"So!" I shouted right back.

Oliver turned his attention to Aaron. He began to cuss him out and called him names just before pushing Aaron out the way and leaving, slamming the door behind him. Later that night Oliver came back to get his things and moved out. "I'm moving in with my sister," he informed me. I saw the hurt and disappointment in his eyes.

I continued to see Aaron and Oliver for months. Aaron came over during the day and Oliver came over at night and on the weekends. Both knew I was still seeing the other one; they didn't care and I didn't care.

CHAPTER 25

Valencia finally called. She said she had gotten my number from directory assistance. I was glad to hear from her. She told me that she and her husband couldn't reconcile their marriage and were getting a divorce. "Mama can me and the kids come live with you in LA for a while until I can get on my feet?" she asked. I was overjoyed at the question; I missed her and my grandchildren. "Yes! You can come live with me!" I yelled with excitement.

Aaron overdosed while at home and sadly had passed away; Oliver found another woman and had moved on. It was just the boys and I in the house; the thought of Valencia and her children coming to stay with us was delightful.

Valencia and the grandkids flew in from Houston a week later. It was great having them in the house. Valencia and I stayed up late laughing and talking about everything; it felt really good to bond with her. We even starting going to clubs together; we went out all the time. Boy did we have a lot of fun! We got drunk, danced, and picked up men. Everyone thought we were sisters; they had no idea that we were mother and daughter. My daughter picked up a lot of men; more than I did, but I didn't get jealous because I had my share of them, too. I just wished that I was skinnier; I had gotten pretty big; weighing nearly 300 pounds. I thought skinny women had more of a chance of being noticed and getting the fine good men. I was ashamed of being fat, but I didn't let it stop me; I did whatever it took to make a man notice me. I'd tell him, "If you just give me a chance, you'll see that I have more to offer than those boney toothpick women that can't keep you warm at night." Clyde took me up on my offer.

Clyde was hypnotic; I was instantly crazy about him. Aside from his cocaine habit, he had all the qualities I liked in a man, tall, fine and *young*. I couldn't believe that a man as fine as Clyde would want a woman like me. I was determined not to lose him, so I did everything he wanted to keep him happy. The night we had met at the club, I was out partying with my daughter and some girlfriends. I used my money to buy all the drinks; anything Clyde wanted I bought. He came home with me that night, and has been here ever since.

Clyde had a seriously bad cocaine habit. He did a line of coke as soon as he woke up, did several lines throughout the day, and he drank large quantities of liquor. The fighting started almost immediately after he moved in.

I was awakened from my sleep one night by the muzzle of a .45 pistol tapping on my forehead. I jumped up terrified, as Clyde stood over me sweating profusely. "I need some money!" he said, sounding out of breath, "and I ain't got time to beg for it."

I reached for my purse and took out my wallet. "All I have is twenty dollars," I said, my hands were shaking as I handed him the money; he snatched the money out of my hand and walked out the room.

Clyde had a short fuse, anything set him off. He was snorting coke and drinking all the time; I stayed drunk all the time, too. My kids were sick and tired of both of us. All we did was get high and fight; for years.

Valencia finally couldn't take the drinking and fighting anymore so she moved out. She and her children got an apartment on Lemoli Avenue in Gardena. She even stopped going out to the clubs with me. She claimed she couldn't take anymore of my outrageous behavior and drunkenness. I didn't want her to stop going to the clubs with me, we had too much fun together; I thought we were bonding like mothers and daughters were supposed to do.

"Please don't go!" I begged her.

"I hate Clyde!" Valencia said. "He's a dope head and I can't stand to see him beat you up anymore. You need to leave him Mama before he kills you!" I pleaded with Valencia not to go, but she and her kids moved out anyway.

At least, Travis and Junior were still living in the house, although I rarely saw them. They were fifteen and sixteen, into girls and doing their own thing. They hated Clyde just as much as Valencia did, if not more; which was their excuse for staying away from home for long periods of time. I hadn't heard from Sandra in months; she never called nor did we have her telephone number. I hoped she was happily married, living with her three children somewhere in Los Angeles.

Sometimes my neighbor Cassandra would hear me and Clyde fighting; she would wait until she knew he was gone; then she would come over to check on me. I liked Cassandra; she had always been compassionate and nice; her sons were nice too. My boys would hang out with her two boys and she would come over and hang out with me. We would drink, and sit and talk for hours.

One of the days she came over to check on me, I was sitting in the living room nursing two black eyes; blood was oozing from my ear. "Girl, you need to leave Clyde, he's crazy!" she said. "He's always beating the mess out of you! He's a bastard!" Cassandra said as she reached for some tissue to help clean my face.

"Cassandra don't talk about my man like that! I love him! It's my fault because I keep pressuring him about the bills in the house and about money, when I know he doesn't have a job. I need to quit bothering him when I know he's trying to get things together."

Cassandra looked at me in amazement for defending Clyde. "Get what things together? Everything he has you bought, even his cocaine," Cassandra shouted. "You're helping him to beat your ass!"

"I just need to do more to please him," I said. "Then he'll be happy again. If you can't understand that then you can get out! I love Clyde and I don't care what anybody thinks."

Cassandra stood up and headed for the front door. "Well his ass don't love you!" she said as she walked out, slamming the door. Cassandra and I never spoke to each other again.

Clyde's cocaine habit was out of control and becoming too costly; I went out and found a job. I got hired at Jordan's Soul Food Restaurant on Wilmington & 113th Street. Mr. Jordan agreed to pay me under the table so I could keep getting my welfare and social security check. That was my kind of job. I washed dishes, bussed tables, cooked and ran the cash register. I was diligent and always on time. I even worked double shifts and split shifts, day or night. Mr. Jordan would tell me often that I was one of his best employees;

despite my drinking problem, that he was quite aware. I *had* to have my drink. I hid several bottles of Hennessey, my drink of choice, in the back storage room; I kept my drink hidden in a Styrofoam cup, and sipped it through a straw. Everyone at the job knew I drank, but I was a good employee; so it was overlooked.

Sometimes, if I was too drunk, Mr. Jordan would have to send me home. Every evening after work, I'd go to the liquor store, get drunk in the park, and then go home. Clyde was always there when I got home; with his hand out or passed out. As soon as he woke up, the fight was on, because he would be expecting his next fix.

Things never got better between Clyde and I; they only got worse. He continued to beat me up and take all the money. I never understood why all the love I had for him never made him love me back the same way. I was cooking in the kitchen one day, when Clyde walked in and punched me in the mouth, for no reason. As I lay on the floor wiping blood from my busted lip, I saw him reach into his pocket, pull out a small bottle; opened it, and put three drops of something into a glass of wine he had just poured. "Here baby," he said, handing me the drink while I was still on the floor. I was hesitant to take the glass, but was scared that if I didn't we would fight some more. "Drink it." he instructed. I reluctantly drank the glass of wine. I woke up a day later in bed, naked, very sore and unsure what Clyde had done to me. I mustered up enough energy to get out of bed, put my robe on, and reached under the mattress for the .45 pistol that Clyde kept under it. I put the gun in my robe pocket and slowly limped out of the bedroom and into the living room; Clyde was sitting at the dining room table rolling joints.

I limped over to him, and pulled out the gun. "What did you put in my drink?" I asked as I pointed the gun at him. He dropped the joint he was rolling.

"Nothing baby, it was n-n-n-nothing," he stuttered holding his hands up.

"You're lying! I know you've been putting something in my drinks and taking advantage of me! I know you've been doing it for a while!" I stepped closer to him and pulled the trigger back on the gun.

"No baby, you got it all wrong, I love you."

"You're not fit to live!" I said as I walked even closer, still pointing the gun at him. Clyde looked terrified as he anticipate what my next move would be.

I stared at him. Then I heard a voice, that didn't sound like Freddie's voice; it was God. "Don't kill him Priscilla, think about your children." I was used to Freddie talking to me; this was the first time God had ever spoken to me. I lowered the gun and said "If you ever hit me again, I will kill you. Now get out of my house!" I ordered. Clyde scrambled to grab his marijuana and hurried out the front door. That night, I packed all of his belongings and set them outside on the front porch.

The next day, Junior came home to find the house in total disarray, as if a cyclone had gone through it. Clyde had showed up wanting money; too high to remember that I had put him out the night before. He banged on the door; hard and loud, until I answered it. "I need some money" he demanded. "I ain't got no money!" I yelled. Clyde hit me so hard that I fell on the coffee table and broke it. As I tried to get up, he picked up one of the broken table legs, and hit me again; so hard that I soared in the air and landed in the chair. I got up and I ran into the kitchen as blood poured from my head. I threw dishes, pots, pans or whatever I could get my hands on to try and stop him, but Clyde was acting like a crazed animal. He kept charging at me with this demonic look in his eyes. "I don't have any money!" I kept screaming, but he didn't believe me. He grabbed me by my hair, punched me several times in my face and then dragged me into the bedroom by my arm. I kicked and screamed, but couldn't get away. Junior walked in the house just as screams were coming from the bedroom.

"Where's the money! I know you got some money!" Clyde screamed as he continued to punch me. Junior burst through the bedroom door and grabbed Clyde by the neck. He started beating him up; stomping, kicking and beating him down on the floor.

"No, Junior don't hit him!" I screamed. I started beating up Junior for beating up Clyde.

"What are you doing Mama?" Junior yelled as he tried to block my punches.

"Leave Clyde alone, don't hurt him!" I yelled back.

"Mama! This man is trying to kill you. Look at the blood all over you. He's beatin' you to death because you didn't give him money for drugs, and you're hittin' me, for hittin' him, because he's hittin' you? What's wrong with you?" Junior stared at me, shocked that I was defending Clyde.

"I love him, please don't hurt him anymore." I said. Clyde lay on the floor holding his stomach and bleeding from his nose, lip and eyebrow.

Junior took a couple steps back and pointed his finger at me. "You're crazy and he's crazy! I'm outta here!" he said. "Let him kill you for all I care!" Junior ran out of the house.

Clyde got up off the floor. I tried to help him, but he pushed me away. He limped out of the house, loaded his few bags in his car; that were sitting on the porch and drove off.

I tried to stop the bleeding from my forehead, but I couldn't get it to stop. In a panic, I ran out of the house, looking for someone to help me. A man at the corner was just getting out of his car; I ran up to him and asked for help; blood poured from my forehead like water. The man popped the trunk of his car and grabbed some rags and an ice pack from his first aid kit; he helped me to get into his car; then drove me to County General Hospital. I was immediately examined and whisked straight into surgery; Clyde had broken a blood vessel in my forehead. After the surgery, the doctors told me that if I had waited a few minutes longer to get help, I would have died. I stayed in the hospital for almost a week. I didn't call anyone, not even my kids.

I never saw Clyde again and I hadn't seen or heard from Junior in months; until I got a phone call that he was in jail. Junior was *always* into things in the neighborhood, getting into trouble with the law, experimenting with drugs, *or something*. This was the fifth time he had been arrested. It turned out that Junior had decided he wanted to be in a gang; for his gang initiation, he had to assault someone using a gun. At Junior's arraignment, the judge set his bail at $50,000. "You're seventeen years old son, and facing 25 years to life in prison for assault with a deadly weapon," the judge said. "Do you understand the seriousness of these charges?" Junior hung his head down and cried.

"Mama, please help me!" Junior begged while on the telephone later that day. "I don't want to go to prison," he cried out. I did not have any money to pay for Junior's bail or a lawyer. All I could do was to pray to God for help. It had been a while since I had been to church, but I always read my Bible and I always believed in God. I believed if I prayed God wouldn't let Junior go to prison. After hanging up the telephone, I got down on my knees and prayed like I had never prayed before. I blamed myself for Junior being in jail.

Junior's hearing was two month later, in the Los Angeles County 325th District Court. Judge Joe Brown was the presiding judge. I sat with Travis, Valencia and the grandchildren in the courtroom. As we waited for court to start, I thought about a conversation I had with one of my drinking buddies in the park; something that I didn't want to hear at that time.

I was sitting in the park drinking with Wanda when she asked me how old my kids were. I had to think for a minute because I was so drunk. Their ages finally came to me; I remembered they were all teenagers.

"Why?" I asked.

"It must be tough raising four kids," she said. "That oldest boy of yours, Junior, I see his bad ass in the neighborhood getting into stuff all the time. I bet he stays in trouble," she continued.

I looked at her, wondering where she was going with this conversation. "Junior knows I don't want him getting caught up in these streets, but he got his own mind. I can't tell him nothing, he don't listen to me. When he was five years old he spit in my face and called me the devil."

"Well what do you expect?" Wanda asked. "Look at his mother!" She swallowed a big gulp of the Cool Breeze she was drinking and lit a joint. "*You* always drunk, *you* ain't never at home and *you* always in the street. Hell, you in the park gettin' drunk more than you at home taking care of your kids." I stopped drinking my can of Old English and looked at her; appalled at her judgmental attitude. "You know how I know?" she asked, looking up at me with blood shot eyes. "'Cause I'm always out here with you. I got six kids and I can't tell you nothing about them; I don't know any of my kids, and they don't want to know nothing about me. A drunk mother ain't no mother, and damn sure ain't no role model!" Wanda took a puff of her joint.

I got mad and walked off.

Remembering that conversation convinced me that if I had been a better mother my son wouldn't be facing prison. It *was* my fault.

I got nervous when the judge walked out; I prayed under my breath. Junior entered the courtroom wearing an orange jumpsuit, handcuffs with shackles around his ankles. The bailiff walked him in front of the Judge's bench and left him standing beside his court appointed attorney.

"What's the problem son?" Judge Brown asked. "You're being accused of assault with a deadly weapon. Do you want to go to prison?"

"No sir," Junior answered, hanging his head. "I don't want to go to prison."

"You're a seventeen-year-old young man. Do you have any idea what would happen to someone your age in prison facing 25 years to life?" Junior shook his head no. "According to our records you've been in and out of trouble for the last 10 years. Is your father living in your home?" Judge Brown asked.

"No, Sir. Not since I was little," Junior answered.

"Hmm," Judge Brown said as he leaned back in his chair. "Are you still in school?"

"Yes, Sir."

"What grade are you in?"

"Twelfth," Junior answered.

"I'll tell you what young man I'm going to give you a break; I don't know why; I just feel compelled to do so. I want to believe that you know you were stupid to try to join a gang, something that would surely land you in prison or in the morgue." Junior stood looking at the Judge and wondering where he was going with his statements. "It's October and you should be graduating from high school in May of next year. If you can finish high school and graduate, I won't send you to prison. When you bring me your official high school diploma, I will dismiss all the charges against you. Now *your* freedom and *your* future are in *your* hands". Junior looked up at the judge with a puzzled look on his face.

"Sentencing is pending this young man's high school diploma." Judge Brown said. "This case will be reviewed in 8 months at which time, if the high school diploma is presented all said charges will be dismissed; if the high school diploma is not presented, the defendant will face the maximum sentence for the crime he committed." The Judge banged his gavel and Junior was led away to be processed for release.

I was stunned at the Judge's decision. I realized it wasn't Judge Joe Brown who made the decision, but God. I thanked Him for answering my prayers.

CHAPTER 26

It was lonely at home. Junior graduated high school and moved out to live with his pregnant girlfriend. I hadn't seen him since May. Even my sixteen-year-old, Travis, moved out. He said he was discovered by Coca Cola when he entered a talent search, and was going to be doing commercials, and would become this big-time actor. As excited as he was, I couldn't be happy for him; I was too down and out inside.

I had no one left except Freddie and the people I worked with. I missed Clyde so much. "Why couldn't he be good to me and love me like I loved him?" I asked Freddie as I swallowed some aspirin with a glass of vodka.

I didn't like living by myself. Valencia was glad I got rid of Clyde so we started talking again. I spent a lot of time at her house, I liked that. Valencia had a fiancé now and I resented him. I thought that if she married him, she wouldn't have time for me, and he would come between us. I begged her not to marry him for my own selfish reasons. She married him anyway. Just as I thought, her time became occupied with her new husband.

Travis finally called after a year of being away. "I'm doing a television interview on Good Morning LA, Tuesday on Channel 8," he said. "I want you to watch it." He sounded so excited and I was excited for him. I told everybody I knew to be sure to watch the morning show because my son was going to be on it. I still worked at Jordan's Soul Food Restaurant, so on the morning of the interview Mr. Jordan brought a television to work so we all could watch it. We all crowded our chairs around the television when the show came on. I clapped with excitement to see my son on T.V.

Towards the middle of the interview, the interviewer asked Travis about his childhood. "My mother is a drunk. I had a horrible and dysfunctional childhood. My mother has been an alcoholic all my life. She made it impossible to love her," he answered. My mouth fell open and my co-workers all burst into laughter. I felt humiliated and embarrassed. I stood up and walked away from the television. I didn't want to listen to the rest of the interview. If I had known he would say such terrible things about me on national television, I never would have told anyone to watch. I began to cry. My co-workers stopped laughing when they saw how upset I was. I left work and went to the park.

My drinking was out of control. I started going to church even though I continued to drink. Most of the time when I went to church I was drunk or had been drinking, but I loved the Lord. I begged God to help me. I had so much pain inside of me and just wanted to be delivered from it. Every now and then, I even tried to stop drinking. I even went to some of the local AA meetings that were held at the church that I was attending. But, I couldn't stop drinking. I prayed to God and I drank at the same time.

Valencia was tired of me coming to her house and drinking. If I ran out of liquor and she wouldn't go buy me some more I would go off and cuss out everybody in the house. Valencia finally limited my visits to her house. Travis *obviously* was disappointed with my drinking, considering what he said about me on TV and I hadn't seen him in over two years. Sandra lived somewhere in LA, and she rarely ever called. I found out that Junior lived only a few blocks away from where I lived and I never saw him either.

I missed my kids, and I had grandchildren that I hadn't even seen yet. *I'm going to try to do better, I told myself.* I started going to church more and I went to AA meetings all the time. My family was proud of me. Valencia and her husband fell on hard times so they ended up moving in with me in my one bedroom apartment. Even though I didn't like her husband, I liked having Valencia and the grandkids live with me. It was wonderful and I felt complete and happier. My other children were even communicating with me more and letting me see my grandchildren. I was even trying not to drink, *as much*.

I'd lay awake at night trying not to want to drink. Then I would get up to go find a bottle of liquor that I had hidden in the apartment. I tried hard not to want to drink it, and sometimes I would even pour it out. Occasionally, I would throw the bottle in the trash. But, I always ended up going outside to get the bottle or finding another bottle that was hidden. I tried to hide my drinking from my family because I didn't want them to leave me again.

I tried really hard to listen at my AA meetings, but I kept having trouble concentrating and having panic attacks. My nerves bothered me and my legs hurt from picking at the chronic dermatitis on them. I was lonely and needed the comfort of a man. I was lying to the AA counselors and my family telling them that I wasn't drinking when I was. I felt God had abandoned me, because he hadn't delivered me from this disease. I felt it was just a matter of time before it killed me, because I had to be drunk to do anything. I was scared all the time.

There wasn't an AA meeting that I attended where I didn't cry. I heard so many sad stories about being an alcoholic's wife or an alcoholic's husband, losing jobs, wrecking cars, being ostracized from the family, or killing someone. The stories were difficult and too painful to listen to, so sometimes I would get up and leave.

There wasn't a church service that I didn't cry at either. I threw myself on the altar nearly every Sunday begging God to deliver me from my addiction…afraid that my family was going to disown me… afraid to be alone…scared I was going to die.

I was at work and Freddie told me to leave work, go to the liquor store, buy a bottle of Champagne, and drink the whole bottle. I was already hung over from the night before, but I didn't question Freddie. "I need to go home right now," I told my co-worker. I called a cab to come pick me up. When the cab arrived, I instructed the driver that I was going home, but I would be stopping at the liquor store on the corner of Central Avenue, which was a block away from my house before he took me home. The driver did as I asked and stopped at the liquor store. I got out of the cab, walked into the liquor store and bought a bottle of Champagne. Carrying a brown paper bag with the Champagne in it, I jumped back into the cab and the driver proceeded to drive the rest of the way to my house. I noticed the cab driver watching me in his rear view mirror. He looked to be in his late twenties. I was forty-eight, but looked fifty-eight and felt every bit of sixty-eight. I felt embarrassed that my self-esteem was low and I wasn't looking my best.

"Why do you keep looking back here?" I asked the cab driver.

"I was wondering if you were going to be celebrating alone." I smiled at his flirtatious comment. "I see you bought a bottle of Champagne," he continued.

"I'm not celebrating; I'm just drinking it because that's what I want to do."

"Are you drinking by yourself?" he asked curiously.

"Why?" I asked, wishing he would hurry up and get to the real reason he was asking so many questions.

"I wanted to know if you desired some company."

Flattered at the invitation, I said, "Sure, if you want to join me." We finally reached my house and he parked the cab. I stuck my hand into my purse and pulled out money to pay him. He reached for the money and rubbed my hand. I cracked a faint smile. I pulled my hand away and opened the cab door to get out. With my purse in one hand and my bottle of Champagne in the other, I used my hip to shut the door. Then I bent down and looked at the cab driver through the passenger side window.

"So what are you waiting for, are you coming?"

He smiled and quickly hopped out of the cab. We walked into the apartment and went straight to my bedroom. Valencia, her kids and her husband were watching television on the couch. I didn't even speak. The cab driver spent the night. The next morning he told me his name was Nathaniel and that he was 29 years old. I told him my name was Priscilla and I was 48 years old. "I don't care," he said, "I figured you were around that old anyway." Nathaniel came over every night for months. Every time he came, he brought something to drink with him. He eventually moved in.

Things between Nathaniel and I were going great until he started becoming controlling and bossy. *Where you going? Who you going with? How long you going to be gone?* I heard these questions every day. I felt like I was with Mr. Murray again. Nathaniel was very jealous, more so than any other man I had ever been with. He was driving me crazy. He was so jealous that he didn't want me talking to my own children. He wanted me to talk only to him, to leave the house only with him, and to do things only with him. I was being smothered and feeling trapped. We fought and argued all the time.

It was getting close to Mother's Day in 2005, and my children had been acting suspicious and secretive. I knew they were planning something but I didn't know what. A few times I asked what they were planning, but no one would tell me. I was still hiding my drinking, only drinking heavily in my bedroom and moderate to none around my children. I had stopped going to the clubs, and the bars, and hanging out at the park. I spent more time at home, other than when I went to work. Since Nathaniel lived with me, I had no choice; he wouldn't let me do much anyway.

Sandra and her husband came to visit Thursday night. When I saw her I knew something was going on. She rarely ever came to visit. "Mama," Sandra said after we sat down on the couch. "We have planned a big surprise for you for Mother's Day. You're going to be on the Oprah show tomorrow!" she blurted out excitedly.

"For what?" I asked feeling unimpressed.

"It's a big surprise and I can't tell you why," Sandra continued, almost exploding with enthusiasm.

"I don't want to go on the Oprah show," I said as I looked up at Nathaniel who appeared to be fuming with anger. He turned and walked into the bedroom.

Ignoring Nathaniel's behavior, Sandra continued, "You really need to go Mama, your flight leaves in the morning. I'll pick you up to go to the airport because I'm going to go with you," she continued.

"I don't want to go," I said again.

"Mama, *please*! Please be ready by 9 o'clock in the morning." Sandra got up to leave. She gave me a hug just before walking out the door.

Nathaniel and I argued all night long. He didn't want me to go. "I hate your kids because they are trying to come between us," he yelled. "They're taking you on that show to set you up with another man because they want to break us up and Oprah's in on it too! That's how those talk shows are, and Oprah's show ain't no different! You see they didn't invite me to go!" he screamed.

My nerves were frazzled all night. If I went, Nathaniel was going to be mad, and I was scared that he'd break up with me. If I didn't go, my kids would be mad; I was scared they wouldn't speak to me again. I didn't know what to do. I drank an entire bottle of

Hennessey, popped two pain pills and had one beer before I finally made up my mind. I was going on the Oprah show.

The next morning my nerves were still bothering me. I chose not to drink anything since I had so much to drink the night before, but I did take two nerve pills to calm myself enough to get on the airplane. I had never flown before and I was panicking. Nathaniel didn't speak to me all morning, other than to call me names and bad mouth my kids. I ignored him and was ready when Sandra came to pick me up.

The flight to Chicago seemed very long, and I was nervous the entire way. About half way through the flight I took a nap. When we landed, a limo was waiting to pick us up and drive us to Harpo Studios. I didn't talk much because the anticipation of the surprise was rattling my nerves, and I was also trying to come off a high from the night before.

The show was a Mother's Day special where celebrities were presenting their mothers with special gifts. Among the celebrities who came up with an original way to celebrate Mother's Day were Giselle Blondet and Paola Gutierrez whose mothers had opportunities to live enchanting fantasies with their daughters.

Puerto Rican actress and Univision TV host, Giselle Blondet, decided to give her mother a different kind of gift than what she usually received every year. She treated her mother, Alba Gomez, to a day of fame with a Hollywood makeover in preparation for a movie star photo shoot, directed by Mickey Mouse and Minnie Mouse at Walt Disney World's Hollywood Studios.

Meanwhile, Paolo Gutierrez, a correspondent for the morning show "Despierta America", and her daughters Antonella and Isabella went all out and brought grandma Norma San Martin from their native Bolivia, so that she could be Queen for a Day in the Magic Kingdom, with a special magical moment hosted by Cinderella, Snow White and Belle.

The Oprah Team had video-taped their experiences. They looked like they were having so much fun, I thought, as I watched the videos.

The Oprah show captured a huge amount of good will for the Mother's Day weekend activities in support of research for a cure for breast cancer, including the highly publicized Revlon Run/Walk. Top celebrity chefs were participating in "Cook for the Cure" presented by Kitchen Aid; an effort by the culinary community and cooking enthusiasts, to support and raise funds for the Susan G. Komen foundation. I was inspired to know that Nancy Brinker promised her dying sister, Susan, she would do everything in her power to end breast cancer forever. In 1982, Nancy's promise became the Susan G. Komen for the Cure foundation and launched the global breast cancer movement. Listening to her talk about her sister brought tears to my eyes.

Several well-known chefs appeared on the show to raise awareness and give credit to the women who inspired them: their mothers. All the chefs signed the popular pink Kitchen Aid Artisan Series Stand Mixer, which was being auctioned on a show called *Charity Folks*.

In order to create breast cancer awareness, the celebrity chefs and wait staff wore pink aprons during the holiday weekend. The aprons read *"I cook for Mom."* Oprah had her wait staff wearing the pink aprons, and bringing out samples of food for the audience. The food was delicious.

Several other celebrities sent their well wishes to their moms on the show. Jason Sehorn, a former player for the New York Giants, who proposed to his wife Angie Harmon on The Tonight Show with Jay Leno in 2000, was also a guest on the show. In a touching moment, he surprised a single mother by providing the down payment on a new home. I, along with several audience members, was very touched and became teary-eyed.

During the commercial break, the show's director invited me to sit on Oprah's couch. I nervously obliged and walked onto the stage. My stomach knotted up with jitters. The show continued with my son Travis on the video screen. Oprah asked everyone to watch Travis on the screen.

"Happy Mother's Day, Mama!" he shouted with his usual big grin on his face. "Let me present to you *your* special Mother's Day gift," he pointed behind him. "It's a beautiful, four-bedroom, three-bath, home here in Tuscany Hills, California." The camera showed Travis standing in front of a two-story brick house surrounded by a quarter-acre of land inside a gated community. Ahhs, ooohhs and applauds rang out from the audience. Sandra put her arms around me, leaned her head on my shoulder and cried tears of joy. I cried tears of joy and relief because the suspense of not knowing what to expect had been killing me. I was overjoyed and surprised, covering my face with my hands to hide my tears.

"Look behind you," Travis said. Oprah pointed to the left of the stage. I looked up, removing my hands from my face and wiping the tears out of my eyes. My other children, Valencia and her husband, Junior and his girlfriend, and all my grandchildren came walking out from behind the curtain. Junior was carrying a bouquet of flowers.

"The whole family is here!" Oprah shouted.

I was overwhelmed and could not stop crying. My kids and grandchildren hugged and kissed me. After a few moments we all turned to watch as Travis gave us a narrated tour of the house.

"In your 3,000 square-foot home I chose an African décor. I wanted to give the feeling of being in exotic Africa no matter how far away we are from it. One of the most important features that I chose in decorating the house was indigenous artwork. Most of the art was purchased from an authentic dealer, but some are replication pieces. African art is filled with meaning. The hand-carved statues you see," he said as he walked throughout the house and pointed to several wall hangings and other pieces of art, "are said to bring peace, fertility, health, money, longevity and more. The hand-carved vases and flatware with symbols are of different African tribes. The prints on various chairs and furniture are fabrics that are associated with particular tribes or regions of Africa. I wanted to find art that would mean something to you and to our family. I wanted the house to look unique." He continued the tour, "You have a state-of-the-art kitchen, complete with appliances, dishes, flatware, glasses and pot and pans. Your cabinets and refrigerator are completely stocked with food."

The audience was going crazy with excitement. I was impressed with how much thought and detail he had put into the house. I couldn't stop crying, even Oprah was crying.

He walked up the marble staircase and continued the tour. "Your bedroom is the biggest bedroom in the house; the master bedroom is nearly 800 square feet, and is complete with a king-size bed and television." Travis walked over to a huge walk-in closet. "This is your closet and it's full of thousands of dollars of brand new clothes just for you. The bathroom is also huge. The shower is separate from the eight-jet spa bathtub. Your vanity table is stocked with all kinds of toiletries and perfumes. The closet is full of towels and bed linens.

Now let's go back downstairs and see what's outside," he said grinning. The camera cut to him standing outside on the patio. "This is your new patio set along with a brand new barbeque grill. The freezer inside is full of meat for you to grill."

I sat continuing to wipe tears from my eyes. I looked over at Oprah and she was still crying, too. I looked at my family and they all were crying, too.

"I have one final gift for you, Mama," Travis said. *What more could he possibly give me, I wondered.* The camera followed him around to the side of the house, showing the beautifully manicured yard along the way. On the side of the house was a brand new, tan, Dodge Quest 7 passenger van, complete with a big red bow on it. At that point, I lost it. I screamed and boohooed like crazy. Oprah screamed, hugged me and cried with me. The audience went crazy, too. My family was jumping up and down with joy.

"Happy Mother's Day!" Travis shouted. "I love you and I'll see you at the house after the show."

The monitor went off. The show went to commercial break. The show's director walked me back to my seat in the audience. I sat in awe, crying on my daughter's shoulder. The gifts were more than I expected; more than I deserved.

After the show the entire family flew back to LA together. A limo picked us up at the airport and drove us to the new house. If only I had a drink, I thought. Then I could handle all this excitement. My craving for a drink was so bad that I was starting to shake. My family didn't notice and if they did they probably thought I was shaking from all the excitement.

When we arrived at the house, we found a large crowd gathered. Travis had bussed in all my friends and neighbors from the old neighborhoods in Compton and Watts to celebrate Mother's Day and the house with me. There were friends I hadn't seen in years, it was like a huge family reunion. Travis had left no stone unturned. There was media coverage, food, music and a giant cake that read "Happy

Mother's Day to the Best Mother in the World." Everybody had a great time for hours. I felt better when I was able to break away and have a drink, because I sure did need one.

CHAPTER 27

I liked the "Big House" as I called it, but it overwhelmed me. It was very beautiful. Most people would dream of owning something like this in their lifetime, but I never had. I had no dreams in life, no desires and no ambition. I was happy because my son was happy for giving me the house, but I would have been just as happy in my one bedroom apartment sleeping and sitting on my second-hand furniture, drinking out of a mayonnaise jar and wearing the same crappy tee shirts and pants. I wasn't used to all this stuff: the daintiness of the designs and custom this and that, the designer this and that, all these brand new clothes. It was too much.

Freddie was the only one who understood how I felt. He helped me cope with the anxiety I was feeling by telling me to have a house party. Travis had started giving me a weekly allowance and I used every bit of that money to furnish the liquor supply for my party. I bought every kind of alcohol imaginable. Hennessey, which was my favorite drink, vodka, 2-11, gin, Cool Breeze, Jim Beam, Wild Irish Rose, Madd Dogg 20-20, White Lightning, scotch, brandy, wines and all types of beers. We were loaded down with liquor. I invited everybody I knew to come to the Big House party. Because Travis had bused in the entire Watts and Compton neighborhood to see the house, everybody knew where I lived. I even invited people from my AA meetings to come to the party too. My kids came with their friends; everybody except Travis. We had a good time. We got so drunk and partied all night long. I had so much fun that night that I decided I was going to have a party in the house every night.

I started letting people spend the night. I'd let them stay as long they wanted to. Junior moved in with his girlfriend and kids, Valencia was divorced now so she moved in with her kids, and Sandra moved in with her husband and kids also. I was happy having people in the house because I hated to be alone. Nathaniel and I fought all the time, but once he realized he couldn't control me, he finally stopped trying. He got drunk every day, too.

The house no longer looked like it did when Travis first gave it to me. Several pieces of furniture were broken from people getting drunk and fighting. My sofas and chairs had liquor stains all over them from people spilling their drinks or had burn holes where people dropped cigarette ashes or marijuana butts on them. Most of my African artifacts, expensive what-knots and kitchen appliances that could be easily lifted were stolen; two out of the three toilets were broken.

The Big House was in a gated, upscale community, so my activities were constantly scrutinized by the neighbors and the home owners association. They complained of the music being too loud, people fighting, people getting drunk and wandering into someone else's yard, or driving crazily through the neighborhood. The community security guards and the police had been called several times. They said we were disturbing the peaceful neighborhood and we needed to get ourselves under control. But, we never got under control, things were extremely out of control, and didn't seem to be getting better any time soon.

One night I spent the night drinking at Kathy's house because I was pissed off that nobody at my house had any money to buy liquor. I was tired of everybody always drinking up my liquor and never replenishing my stash. After I cussed out everybody at the Big House, I left and drove to Kathy's house. Kathy was my co-worker from Jordan's Soul Food restaurant. I knew she had something to drink at her house because she liked to get her drink on like me. Kathy lived with her boyfriend, so we all stayed up late, playing music and drinking. I drank Old English and gin mixed together all night and got sloppy drunk. Kathy passed out early, in the chair, but her old man, Tommy, and I kept the night going. By morning I hadn't slept a wink and I was so drunk I could barely stand up.

Kathy woke up and saw Tommy and I sitting on the couch. She jumped to conclusions and went off on both of us. "You whore!" she yelled. "You slept with my man while I was passed out drunk, didn't you!" She continued cussing and acting irately.

I was drunk, but not so much that I couldn't comprehend her accusations. "I didn't sleep with your man!" I said as I struggled to try to stand up.

Kathy pushed me back down on the couch; then stuck her finger in my face. "You're a whore and a no good friend, get out of my house!

"I told you I didn't sleep with your old man," I said as I stumbled to the door. Tommy had fallen asleep on the couch, so he was oblivious to what was happening. Kathy shoved me out the door and slammed it. Kathy and I had been friends for awhile and I was disappointed that she would accuse me of doing such a thing.

It took me a minute to remember where I parked my car. I had an old Toyota that I bought from a crack head a few months before Travis bought me the van. It was different having a car since I was used to riding the bus or walking everywhere I went. Once I finally found my car, I got in it and sped off down Avalon Boulevard. I don't remember if it was minutes later or hours later, but I was being arrested for crashing my Toyota in somebody's front yard on West Manchester Avenue. The car was totaled and gasoline was spilling onto the ground. My head was bleeding and I had cuts on my face and arms. The police took me to the county hospital to get bandaged up and then to the police station to be booked for DWI.

The police kept me at the police station for a few hours and then released me. "Priscilla Murray, you're free to go", an officer called out as he stood holding the cell door open. "What?" I said under my breath. Clearly, I was drunk; I had even urinated on myself. I know my blood alcohol level had to be well past the legal limit because I had been drinking all night. I didn't understand why the police decided to let me go and I didn't ask any questions. Fortunately, I slept off some of my high while I was in the holding cell. I thanked God for not letting me get booked for the DWI as I walked out of the police station. I walked to the bus stop and rode the bus back to Tuscany Hills.

I couldn't remember where my car was so I told my kids somebody stole it. Because I couldn't hide the cuts and bruises I exaggerated the story and told them that I was assaulted. Fortunately, I had another vehicle, the Dodge Quest van that Travis had bought me. After I told the kids what happened, they told me I needed to quit drinking. I cussed out every last one of them. Sandra couldn't take it anymore so she and her kids moved out. She was upset at my behavior and how my actions and friends had trashed the beautiful house in less than a year.

Later that night at the house party, Nathaniel and I had another fight. I grabbed the keys and ran outside to jump in the van. Before I could close the driver's side door, Nathaniel punched me in the face and shoved me to the passenger side. He got in the driver's seat, started the vehicle and headed in the direction of the community clubhouse.

"Let me out!" I screamed. "I don't want to go with you!"

"Shut up!" he yelled, cussing and calling me names while he continued to punch me. Nathaniel was driving like a mad man through the community. He was driving so fast and erratic that I was being thrown around in the car, I didn't have my seat belt on.

"You're crazy, let me out!" I continued to scream.

Nathaniel would not stop the car. He was so drunk; I don't think he knew where he was going. Finally, I opened the car door and jumped out. I rolled over and over and over on the asphalt. I finally stopped rolling when I hit my head on the curb. My face, arms, and legs were severely skinned up and bleeding. Nathaniel never stopped the car he just kept driving. I lay on the ground in agonizing pain until I gathered enough strength to stagger my way back to the Big House. It seemed like it took me forever to walk back. I kept stopping to catch my breath; and sitting down on the ground for a few moments. When I finally made it to the house, I walked in and nobody paid me any attention. I was bloody and my clothes were dirty and torn. I went straight to my room, laid down on my bed, and went to sleep.

The next morning, I woke up in excruciating pain, in the same torn, dirty clothes, and still covered in blood. My bed linens had bloodstains all over them from going to sleep without bandaging my wounds. I looked myself over, I was a mess. Skid marks and scars were all over my face and body. The white meat was showing on the side of my face and on my arms and legs. Some of my cuts were deep and still bleeding. I needed to go to the hospital. I went in the living room and asked one of the guys who was living with me to take me to the emergency room. He had to drive his car because Nathaniel had taken my van.

When I arrived at the emergency room the doctor asked me what happened to me. "I fell down the hill behind my house." I said. I didn't want to tell the truth, that Nathaniel beat me up and I jumped out a moving vehicle that was going at least 60 miles an hour. They would have had him arrested. The doctor stitched me up in a few places and bandaged me up in others, then gave me a prescription for pain pills.

After we left the hospital, we drove around looking for Nathaniel and the van. We didn't find Nathaniel, but we did find the van; wrecked and parked illegally on Willow Brook Avenue in Compton. Fortunately, it started so I drove it back to Tuscany Hills. Nathaniel never came back to the Big House.

A few days later, the sound of someone screaming woke me up. I was sitting inside my wrecked van, parked in front of somebody's house. I couldn't remember how I got there or how long I had been there. The last thing I remembered was finding the van in Compton. The windows were down in the van and empty liquor bottles and beer cans were in the seats and on the floor.

Trying to focus, I looked around to see who was screaming. The garage door was open at the house that I was parked in front of, and I saw an elderly white lady standing inside screaming. I got out of the van and stumbled towards her.

"What's wrong, why are you screaming?" I asked.

"It's a snake!" she said pointing to a corner in the garage. I looked to where she was pointing and saw what appeared to be a twelve to fifteen inch reddish-brown snake with dark blotches and smooth shinny scales coiled up in the corner. Her husband came into the garage; "It's a snake!" she shouted again showing it to him.

"I'll kill it," he said as he rustled around the garage trying to find something to use to kill the snake. I walked over to the snake and picked it up with my bare hands. The snake bit me on my hand between my thumb and first finger. I screamed, the old lady screamed, her husband screamed; then he ran to get the telephone to call 911. With my other hand, I pried the snake's fangs from my hand and threw it as far as I could. "Call 911!" the old lady demanded of her husband, who was already dialing the telephone. I walked out of the garage without saying a word and headed east down the street. I ignored the old couple's pleas to stay and wait for the ambulance. I left my van parked in front of their house and headed back to the Big House. It was too wrecked to drive.

Tension was thick in the Big House. Besides the house being filthy every day, Valencia and Junior were on my case all the time about my drinking. "You need to stop drinking!" Junior would yell.

"I ain't never gonna buy you no more liquor and don't ask me to go to the store anymore! You drink too much and you need to stop! I mean it Mama! Ain't no sense in you cussing me or Valencia out anymore because we won't buy you any liquor, or because we won't give you any money to buy any liquor or because we won't take you to the store to buy you some liquor!" he continued.

"Yeah, Mama! We don't even know you when you are drinking. Our kids don't even want to be around you! You've been drinking all our lives and we are sick of it!" Valencia added.

"I don't give a damn what ya'll sick of! I'll drink if I want to, so leave me the hell alone!" I screamed back. At that point, I started spending most of my time in my bedroom. I bought a microwave oven for my room, a hot plate and a small dorm-size refrigerator; and that's where I stayed, in my room. I cooked my food in my room, ate in my bed and watched television, 24 hours a day. Fortunately, I had a bathroom in my bedroom. I rarely ever came out of my room. I had no idea what was going on in the house.

I heard a commotion in the middle of the night coming from downstairs. I climbed out of bed to see what was going on. It was Valencia and Junior arguing, again. They never seemed to get along. Raymond jumped in the middle of the argument and Junior punched him in the face and started beating him up. I came down the stairs just as Valencia jumped on Junior's back in an attempt to defend her husband. Junior threw Valencia off his back and slapped her across the face. When I saw Junior slap Valencia, I got mad and slapped him. "Why are you hitting me?" Junior yelled, holding his face. Before I could answer, Valencia punched Junior in his face. I grabbed

Junior and wrestled with him to keep him from going after Valencia, who ran to the telephone and dialed 911. Junior, mad because he couldn't get to Valencia, turned his attention back to Raymond and they began to fight again.

There was terrible mayhem. Valencia had been drinking and Junior was high, so it was hard to calm either one down. By the time the police arrived, Junior and Raymond had busted down the front door and were fighting in the yard. The police broke up the fight.

"Junior beat up my husband and he slapped me!" Valencia screamed. "I want him arrested! I want to press charges!" she continued.

"What?" Junior yelled, surprised that his sister would want him arrested. The police grabbed Junior and put him in handcuffs. "You're being arrested for assault, sir," the officer told Junior as he placed him in the police car.

I watched with tears in my eyes as the police drove off with Junior, handcuffed in the back seat. Everything had happened so fast and now Junior is being arrested. I was flustered and my nerves were in a tizzy. Valencia continued to mouth off, cuss and complain about the incident. "We're moving out!" she threatened. "We ain't staying in this raggedy, filthy house no more, especially if Junior is going to be living here."

Junior had almost completed his two-week jail sentence before Travis heard about what happened. He called the Big House upset about the incident, and said he was coming to the house to talk to Valencia and me. Travis hadn't been to the Big House since he gave it to me almost a year ago.

Travis pulled up to the Big House in his Cadillac Escalade later that same day. I saw him drive up so I came out the house to meet him. I could see the expression on his face through the windshield as he arrived and it made me uneasy. He looked pissed.

He brought his SUV to a screeching halt and jumped out. "What the...!" he asked as he looked at the Quest van parked in the yard with a smashed windshield, and its front end wrecked so badly that it looked like a Yugo instead of a seven passenger van. He walked into the house without saying a word. The front door was scratched, dented and hanging on one hinge instead of three. The house reeked of an indescribable stench and Travis cuffed his hand over his nose. One of my friends was lying on the couch and another was sitting in a chair watching television. Travis ignored both of them. He continued to look around the house without saying a word to anyone. He just walked and looked with an astonished look on his face. Watching his facial expressions and his demeanor, I knew he was mad. I suddenly became terrified, so I ran to my room and hid in the closet. Travis continued to walk into every room in the house, upstairs and downstairs. Valencia and her husband were in their bedroom, they didn't speak nor did they come out of the room. The grandchildren were running around playing in the house. Travis ignored them too and just continued to look around the house without saying a word, rubbing his hands across his brow and mouth.

"What the *hell* happened to this house?" he finally yelled out. "Mama!" he screamed as he opened the door to my bedroom. "What the hell did you do to the house?" I pushed my way further back into my closet; too scared to speak.

The carpet throughout the house was ripped and stained. One toilet was completely broken, but apparently, someone kept using it. The other toilet was rigged to flush after someone broke the handle and the lid. Doorknobs were missing from most of the doors and some doors were missing. There were holes in the walls. Somebody started to paint a few of the walls, but stopped before finishing. Half the furniture was missing and what was left was ripped, broken, stained and dirty. The expensive paintings and wall hangings were gone along with most of the African artifacts and sculptures and decorative what-knots. Only the refrigerator, which had a huge dent in it, the stove which had only one eye working and the dishwasher, which was broken, were left in the kitchen. All the other small appliances, like the microwave, the toaster, the can opener and the mixers were gone. In my bedroom where I had been cooking, there was food and grease stains everywhere. The walls and the carpet were ruined. Trash was piled up in the kitchen and trash cans were overflowing all over the house. Flies were everywhere, inside and outside the house.

"Mama!" Travis screamed out again. "Oh my God!" I heard him say in agony. "Ya'll have turned this house into the ghetto!" he said as he stared out the window into the back yard. Bags of trash lined the outside patio. There were broken down cars in the yard with spare parts scattered around them. Toys were everywhere. The barbeque grill was on its side. The grass looked like it hadn't been cut in months.

"Mama!" he screamed again, this time sounding even more aggravated. By now, he was standing in my bedroom. I came out of the closet trembling and crying. Travis turned his attention to me. He looked like a dragon ready to spit fire. I had never seen an expression on his face like the one I was seeing now. "What the hell did you let happen to this house?" I just looked at him, unable to speak. "I gave you this house because I love you and I wanted you to live comfortable! You have turned it into the projects! You know what?" he screamed, throwing his hands into the air, "All of ya'll gettin' the hell out!" I looked at him as he walked out the bedroom and down the stairs. I followed him.

"Travis, you gave me this house! You told me it was mine! So if it's mine I can do what the hell I want to do with it!"

He was almost down the stairs, and then he suddenly turned to look at me with a look that was so scary that I thought he was going to smack me. "No the hell you can't!" he yelled back. "You, your kids and your drunk ass friends are gettin' the hell out of this house! This is Tuscany Hills, it ain't the damn projects!" he continued.

"You always trying to control everything. If this house was a blessing from God, why are you trying to take it away? God don't take away nothing He gives you!" I screamed as I ran behind him with tears streaming down my face.

"I said what I had to say!" Travis said. "I want everybody including *you* out of this house in one week!" He pushed through the hanging front door and headed for his vehicle.

Valencia's husband Raymond came running out the house. "Say man! We ain't got to go nowhere! This is your mama's house!" Travis turned to him. He walked over to Raymond and hit him in his mouth. Then he grabbed him by his neck and started beating him up. Valencia and I started screaming. He wouldn't stop hitting Raymond. Raymond was trying to fight back but Travis was acting like a mad man. Finally, they stopped fighting. Raymond lay on the ground panting. Travis stood up and dusted the grass and dirt off his clothes. He got in his Escalade and drove off, burning rubber out the driveway.

We stayed in the house a little longer than a week, but eventually moved. My two friends, Joey and Peter, went back to the South Central Shelter. Valencia, Raymond and her kids moved into a one bedroom apartment on Van Ness Avenue; I moved in with them. Travis sold the house.

Valencia, so angry with Travis for throwing us out of the Big House, called the tabloids and told them what he did. Of course, she didn't tell the entire story, only enough to make Travis look like the bad guy. As a result of going along with what Valencia did to her brother, the guilt began to eat at me. I started drinking more and more to try and ease the pain of the shame I was feeling.

CHAPTER 28

The apartment was small and cramped. Between the three kids, Valencia, her husband and myself; we hardly had room to move. The apartment had one bedroom that Valencia and her husband shared a kitchen, a small dining area, a living room and one bathroom. I slept on the couch and the kids slept on the floor.

It had been two months since we moved and I had been feeling very depressed. Travis wasn't speaking to me, Junior was mad at me, and Sandra hadn't called me in months. All I did was lie on the couch, drink my liquor and watch television. Some days, I didn't have the energy to take a bath or brush my teeth. I had gained so much weight and my legs hurt so bad that I never wanted to leave the house. The only time I left the house was at the first of the month when I got my Social Security check. I'd get out to cash my check; give Valencia money for half the rent; then have her take me to the liquor store to buy a month's supply of liquor. Once I got back home, I never left again, until the next month.

Valencia had begun to get irritated with me so we argued all the time. She resented me living with her and had no problem expressing how she felt about it. She cussed and complained all the time. The pressure and verbal abuse from Valencia was becoming unbearable. I tried to make an attempt to get up and do more around the house in hopes that she would let up but she never did. I had become complacent and used to my behavior for so long that the more I tried to do better the more I realized I couldn't. I was confused and even more depressed.

Junior and Valencia finally made up; probably because he was getting a disability check that the State of California had issued for him, in my name as his legal guardian. As a teenager, Junior had a bad reaction to some drugs he had been experimenting with. It landed him in the psychiatric ward at the county hospital. After his release into *my* guardianship, the State issued him a monthly disability check. Junior knew he was going to have to come to Valencia's house to pick up his money, after I cashed his check.

It was the first of the month and Junior had come over with his girlfriend, Shaniqua and their new baby. I had been drinking and my nerves were frayed, more than usual; I felt a lot of anxiety. I sat up on the couch to make room for someone else to sit down. My grandchildren were playing dolls with one of Shaniqua's other children from a previous relationship; in the corner near the television. I heard one of my grandchildren say, "Look at grandma, she drinks all the time, she's just an old drunk." The kids pointed to me and started laughing. I looked at them and ignored what they had said; they had said things like that to me before.

Junior had a beautiful baby boy. I bent down to pick him up from his infant seat. "What do you think you are doing?" Shaniqua, asked with an attitude.

"I'm getting ready to hold my new grandson," I answered.

"No the hell you ain't!" Shaniqua yelled, grabbing her baby out his seat before I could get him. "Your drunk ass ain't touching my baby and I don't care if you are his grandmother!" Everyone in the house got quiet and turned their attention to the scene Shaniqua was making. I said a few cuss words back to her, and then leaned back on the couch, expecting Junior to say something to her about speaking to me in this manner. Junior didn't say a word. Neither did Valencia. Shaniqua continued. "You're drunk right now and you stink! You ain't never picking up my baby!" I started crying and ran to the bathroom; my feelings were very hurt.

Freddie talked to me in the bathroom and told me that no one cared about me. He convinced me that if I killed myself they would care; then they would be sorry. I believed him, so I looked in the medicine cabinet and pulled out several bottles of prescription drugs. I swallowed about 15 to 20 pills and chased them with a bottle of Robitussin cough syrup; that I had found in the cabinet.

I walked out of the bathroom, grabbed the telephone off the kitchen counter; and then went back into the bathroom. I called 911 and told them I was *going* to kill myself. Before long, the paramedics were breaking down the bathroom door. Since the bathroom was rather small, and I weighed about 300 pounds, it was a struggle getting my body out of the way, in order to get through the door. I had no idea what my family was doing at this time; all I remembered was a tube being shoved down my throat, throwing up on the bathroom floor, and waking up in the mental ward of the Martin Luther King County Hospital.

"Why did you try to kill yourself, Priscilla?" the psychiatrist asked the next morning when I met with him. "I didn't feel loved. I want to be loved and respected by my family, but they disrespect me; they talk to me crazy; they let their kids and their friends talk to me crazy; they all disrespect me. I feel like nothing!" I put my head in my hands and cried.

The psychiatrist released me a week later with a slew of prescriptions from depression pills to sleeping pills. We never discussed Freddie. I felt rested after my stay at the hospital, although I was a little sad that no one came to visit me.

Valencia did however, pick me up from the hospital, and took me back to her apartment. As soon as I set foot back in the apartment, the anxiety came back. That same day, I started back drinking, while taking my prescriptions drugs.

I tried to stay out of Valencia's way, but it was no use. The apartment was just too small, and according to her, I couldn't do anything right. I don't know if Valencia was having a bad day or what, but she was short-tempered more than usual. She had been snapping, yelling, and cussing at everyone all day. I was tired of her yelling and cussing, so I decided to yell and cuss back.

"Get the hell out of my house!" Valencia yelled, as she walked over to the door and opened it.

"What?" I yelled back. "What you mean get out! Where the hell am I supposed to go at 10 o'clock at night?"

"I don't care where you go, but you're getting the hell out of my apartment!" Valencia continued. She went to the telephone and called the police. "Hello, my name is Valencia Wilson, my mother is crazy, and is no longer welcome in my house!" I looked at her in amazement that she would call the police on her own mother, and put me out her house. "She's an alcoholic," Valencia continued, "as a matter of fact she's sloppy drunk right now, and incoherent; I want her out of my house, now! Can you please come and remove her from my apartment!" Valencia hung up the telephone. "Mama you ain't nothing but an old drunk and you ain't never gonna change!" Valencia continued. "All you have ever been is an alcoholic!"

"God is gonna heal me one day, because He still loves me! I don't care what you say, you ain't my judge and you ain't got no Heaven or Hell to put me in! God loves me!" I shouted back.

"God don't love you! He ain't gonna do nothing for you because you're crazy! You're an alcoholic and you gonna die an alcoholic!" Valencia shouted. Her words cut me like a knife. I grabbed Valencia, and we started fighting. Valencia and I had many fist fights over the years, but this time we fought like strangers on the street. The kids started screaming and crying. Raymond finally broke us apart; we had destroyed the living room.

The police arrived soon after. "My mother is drunk and she's crazy!" Valencia shouted to the police. "I want her out of my house!" The police looked at me, noticing my inability to stand up and my torn clothes; they grabbed my arm and escorted me out of the apartment. I *was* very drunk, but I still felt the pain of my heart breaking as they led me outside.

"How could she throw her own mother out on the street?" I asked the police officers as we headed down the hall to leave the building. I was crying hysterically. "How can she say such cruel things to me and be so heartless? God didn't forget about me," I continued. "I'm still waiting for Him to help me. He's gonna help me!" I said with assurance. Neither of the officers made a comment.

The police left me standing outside the apartment on the sidewalk. They instructed me not to return to the apartment or they would be forced to arrest me for trespassing. I tearfully staggered my way down the street, unsure where I was going.

I had no money, no direction, and no one I could turn to. I walked and walked for what seemed like hours. I passed several prostitutes hanging out on corners; giving favors in alleys and cars. I observed several drug transactions, witnessed a few fights, and I even saw a police chase. My legs hurt from all the walking, so occasionally

I had to stop and rest on a bus stop bench; sometimes I fell asleep. When I woke up, I started my journey again; still unsure where I was going. During one of my bus stop breaks, a car pulled up in front of me. It was Al, one of the security guards from Tuscany Hills. He had recognized me as he drove by, he decided to turn around, to come back to see if I needed a ride somewhere. Al, a slender, short white man, with leathery skin, looked like he had been smoking all his life; he also had a bad smoker's cough.

"Priscilla?" he called out, as he pulled up in front of me. I looked up, recognizing him. "You need a ride somewhere?" he asked. I briefly explained my situation and told him I had nowhere to go. "Get in," he said, "you can stay with me, my brother and his wife in our mobile home in Lake Elsinore."

Knowing I had no other options, I took him up on his offer. I got in his old Chevrolet Impala and proceeded to ride with him to his house. During the ride, we talked about the Big House, all the fun parties I had, and all the crazy stuff that happened while I lived there. We even joked about all the times he would sneak up to the Big House and get drunk while he was supposed to be on duty in the community. Al told me he was still a security guard at Tuscany Hills and that the Big House had been sold. I knew the house had been sold, and I felt sad about it.

We discussed the living conditions at Al's house. "My brother and I smoke that stuff, get drunk all the time and sometimes we fight, but we love each other," he said in his country twang, laughing. I looked at him and laughed too. "My home ain't much," he continued. "We ain't got no running water, no electricity and only two beds, but you welcome to sleep on the couch and stay as long as you want." After Al mentioned getting drunk, I was oblivious to everything else. I couldn't complain; anything was better than sleeping outside, or being with a family that didn't want me, and who saw me as a despicable drunk, unworthy of their love.

I slept the rest of the night and most of the day after arriving at Al's home. When I finally awoke, I felt delirious. I sat up on the couch trying to get my bearings. I looked around the room, the mobile home was small and run down; it was actually a camper that could attach to a vehicle; there was trash and junk everywhere; it looked like it had never been cleaned. I heard voices coming from outside; I walked to the opened front door. Al, what I assumed to be his brother and his brother's wife, were sitting outside in lawn chairs drinking beer. I went outside. My eyes were having trouble focusing because of the bright sun. The camper was parked in a trailer park with about thirty other trailers; next to a Wal-Mart store. I looked up in the sky, the day was almost gone and the sun was beginning to set.

"Good morning or should I say good evening," Al said, laughing showing the 3.5 teeth in his mouth.

"I must have been really tired," I said.

"I guess so." Al said. He introduced me to his brother, Hank, and Hank's wife, Becky, who offered me a beer. Hank was taller than Al, had greasy, matted hair and was missing his front teeth. Becky was frail and very skinny; she looked to weigh around ninety to one hundred pounds; her hair looked as though it hadn't been washed in months and unlike Hank, she had teeth, but they were rotten in the front.

I sat down to drink my beer. "What day is it?" I asked, feeling confused that I couldn't remember the day of the week.

"Saturday," Hank answered.

My stomach growled from hunger pains. "Is there something I can eat?" I asked. Al stood up, led me back inside the camper and offered me some Vienna sausages and crackers. "My brother and his wife don't work," he said. "He stays too drunk to keep a job and his wife's a dope head. I'm the only one with a job and it's part-time. We go out every day begging for money and food; when we get money, we buy booze and dope. You gonna have to carry your own weight around here, and we share everything." Al stated.

"Okay," I said. I went back to the couch and sat down to eat my food.

After I ate, I decided to walk to Wal-Mart. I looked around the store, then I took some underwear and a shirt off a rack. I went into the bathroom, locked the door and began to wash up in the sink. I changed into the new underwear and the shirt. I washed my old underwear and shirt in the sink and put them into the large canvas bag I was carrying.

I came out of the bathroom feeling a little nervous, hoping that no one saw me. Confident that they didn't, I walked throughout the store, stealing various things, food and liquor. I stuffed what I could in my pockets, and clothes, and into the bag I was carrying. The liquor I hid under my arm. I walked out of the store. No one paid me any attention.

The next morning I did as Al, Hank and Becky did every day. Going our separate ways, we went out and begged for money. I stood at corners and near intersections to panhandle, I approached people at gas stations; and I walked up to people as they came out of the grocery store or the 7-11. When I got tired, I used the money that was given me to eat at a diner or a local fast food restaurant. On my way home, I stopped at the liquor store and bought whatever alcohol my money could buy; I walked back to the mobile home.

Once I got the begging concept down, I established a routine. I went to Wal-Mart every other day, I didn't want them to notice me coming in the store all the time, for fear they might catch me stealing. Every night we got drunk. I got used to my way of living.

I lay on the couch asleep, dreaming the same reoccurring dream that I had been dreaming since I moved into the trailer park two months ago. I dreamed about my funeral, I saw myself in the casket, and I saw all my children at the funeral except Travis. Where was Travis? Every time I dreamt the dream, I'd wake up in a panic, sweating and hyperventilating; then I would pray to God and ask where my son was. God never answered me. I had that dream so much; that I tried to do all I could to stay awake. I took speed, No Doze pills and other over-the-counter medications, that I stole from Wal-Mart, to keep me awake. I was very sad and very depressed; I couldn't stop thinking about that dream. I cried often, worried that something had happened to my son, and wondering where he was. I kept asking God to please help me! "Why won't *you* help me? Don't you hear me?" I asked. I never got an answer, until one night there was a knock at the door.

Bam! Bam! Bam! Bam! Bam! Someone was frantically beating on the front door. I was the only one in the living room, and I was too scared to open the door. I ran to get Al; I didn't know if it was the police or a drug dealer. Al opened the door; it was Travis.

"Do you know a lady named Priscilla? She's black, about 5'4, short hair, 50 years old," Travis asked, his voice sounding panicked; as he held up a photo and tried to catch his breath.

"Yeah I know Priscilla," Al said. He opened the door wider; Travis saw me standing near the couch. He let out a long sigh of relief, as his eyes welled up with tears; that streamed down his face. "I found her!" he shouted to someone outside. "I found Mama!" He ran past Al and hugged me tight, crying tears of joy on my shoulder. A few seconds later, Junior and Sandra ran inside the camper. They were crying too. "We found you!" they both shouted simultaneously, as they ran to hug me. The moment felt like a scene out of a movie. I had asked God where my son was, and He brought my son to me. God had finally answered my prayer; I knew He loved me; I knew He heard my prayers. I broke down crying uncontrollably, we all cried, and we hugged each other for a long period of time. "Let's go," Travis finally said, as he wiped his eyes. "Come on, Mama, you're coming with us," he continued. I didn't resist. I said goodbye to Al and the others, then followed my kids out of the camper. Travis opened the passenger door of his Escalade for me; that was double-parked in the middle of the trailer park, and he helped me to climb into the seat. Junior and Sandra climbed into the back seat; we all continued to cry. "Are you hungry?" Travis asked. I nodded my head, yes. Denny's restaurant was nearby, so Travis pulled into the parking lot. Junior helped me out of the car, and Sandra held my hand, as we walked into the restaurant.

"Mama, we have been in that trailer park looking for you for hours," Travis said, after we were seated at our table. "We knocked on every door looking for you, we found you in the very last trailer."

"How did you know where I was?" I asked curiously.

"One of my home boys saw you at Wal-Mart," Junior said. "He told me he saw you walk to the trailer park across the street. So, we put two and two together, and came looking for you," he continued. I hung my head and started crying again, so did everyone else.

I felt embarrassed about the way that I looked; my shoes were raggedy, my clothes were filthy, I hadn't brushed my teeth, washed my hair, or had a bath in days. I was also embarrassed when my food arrived; I was so hungry, that I devoured my chicken-fried steak meal, before the kids could get through half of their meal.

"Mama we love you. You are going to die if you don't stop drinking," Travis said sincerely, as he continued to cry. "I have been busting my butt trying to make you happy; trying to keep you from dying an alcoholic! How many times have you failed AA? How many times! Mama?" he asked raising his voice.

I looked up at him. "A lot," I said sadly.

"We feel like we can't do anything for you, because you don't want to stop drinking. When will you be ready to stop? When you're dead?" Sandra and Junior started sniveling.

"I'm sorry," I said sorrowfully.

"Yeah, yeah; we've heard that a million times Mama!"

"You don't know what I go through every day," I rebutted. "You don't have a clue! I am tired of my life being like this! I want to stop drinking, but I can't stop!" I said.

"You know what Mama, you're just like your mother!" Travis said. When he said that I sat up in my seat, and I looked at him. Travis looked more like me than any of my other children, and looking at him when he said those words, was like looking at myself in the mirror; hearing myself say those horrifying words. *'You're just like your mother!'* I repeated in my mind. Those words cut through me like a double-edged sword. Out of all the people in the world, my mother was the one person I *never* wanted to be like; but at that moment, I realized Travis was right; I had become my mother.

"What is wrong with you Mama? Why do you think I've been calling you Mommy Dearest, ever since I was a little boy? It's because you drink just like that lady in the movie, and you act like her too! Why can't you stop drinking?" He started crying extremely hard.

"I don't know how to stop!" I said, putting my head down on the table; still crying. "I'm scared!"

"You're scared? Mama, you've scared us to death for years, wondering where you were, not knowing if you were dead or alive; what did you think could happen to you living in these streets?" Do you want to die? Junior asked, crying out with loud sobs.

"I'm going to stop drinking, I promise. I'm going to stop drinking! I don't want to be like my mother," I cried out loudly. I put my head down on the table again, and began to pray silently, *'God in Heaven, please hear my cry. I am an alcoholic, and I have become just like my mother. If you deliver me from this alcoholic disease, I promise I won't ever take another drink for the rest of my life. I want to live and not die.'* When I opened my eyes, my kids were staring me and still crying, I looked at all three of my kids and said, "I'm ready to be helped, I don't wanna die."

"I'm going to find you the best treatment in the world and I *don't* care how much it costs," Travis said. "We ain't never, never, *never* gonna leave you alone again."

Sandra, who had been sitting at the table, silently crying, squeezed my hand and said," I love you Mama." We stood to leave; Sandra, Junior, and Travis hugged me again; they didn't seem to mind my dirty clothes or my horrendous body odor.

"I love all of ya'll," I said. "I'm sorry. It will never happen again."

"You make it impossible to love you, but we love you anyway," Travis said with a smile. "We always have and we always will."

CHAPTER 29

The peace and quiet of the Hilton Hotel was indescribable, and wonderful. I took long hot baths and ordered a lot of room service; the rest had served me well. I had been here almost a week, after my kids had found me, but the urge to drink was very powerful and still there. I was tempted several times to walk out and go find something to drink. I tossed and turned in my bed; most of the time, I couldn't sleep. I had night sweats, body aches, shakes and bad dreams. I fought hard to get through every one of them. I kept telling myself that I could do it, that I wasn't going to be like my mother anymore. I even ignored Freddie. Freddie wouldn't stop talking to me. He kept reminding me of how much I loved liquor and how it made me feel good. "What about your friends on the streets, don't you miss them?" he asked. I didn't answer. I did miss my friends, but I didn't miss living in the streets.

"The First Step Rehabilitation Center in Houston, Texas is where I'm going to send you," Travis told me on the telephone that Monday morning. "It's the largest chemical dependency treatment center in the Southwest; it's state-of-the-art, and it's recognized by addiction professionals as the best. Mama, I want you to *have* the best," he continued. "My friend's mother went there for her alcoholism treatment too; so this treatment center came recommended by someone I know. I know this place can help you," he said with an assurance. I didn't make any comments. I had a rough night. As a matter of fact, every night had been rough, but I wasn't going to tell anyone about them.

Travis made sure that I had everything that I needed for my stay in the rehab. His fiancée, Kendra, was very helpful. She picked out all my new clothes. I was very appreciative, but embarrassed that she had to see me in this manner. She was a lovely, pretty girl and I wished we could have met under better circumstances. I found myself crying and apologizing to her constantly in hopes that when I got better she wouldn't hold this against me.

A limo came later that day to take me to the airport. Rebecca, Travis' assistant, rode with me to the rehabilitation center in Houston. Cleveland Browns quarterback Dominic Henderson's mother, Mary, rode with us also. She was Travis' friend's mother, and a recent graduate of The First Step. Travis thought it would be helpful if I met someone that had gone through what I was about to experience. He also told me he couldn't make the trip, and that Rebecca and Mary would be joining me to help get me settled. He promised he would call me often.

After arriving at the center, the three of us sat in the reception area until they called my name. I was terrified. My nerves were disconcerted, and my head was hurting. I sat quietly pretending to listen to Mary talk to me about what things to expect and how The First Step program worked, but I wasn't listening. Her lips were moving but I couldn't hear anything. All I heard was Freddie talking to me and pleading with me to leave. He had been doing that ever since I was in Los Angeles at the hotel, but I was determined not to listen. I realized my first night in the hotel that Freddie was a liar, and that he wasn't my friend. He kept trying to convince me that my kids where trying to change me into something that *I* could never be; that they didn't love me, and that the tears that my kids shed weren't real. But, he was wrong and he wasn't my friend. A real friend wouldn't say mean things like that. It was because of Freddie that I did a lot of the terrible things that I did. Every time I didn't want to do something, he always convinced me to do it. Our friendship ended that night in September 2005. I chose not to listen to Freddie anymore; I was going to start listening to God instead.

When I heard my name called, I stood up. A nurse summoned me to follow her into one of the counseling rooms. Rebecca carried my bags. "It's our policy that all bags are searched prior to admittance." The nurse said. "Are you ok with that?" she asked looking at me. I nodded my head ok, but I wasn't really ok with that. She searched every inch of my luggage; she took away my nail kit and my shoe laces. "Now let's get you settled into your room," the nurse continued. "Ok ladies," speaking to Rebecca and Mary, "this is as far as you go." I started to cry. "Priscilla will be in detox for a while and unable to receive telephone calls. She will call you when she is able to make phone calls." Rebecca and Mary hugged me and wished me well just before leaving. The nurse led me to my room; the place I would call home for the next four weeks.

Later that day I met with one of the directors, John Lucas. Mr. Lucas played Point Guard for the Houston Rockets basketball team in the late 70's to early 80's. He became addicted to drugs and alcohol for years. He is also an Alumni of The First Step program. After his recovery, it became his mission to help addicts recover the way that he was helped.

"Mr. Lucas, do you understand that I have been drinking for twenty-seven years! My sons were 2 and 3 years old when I started drinking; and my girls were 6 and 8! All they know is their mother was a drunk. I had to get drunk to do anything," I continued. Mr. Lucas sat behind his desk listening and letting me vent. "I was hanging out in the park one day, a place I *loved* to be more than I loved to be at home. A drinking buddy of mine told me that a drunk can't be a mother because they're incapable of being a role model. I always believed that even though I drank, I was still a good mother; I took care of my kids; I was there for my kids." I hung my head and started to cry. "They have never been without a place to lay their heads and they ain't never went hungry. Don't that count for something?" I looked up at Mr. Lucas who had leaned back in his chair.

"Today is the first day of the rest of your life Priscilla. Your kids obviously love you, because they brought you here," he said.

"My friend in the park was right; a drunk can't be a mother or a role model. For years I convinced myself that I was a good mother, but I wasn't, I never was. I was a terrible mother. I didn't show my kids love, I didn't show them appreciation; I didn't teach my kids how to be anything except how to not be like me." I wiped tears off my cheeks as I cried harder. "Do you think they will ever forgive me? Will they ever let me be a mother to them now, years later?" I asked sadly.

"They already have," Mr. Lucas said with sympathy. "Your kids loved you enough to find you on the streets. If that's not love, then I don't know what is."

After our meeting my heart was so full. It felt good to express how I really felt about being a mother. If only I could turn back the hands of time. There were so many things I would do differently.

By day two I was in the corner shaking and crying. The counselor came in the room looking for me. "Priscilla, are you alright?" she asked. "I need to call my son to come and get me. I can't do this! I want to go home. Please let me call my son to come and get me." I begged. "You know I can't do that, Priscilla." The counselor said softly as she helped me get up off the floor. "Give it time, today is just the second day, you can do it." I hugged her and continued crying. "Things will get better." She encouraged.

The rest of that week, it didn't get better. It got worse. My stomach cramped, I couldn't hold any food down, my head hurt and they still wouldn't let me call my son. I was miserable. By the beginning of the following week, I started to feel better. The counselors said I made it through the hard part which was detox. I was fifteen days sober if you count the days in the hotel.

CHAPTER 30

During my second week, it was all about routines. It was up at 7:00 every morning and lights were out by 10:00 every night. We received 30 minutes of free time or outdoor time, whichever we chose once in the morning and once in the afternoon. We had to be at breakfast, lunch and dinner at our scheduled times. We were also assigned chores. I was given the responsibility of keeping the laundry room clean. I was not used to a domestic regimen, so I rebelled and became argumentative.

I had a lot of counseling sessions; as a matter of fact too many counseling sessions, group sessions and individual sessions. Everybody wanted to get to know me, or wanted to know about me. I didn't know me, so how were they going to know me. I didn't even want to know about them. I was tired of talking about me, and I was tired of talking about my alcoholism. I wanted to be left alone and I was ready to leave.

This was the week that my psychiatric visits began. I had already seen several psychiatrists in the past and they couldn't tell me what was wrong with me, so I didn't expect this psychiatrist to be any different. All I ever got was pills and more pills. They never fixed what was really wrong with me.

I sat on the couch across from the psychiatrist and told him about my anxiety and Freddie. "When my kids found me on the streets and took me to the hotel, Freddie kept telling me to leave and runaway. He kept reminding me of all the fun that we had when I was drunk, but I wouldn't leave the hotel. That was hard for me. It took all the strength that I had, which wasn't much not to leave. Liquor and men are what I loved the most in life and Freddie knew that. I realized back in the hotel that he wasn't my friend. He tried to convince me that my kids didn't love me, and I knew that was a lie! So, now I won't listen to him. I guess Freddie's mad at me now, because he hasn't talked to me in over a week."

"Priscilla, do you believe that Freddie is a real person?" Dr. Phillips asked.

"I know he is not a real person, but he talks to me like a real person, and he sounds like a real person."

"Priscilla, Freddie is an alter-ego that you created inside your head. He isn't real. I believe you created Freddie as a way to escape from stressful situations in your life. I believe you suffer from Dissociative Identity Disorder, otherwise known as Multiple Personality Disorder." I repositioned myself on the couch to concentrate on what Dr. Phillips was saying to me. He continued, "Theoretically, DID is believed to be linked with the interaction of overwhelming stress, traumatic experiences, insufficient childhood nurturing, and an innate ability to dissociate memories or experiences from consciousness. Prolonged childhood abuse is frequently a factor, including sexual abuse, all of which are in your past. A Dissociative Identity Disorder sufferer's personality divides into sub-personalities, known as alters. The alters have their own memory. Consequently, the sufferer has episodes of amnesia, which explains your blackouts or the lost periods of time you reported to me; and your chaotic behavior during alcohol intoxication. Priscilla, many DID patients abuse drugs and alcohol or both."

For the first time in my life, somebody knew how I felt. I sat listening to Dr. Phillips speak to my soul and slowly feeling a lifetime of burdens being lifted off my shoulders. I finally knew what was wrong with me. Tears began to run slowly down my face.

"Priscilla, an altered personality takes over the pain that you yourself cannot handle. It's a defense mechanism that the mind uses to cope with extremely traumatic experiences and stressful situations. In your case you were born to an abusive, alcoholic mother. You witnessed your father abuse your mother. You were raped as a child and sexually abused as a teenager. You married a drug addict who severely beat you. You divorced him and married someone who mentally abused you. All of this is a lot for one person to handle, so Freddie was created. He was created to help you face further stressful situations that sweet, loving, kind Priscilla by herself couldn't handle. When you're stress free and happy and things are good you won't hear from Freddie. Now that you have stopped drinking, you won't hear from Freddie. He only surfaces when pain, dysfunction and chaos are present.

I was crying hard. It was such a relief that someone finally told me what was wrong with me. Now I understood.

"Does your family know about your alter Freddie?" Dr. Phillips asked.

I hung my head. "No. I thought if I told them they would think that I was crazy, and I'm not."

"Does your family know about your history?"

"Some things," I answered. "Some things were just too painful to talk about."

"Well I have good news. There is treatment for DID sufferers, and studies show that after the age of 50, the alters will spontaneously reduce or disappear, but every person is different. You are how old?" He asked, making light because I was already 50. I smiled back.

"I see in your medical file that you have been to several doctors seeking treatment for your nerves and depression, and you're on several medications. It is almost unavoidable that a person will be misdiagnosed for DID. Many will be diagnosed as being depressed because the primary or core personality is subdued and withdrawn, particularly in female patients. They also may be misdiagnosed as schizophrenic or having a panic disorder. Persons with DID are often frightened by their dissociative experiences, and may go to the emergency room or clinic because they fear they are going insane; this could explain your frequent visits to doctors." I continued to absorb all that he was saying.

"While you're at The First Step you'll be treated by a therapist with specialized training in DID. Medication is usually discouraged until your personality has been reintegrated. I want to treat you with alternative treatments that help to relax the body as an adjunct, to psychotherapy and or medications. I'll treat you primarily with herbs that help the nervous system. I also recommend art therapy or keeping a journal, as ways to integrate your past into your present life. You completed the first step which was making the choice to stop drinking. The second step was coming to The First Step to get the necessary treatments to help you continue to your last step. That step is detaching yourself from abusers and situations that may lead to a chaotic and trauma-filled lifestyle, so that you can get your life on the right track."

I sat crying and wiping my eyes until they were red and swollen. Never in all my life had I been so full of knowledge and understanding about myself. Now I know who I am. Dr. Phillips' session was very enlightening. He said we would meet twice a week as long as I was there. I knew I was going to look forward to those sessions.

As I walked out of Dr. Phillips' office, I noticed a display of pamphlets next to the door. To my surprise I recognized one of the photos featured on a pamphlet about Dissociative Identity Disorder. It was Herschel Walker, a running back in the NFL back in the 80's and 90's, and two-time Heisman Trophy winner. *He has DID, too? I wondered.* I read a quote by him on the front of the pamphlet. It read, 'Mistakes should be taken as a training tool to help you to get better'. I continued to read. Herschel said he struggled with DID for years, but had only been treated for it in the last eight years. He even wrote a book about his struggles with the disorder called, *"Breaking Free: My life with Dissociative Identity Disorder."* I was so amazed that someone so famous had a sickness like me. I couldn't put the pamphlet down; I read some more. Herschel wrote about his suicide attempts and how he felt the same disconnect from his childhood that I had felt. Oh, what a relief it was to know someone else had the same thing that I had. I walked out of the office and headed back to my room, carrying the pamphlet, and thinking, *'I'm going to buy his book when I get out of rehab.'*

CHAPTER 31

After my session with Dr. Phillips, I started to see things clearer, but the alcoholic urges were still there. The rehab center had a Christian treatment program that I enjoyed. I wanted to stay as close to God as possible, so I attended often. Ephesians 5:18 was the scripture that the program was based on. *'Do not get drunk on wine, which leads to self-indulgence. Instead be filled with the Spirit.'* I wanted to be filled with the spirit. I attended the daily morning devotions led by Christian recovery advocates, and Christian counselors; also I attended the women's spirituality groups.

One afternoon after a session, I headed to the cafeteria for lunch. In the cafeteria, I saw a few of the staff, counselors, and one of the psychologists hovering over a young teenage girl that I had known to be a heroine addict. They had made a circle around her and had begun to pray. They called out to God on her behalf. Several people were standing around the group that had formed the circle. Some joined in the prayer while others stood watching and crying. It was the most moving thing that I had ever witnessed. I believed that the Holy Spirit filled the cafeteria through the abundance of prayer and emotional energy that was being released in the room.

When they were finished praying, and the group broke up, I ran to my room crying. My roommate, Alexandria, was sitting on her bed. During detox, I had a room by myself; after detox I got a roommate. My roommate's name was Alexandria Pinkerton. She was a thirty-five year old mother of three, and an alcoholic. She, too, had been molested and raped as a child. We shared stories and found that we had a lot in common.

Alexandria didn't know what was wrong with me when I suddenly burst through the door, and knelt down at my bed facing the east wall. I began to pray. "Lord!" I cried out. "God if you help me one more time. If you take these alcoholic urges from me, out of my mind and out of my body, I will tell people about you! I will let everyone that I come in contact with know that you and you alone saved me!" I kept repeating the same prayer over and over again until I was exhausted. Finally, I got up from the floor and climbed into my bed. Alexandria sat quietly the entire time, never saying a word to me. I laid in bed crying until I fell asleep. That night I dreamt I saw an angel at the edge of my bed. I felt the softness of its wings. Then I saw Jesus standing in the corner of my room near the window on the east wall. He called my name. I sat up in my bed, trembling at the sight of Jesus. "Priscilla," Jesus continued, "I have always been here for you, but where have you been for me?" He asked. "I have lived a terrible life, Lord, and I'm so sorry. I didn't know you then like I know you now," I said looking into his eyes. "Please forgive me," I asked sincerely, as I began to cry. "I promise Lord, if you change my life, if you break this alcoholic spell that has kept me prisoner for 27 years, I won't ever take another drink, and only you will be Lord over my life." Jesus looked at me and said, "I will deliver you;" Then He faded away.

I woke up the next morning feeling like a new person. My mind and even my body felt different. I told Alexandria about my dream. "My deliverance has finally come," I said with enthusiasm. "After 27 years, God has broken the spell of my addiction." Alexandria hugged me as we both cried tears of joy.

Four weeks sped by so quickly. This was my last week at The First Step, and I was looking forward to going home. The thought of starting my new life as a sober woman was almost inconceivable. Mr. Lucas called me into his office shortly after breakfast. When I arrived, I found that Dr. Phillips was also in the office. I felt a sudden case of butterflies in my stomach. Unsure what to make of both of them in the office, I hesitantly walked inside and sat down in the chair next to Dr. Phillips. They both smiled at me, and I cracked a faint smile back.

Mr. Lucas leaned back in his chair and opened what he explained was my portfolio from The First Step. "I am so proud of your progress, Priscilla," Mr. Lucas said. Dr. Phillips nodded his head in agreement.

"The reason that I called you to my office is because Dr. Phillips and I feel that you would benefit more from another one of our rehab programs called The Second Step." The smile left my face. I knew very little about The Second Step; just that it was a transitional living program a few blocks from this facility.

Mr. Lucas continued, "Completion of a recovery program is often the most trying and difficult time for those starting out on a life of sobriety. The temptation to slip back into old habits is great, and many people feel they need or would like some extra help in resuming their lives. The Second Step's transitional living program helps those individuals who would benefit from a little guidance after completing The First Step programs. We believe you would be a great candidate for this program."

Mr. Lucas waited for a response from me. I sat thinking. I was disappointed that I wouldn't be going home, but if God saw fit for me to be a part of The Second Step program, then that's where I was going to be. "Alright," I said.

"Great, we'll get you scheduled for your transfer at the end of the week." I thanked them both for their concern and I went back to my room.

My last day at The First Step was very emotional. The few that were leaving were given the opportunity to stand and give a testimonial of how their lives had been changed since arriving at the center. I had been there only a month and I felt like a brand new person. A person I had to get to know.

I sat listening to the testimonies. "I stole from my mother, my family, from anybody. I would have stolen from your mother or your family if I knew them. All I cared about was my next drink. If you think you are living with some morals or you got some principles governing your life, take another drink. I guarantee you; in a short period of time it will take your life and flip it. You will go from being a person who thinks your life is governed by some rules to being ruled. That's the reality of being an alcoholic. The First Step has taught me that I have a choice to say no because alcohol cares nothing about me. It doesn't care about you either. It doesn't care where you came from, what your age is, what religion you are or what color you are. Alcohol is big enough to take us all if we don't stand up and make the choice to say no." Everyone stood and clapped for Sherry. Sherry had entered the program about a week before I did. She had been drinking one night, passed out at the wheel of her car, and totaled it. She is now permanently handicapped and walks with the assistance of a walker. She also lost the sight in one of her eyes.

"My name is Michelle and I'm a cocaine addict. I'm looking forward to moving into The Second Step program. Just take it easy, and slow my counselor tells me, one day at a time, that's what you need to remember she says. There are times that I want to make my own plans and do my own thing, but that's how I got here in the first place. I was always telling myself that I could do what I wanted, when I wanted. But, now I gotta listen to somebody else, and it's hard, it's real hard." Tears trickled down her cheeks. "What I learned here is that I *have* to listen to somebody," Michelle said looking over at the counselors that lined the wall. "Ain't no job harder than being an addict. You wake up in the morning; you got no money, you got no friends and got no family. Nobody's got your back. But, by the time you leave from wherever you are; you know exactly where to go to get your next $5, $10 or $20 to buy your next hit. I have to keep reminding myself that compared to that life," she said wiping tears from her eyes, "this way of living has to be easier." Michelle took her seat as the audience applauded her. I wiped tears from my eyes.

Annie, one of the counselors, walked to the front of the room. "For every ten of you here, only one is going to stay clean." The audience began to moan. "That's the reality. There is a 1 in 10 chance of an addict staying clean. But we are going to change the statistics!" she shouted. Everyone shouted in agreement and applauded. Annie continued, "Is there anyone here that is 6 months clean?" Eight people stood up. "3 months clean?" Four people stood up. "And most importantly, is there anyone here that is one day clean?" Twelve women and four men stood up. Applause filled the room. The other counselors handed everyone standing a coin signifying the number of days clean. I felt proud to receive a coin for being one month clean.

I decided not to give a testimony; I was too nervous and overwhelmed. I told myself that I would wait until I graduated from The Second Step to share my experience.

CHAPTER 32

The Second Step was very different from The First Step. At The First Step the entire building was co-ed. Meals, sessions and everything else were combined with men and women, except the sleeping arrangements. There were no men in The Second Step building, which housed only women, thirty to forty in a two-story building. The rooms were like dorms that slept five women in each room. We *still* had to do chores. We also could leave the premises, as long as we were back by the curfew, and didn't drink or use drugs while we were out.

The morning I arrived, some women were being dismissed from the house because they missed curfew. A couple of other women were being turned away because it was obvious that they had been drinking or were high. I was informed prior to coming to The Second Step that some of the people wouldn't be able to handle the rules; today I was witnessing just that.

My first morning there I had a meeting with the director, Mrs. Kathy. "How are you doing?" she asked as I sat down in the chair in front of her desk.

"I'm fine," I lied. I really didn't want to be there, but I knew it was the best thing for me.

"How are your legs, do they hurt?"

"Yes, but I'm dealing with it," I answered in a somber voice. Mrs. Kathy began to pray to God for the healing of my legs, I joined in the prayer. After she finished, I thanked her and hoped that a healing would come soon; the pain was excruciating. We sat and talked about the rules of The Second Step. I was given the responsibility of cleaning the laundry room, again.

There was a lot of tension, arguing and attitudes rising in the house among several of the women. Every day, there was some sort of confrontation. It seemed as though at least half the women in the house were bad tempered and foul-mouthed, while the other half was pleasant and trying to adjust to their new way of living. I learned early on which people to avoid. I also learned who was using again, and who was not, although some tried to hide it. I stayed out of the way of all the bitter people, the gossipers and the troublemakers. I didn't want any problems with anybody, so I chose to mind my own business; I overlooked the drama in the house and I looked forward to leaving.

By week three, I had learned a lot and was beginning to like it. It was a shame that I learned to like it a week before I was to go home. The time went by so fast. I had just gotten into a routine that was comfortable for me. In the mornings I went to devotional. During the afternoons I would go for walks or sit outside. I also read lots of books and started keeping a journal. Occasionally, I would walk to the store to buy some snacks or something to eat later in the day or at night. My son had written a check for my entire stay at The First Step and The Second Step, and he made sure that I had money in my rehab account, so that I could purchase anything that I wanted to at the local store.

I finally spoke to my family the week that I was to leave. I hadn't spoken to anyone since I had arrived seven weeks earlier. Travis told me that he would send a limo to pick me up at The Second Step, that would take me to the airport, and that a limo would pick me up in LA, to take me to his house when I arrived. "You'll stay with me for a while until the apartment that I found for you is ready," he told me. "I found you an apartment in downtown LA that I think you will like. It's also next to an Alcoholic Anonymous location that you can walk to," he continued. I wasn't given very long on the telephone, but I made sure to tell my son how much I loved him, and appreciated everything that he had ever done, and tried to do for me. I didn't tell him this, but I know now that when he bought me the Big House, what Travis meant for good the devil meant for bad. Now that my life has changed, what Travis means for good is going to stay good. I thought about my daughter, Valencia. I hadn't spoken to her since the night that we had that terrible fight, and she put me out. I loved my daughter, and now I understood how I pushed her to her breaking point. I prayed that God would heal her broken heart and allow her to forgive me. I won't let the devil take the good away from me again.

My last day, I woke up early. I didn't sleep well and I was having major anxiety about leaving. I was scared of the unknown, scared of what to expect outside in this brand new world. I had gotten used to the rehab center and the half-way house, I could function here, but could I function out there? I kept crying, because a million 'what if's' kept running through my head.

I packed my clothes and sat on the edge of my bed crying the entire time. Periodically, friends that I had made during my stay came in to wish me well and offer encouraging words and hugs, but I was still scared.

I wasn't scheduled to be picked up until after lunch, which was almost five hours away, but I wanted to be ready. I tried to occupy my time. Finally, one of my roommates convinced me to go down to breakfast. I didn't have much of an appetite, but I went anyway. It seemed that everyone in the house knew it was my last day, because I was met by well-wishers in the dining room. *If they only knew how terrified I was to leave, I thought.*

Group session was always after breakfast. I was glad to know that there were three other women that were leaving the house, too. I had told myself that when it was my turn to leave, I would stand up and give my testimony. I waited until the other three ladies gave their parting speeches before I stood up.

"My name is Priscilla Gibson Murray. Today is my last day and I am two months sober." Applause filled the room. "Thanks to this program, I now know that I have feelings, and I'm grateful to understand that it's okay to share them. I am not a victim anymore. I am grateful that I finally understand my disease, and I am very appreciative for the help that you gave me in resolving my problems. Before coming here, I never owned my own feelings. Every minute, every hour was about a drink, and about a man. I cared more about my man's feelings than my own or my kids. Whenever the man I was with was down, I was lower. When I was lower, I was beat down even lower, and I got even drunker. Every day when whatever man I was with walked in the door, I waited to see what shape he was in so that I would know what shape I was going to be in and how I was going to feel. I know now that no amount of liquor; or any man is going to make my life better. I can only be made better by God."

I took a deep breath and continued, "I drank my first drink at a very young age, and twenty seven years later I became a certifiable alcoholic. I've been raped, beat up, and homeless. I turned out to be an unfit mother, a liar and a thief. I had to hit rock bottom to realize that my life needed to change. I heard that if you can look up, you can get up. One night as I lay sleeping in my bed at The First Step, I had a dream that I saw Jesus. It was then that I looked up and I got up. That night I gave what I thought was my worthless life to Him and I chose to live, and not die. Jesus delivered me and I am forever grateful. In all my life I will never know the full extent of what my alcoholism did to my children. I know I have to forgive myself for what I put them through, and I pray that they will forgive me. I thought God forgot about me. I had many tragedies and near death experiences, and God sustained me through them all. I know now that He didn't forget me, but He was with me all the time. I'm going to miss everyone here," I said as I wiped away the tears rolling down my cheeks. "Please pray for me and thank you for showing me the right way." The entire room stood and applauded.

I waited downstairs in the lobby until the limo driver came to pick me up. My roommate sat with me. We agreed to keep in touch with each other. After the emotional good-byes, I headed to the airport. My son called me just before I left to tell me how proud he was of me, and that he would be waiting for me in LA at the airport. It was comforting to hear that because I desperately missed him and the rest of my family.

I found my way through Houston's Hobby Airport, with the help of the limo driver. The security check line was extremely long and slow. I made it to my gate just a few minutes before it was time to board the plane. My nerves were agitated and I was very fidgety. I didn't know whether I wanted to sit or stand, go to the bathroom or not go to the bathroom. Finally, everyone boarded the plane.

Once I got settled in my seat and the plane took off, I started to relax. I gazed out of the window as we flew through the clouds, and felt a sense of peace come over me. I thought about all the positive things that I would do that I never dreamed I could do. In my mind I recited Philippians 4:13, 'All things are possible through Christ who strengthens me.' A smile came upon my face. I'm ready now, I can do this. Thank you, God!

The End

EPILOGUE

My name is Priscilla Gibson and I *was* an alcoholic. As of today, January 7, 2009 I am two years, 3 months and 15 days sober. It feels good! On my sober anniversary my friends at the Hemet Valley Recovery Center presented me with a two years sober pendant. I am looking forward to a collection of sober pendants for the years to come. God kept his promise. He delivered me from 27 years of alcoholism. I have no urges to drink, I can pass by a bar, a liquor store or be around liquor at a function or party and the urge to drink is not there. I am also happily single. For the first time I am *really* enjoying my life. I still suffer from the nerve damage in my legs, but I am happily HIV negative! The most wonderful news of all is that my family forgave me and they love me very much.

My life will forever be a living testimony and an example to those who struggle with the disease of alcoholism. God made me a new person and I want the world to know He healed me. That is my promise to keep to Him.

ALCOHOLICS ANONYMOUS
for the
UNITED STATES

ALABAMA

FOURTH DISTRICT CENRAL
OFFICE
P.O. BOX 8091
ANNISTON 36202
256-236-3190
888-489-9554

AUBURN OPELIKA
INTERGROUP
425 WEBSTER ROAD, LOT 224
AUBURN 36832
334-559-0798

BIRMINGHAM INTERGROUP
242 W. VALLEY AVENUE, STE
211
BIRMINGHAM 35209
205-290-0060

WIREGRASS INTERGROUP
P.O. BOX 1931
DOTHAN 36302
334-792-3422

HUNTSVILLE INTERGROUP
3322 MEMORIAL PKWY S.W.,
STE 519
HUNTSVILLE 35801
256-885-0323
www.aahuntsvilleal.org
aacentraloffice@knology.net

MOBILE EASTERN SHORE
AREA
INTERGROUP
600 BEL AIR BLVD, STE 224
MOBILE 36606
251-479-9994
www.mobileaa.org
mesaico@bellsouth.net

MONTGOMERY AREA
INTERGROUP
828 FOREST AVENUE, STE A
MONTGOMERY 36106
334-264-4122
www.centralalaa.org
mgmicco@netscape.net

N.W. ALABAMA INTERGROUP
P.O. BOX 3271
MUSCLE SHOALS 35662-3271
256-386-0663

ARIZONA

RIVER CITY CENTRAL OFFICE
603 MARINA BLVD
BULLHEAD CITY 86442-5414
928-763-4499
800-864-1606
central_office@rcco-aa-org
www.rcco-aa.org

CENTRAL MOUNTAIN
INTERGROUP
2619 UNION DRIVE, STE A
COTTONWOOD 86326
928-646-9428
www.centralmountain.org
aa@centralmountain.org

FLAGSTAFF INTERGROUP
CENTRAL OFFICE
P.O. BOX 31205
FLAGSTAFF 86003
928-779-3569
www.flagstaffaa.org
webservant@flagstaffaa.org

SITKA INTERGROUP
P.O. BOX 2924
SITKA 99835
907-747-8866

AGUA FRIA INTERGROUP
9164 N. 43RD AVENUE, STE 15
GLENDALE 85302
623-937-7836
aguafriaintergroup@netscape.com

KINGMAN INTERGROUP
3696 DEVLIN AVENUE
KINGMAN 86401
928-757-1895
800-864-1606
panair74@yahoo.com

LAKE HAVASU CITY
INTERGROUP
P.O. BOX 1453
LAKE HAVASU CITY 86403
928-453-0313
www.havasuaa.com

OFICINA INTERGRUPAL
2549 SOUTH 6TH AVENUE
520-622-5112

YUMA INTERGROUP
P.O. BOX 4446
YUMA 85366
928-782-2605

ALASKA

ANCHORAGE INTERGROUP
OFFICE
523 WEST 8TH AVENUE, ROOM
101
ANCHORAGE 99501
901-272-2312
www.anchorageaa.org
aaig@alaska.com

FAIRBANKS INTERGROUP
OFFICE
P.O. BOX 73882
FAIRBANKS 99707
907-456-7501
www.fairbanksaa.org

JUNEAU INTERGROUP
BOX 21732
JUNEAU 99802
907-586-1161
www.home.gci.net/juneau-aa
juneau_aa@yahoo.com

KETCHIKAN INTERGROUP
P.O. BOX 9275
KETCHIKAN 99901
907-225-5154

SITKA INTERGROUP
P.O. BOX 2924
SITKA 99835
907-747-8866

KENAI PENINSULA
INTERGROUP
BOX 3744
SOLDOTNA 99669

MAT-SU INTERGROUP OFFICE
P.O. BOX 871944
WASILLA 99687
907-376-4777
www.matsuaa.org

EAST VALLEY INTERGROUP,
INC
1320 EAST BROADWAY
MESA 85204
480-834-9033
www.aamesaaz.org
info@aamesaaz.org

RIM COUNTRY INTERGROUP
408 WEST MAIN STREET, STE
10
PAYSON 85501
928-474-3620
www.paysonaa.org

SALT RIVER INTERGROUP
4602 N. 7TH STREET
PHOENIX 85014
602-264-1341
www.aaphoenix.org
aaphx@aaphoenix.org

OFICINA INTERGRUPAL
HISPANA
2401 N. 32ST, STE 9
PHOENIX 85008
602-957-7457

PRESCOTT AREA
INTERGROUP ASSOC.
240 S. MONTEZUMA STREET,
STE 108
PRESCOTT 86303
928-445-8691/ FAX 928-445-9493
www.prescottaaa.org
prescotta@prescottaa.org

CONCHISE COUNTY DIST 02-
200
SIERRA VISTA 85635
520-456-0031
877-459-0031
www.aa-cochisecounty.org

TUCSON AREA INTERGROUP
INC
840 S. CAMPBELL AVENUE
TUCSON 85719
520-624-4183
520-882-7422
www.aatucson.org
info@aatucson.org

VICTOR VALLEY INTERGROUP
CENTRAL OFFICE INC.
18888 OUTER HWY 18, STE 107
APPLE VALLEY 92307-2315
760-242-9292
www.adesrtcentral.com/victorvalley
vvigco_aa@yahoo.com

ARKANSAS

FORT SMITH AREA
INTERGROUP
CENTRAL OFFICE
1209 NORTH B STREET
FORT SMITH 72901
501-783-0123
www.aa-fort-smith-arkansas.org
sobriety@aa-fort-smith-arkansas.org

INTERGROUP COUNCIL OF W.
CTRL
411 SELLERS STREE
HOT SPRINGS 71901
501-623-6328
800-753-9262

ARKANSAS CENTRAL SERVICE
OFFICE
7509 CANTRELL ROAD, STE 106
LITTLE ROCK 72207
501-664-7303
www.arkansascentraloffice.org
aacentral@direclynx.net

CALIFORNIA

UKIAH VALLEY INTERGROUP
P.O. BOX 482
HOPLAND 95449
707-744-1644
www.aaukiah.org

OFICINA CENTRAL HISPANA
VALLEY
45130 SMURR STREET, UNIT 7
INDIO 92201
760-342-2142

ANTELOPE VALLEY
INTERGROUP
44751 BEECH AVENUE, STE 2
LANCASTER 93534
661-945-5757

LODI 24 HOUR TELESERVICE
LODI 95240
209-339-1201

HARBOR AREA CENTRAL
OFFICE
3450 EAST SPRING STREET, STE
109
LONG BEACH 90806
562-989-7697
www.hacoaa.org
hacoaa@verizon.net

OFICINA HISPANA DEL ESTE
DE LA
6422 ½ EAST WHITTIER BLVD
LOS ANGELES 90022
213-722-4175

LOS ANGELES CENTRAL
OFFICE
4311 WILSHIRE BLVD #104
LOS ANGELES 90010
323-936-4343
www.lacoaa.org

OFICINA INTERGRUPAL
CONDADO VE
545 SOUTH B STREET, STE B
OXNARD 93030
805-486-7616

WESTERN SLOPE
INTERGROUP
P.O. BOX 1434
PLACERVILLE 95667
530-622-3500

OFICINA INTERGRUPO DE
CHINO
898 N. GAREY AVENUE
POMONA 91767
909-629-0493

OFICINA INGERGRUPAL
HISPANA
DEL CONDADO DE TULARE
P.O. BOX 3335
PORTERVILLE 93258
559-791-0920

NORTH CALIFORNIA
INTERGROUP
P.O. BOX 991107
REDDING 96099-1107
530-225-8955
www.aanorcal.org
info@aanorcal.org

OFICINA INTERGRUPAL DEL
ESTE
DE LA BAHIA
1412 MAC DONALD AVENUE
RICHMOND 94801
510-233-6249

OFICINA INTERGRUPAL DEL
VALLE CTR
3744 ATCHLSON STREET, APT
E
RIVERBANK 95367
209-869-1863/FAX 209-869-1693

CENTRAL CALIFORNIA
FELLOWSHIP
7500 14 AVENUE, #27
SACRAMENTO 95820-3560
916-454-1100
www.aasacramento.org
centraloffice@aasacramento.org

OFICINA CENTRAL HISPANA
COSTA NORTE
525 W. ALMA AVENUE
SAN JOSE 95125
408-287-7205

INTERGRUPAL HISPANA DE
SAN JOSE
894 N. 10TH STREET, STE #3
SAN JOSE 95112
408-975-0826
www.aaespanolsanjose.org

CENTRAL COAST CENTRAL
OFFICE
INTERGROUP
3419 MIGELITO STREET
SAN LUIS OBISPO 93401
805-541-3211
www.sloaa.org
mail@sloaa.org

SAN MATEO CO FELLOWSHIP
OF A.A.
2242 PALM AVENUE
SAN MATEO 94403
650-577-1310
www.aa-san-mateo-org
asanmateo@aol.com

OFICINA INTERGRUPAL
HISPANA DEL
AREA DE SAN MATEO
748 MERCY STREET
SAN MATEO 94040
650-679-2374

OFICINA INTERGRUPAL DE
ORANGE
1754 S. MAIN STREET
SANTA ANA 92706
714-541-7225

ORANGE COUNTY CENTRAL
OFFICE
1526 BROOKHOLLOW ROAD,
#75
SANTA ANA 92705
714-556-4555
www.oc-aa.org
ocaa7664@sbcglobal.net

INTERGROUP ANSWERING
SERVICE
SUSANVILLE 96130
530-257-2880

CENTRAL SERVICE OFFICE,
INC
27393 YNEZ ROAD, STE 156
TEMECULA 92591
951-695-1535
www.temeculacentraloffice.org

24 ANSWERING SERVICE
THOUSAND OAKS 91361
805-495-1111

ALL SOUTH BAY CENTRAL
OFFICE
1411 MARCELINA AVENUE
TORRANCE 90501
310-618-1180
southbayaa@earthlink.net

OFICINA INTERGRUPAL DEL
CONDADO DE TULARE
1700 SOUTH K STREET, STE D
TULARE 93274
559-688-0130

24 HOUR ANSWERING
SERVICE
TWAIN HARTE 95383
209-533-1134

NORTH SOLANO INTERGROUP
413 WILLIAMS STREET
VACAVILLE 95688
707-446-2244
www.aasolanonorth.org

SO. SOLANO COUNTY
CENTRAL OFFICE
529 CAPITAL STREET
VALLEJO 94590
707-643-8217
www.aasolanosouth.org

OFICINA CENTRAL
LATINOAMERICAN
7311 VAN NUYS BLVD, STE 3
VAN NUYS 91405

OFICINA INTERGRUPAL
NORTE-ORANGE
330 N. STATE COLLEGE BLVD,
STE 207
ANAHEIM 92806
714-956-7243

NORTH VALLEY CENTRAL
OFFICE
P.O. BOX 1144
CHICO 95927
530-342-5756
www.aabutte-glenn.org

24 HOUR ANSWERING
SERVICE
CHINO 91710
909-628-4428

OFICINA INTERGRUPAL
1177 3RD AVENUE, STE 3
CHULA VISTA 91910
619-476-0288

INLAND EMPIRE CENTRAL
OFFICE
1265 NORTH MT. VERNON
COLTON 92324
909-825-4700
www.inlandempireaa.org

DEL NORTE INTERGROUP
P.O. BOX 1067
CRESCENT CITY 95531
707-464-3411

VALLEY SERVICE CENTER
7000 VILLAGE PARKWAY, STE 5
DUBLIN 94568
925-829-3160
925-829-0666
888-859-3230
www.valleyservicecenter.org
info@valleyservicecenter.org

HUMBOLDT COUNTY
INTERGROUP
P.O. BOX 7102
EUREKA 95502-7102
707-442-0711
www.aahumboltdelnorte.org

OFICINA CENTRAL NORTE
588 DRY CREEK ROAD
HEALDSBURG 95448-8188

A.A. CENTRAL OFFICE OF
KERN COUNTY
930 TRUXTUN AVENUE, STE 110
BAKERSFIELD 93301
661-322-4025
www.kernaa.org
info@kernaa.com

OFICINA CENTRAL HISPANA
13334 RAMONA BLVD, STE E
BALDWIN PARK 91706
626-338-4612

VENTURA COUNTY
CENTRAL SERVICE OFFICE
321 N. AVIADOR STREET #115
CAMARILLO 93010
805-389-1444
www.aaventuracounty.org
vcaaco@verizon.net

SANTA CLARA COUNTY
INTERGROUP C.O.
274 EAST HAMILTON AVENUE,
STE D
CAMPBELL 95008
408-374-8511
www.aasanjose.org
office@aasanjose.org

CENTRAL INTERGROUP
OFFICE OF THE DESERT
35325 DATE PALM DRIVE, STE
134
CATHEDRAL CITY 92234
760-324-4880
www.aainthedesert.org

TULARE COUNTY CENTRAL
OFFICE
628 N. FARMERSVILLE BLVD
FARMERSVILLE 93223
559-747-1277/FAX 559-747-1278
www.aa-tulareco.org
tccof@hotmail.com

OFICINA INTERGRUPAL
HISPANA
520 N. FULTON STREET
FRESNO 93728-3402
559-266-6152

CENTRAL SERVICE OFFICE OF
FRESNO
2812 N. BLACKSTONE AVENUE
FRESNO 93703-1002
559-221-6907
www.fresnoaa.org
fresnoaa@sbcglobal.net

MENDOCINO COAST
INTERGROUP
P.O. BOX 1629
FORT BRAGG 95437
707-964-7726
www.mendocinocoastaa.com

FULLERTON NORTH ORANGE
COUNTY INTERGROUP
1111 E. COMMONWEALTH, STE
D
FULLERTON 92832
714-773-4357
www.aanoc.com
officemanager@aanoc.com

OFICINA INTERGRUPAL
HISPANA
16319 NEW HAMPSHIRE
AVENUE
GARDENA 90247
310 516-8626

SAN GABRIEL/POMONA
VALLEY
CENTRAL OFFICE
849 E. ROUTE 6, STE D
GLENDORA 91740
626-914-1861

WEST CENTRAL OFFICE
2365 WESTWOOD BLVD, STE 22
LOS ANGELES 90064
310-474-7339

OFICINA CENTRAL HISPANA
2607 SOUTH VAN BUREN
PLACE
LOS ANGELES 90007
323-735-2089

LAKE COUNTY INTERGROUP
P.O. BOX 1054
LOWER LAKE 95457
707-995-3316

CENTRAL VALLEY
INTERGROUP
1024 J STREET, ROOM 428
P.O. BOX 185
MODESTO 9353-0185
209-572-2970
866-507-6237
www.cviaa.org
info@cviaa.org

MONTEREY BAY AREA
INTERGROUP
1015 CASS #4
MONTEREY 93940
831-373-3713
aamonterey.org

NAPA COUNTY INTERGROUP
462 COFFIELD AVENUE, APT.
NAPA 94558-5567
707-255-4900

EASTBAY INTERGROUP
CENTRAL OFFICE
295 27TH STREET
OAKLAND 94612
510-839-8900
www.eastbayaa.org
centraloffice@eastbayaa.org

PARADISE INTERGROUP
330 SKYLINE BLVD
OROVILLE 95966
www.aabutte-glenn.org

SALINAS VALLEY AREA
INTERGROUP
9 WEST GABLIAN STREET, STE
11
SALINAS 93901-2723
831-424-9874
www.aasalinas.org
dryandsober1@aol.com

OFICINA CENTRAL HISPANA
INTERGRUPAL - McDOUGAL
BUILDING
5 GAVILAN STREET, STE 216
SALINAS 93901
831-757-8518

OFICINA INTERGRUPAL
DE SAN BERNARDINO
3628 UNIVERSITY AVENUE
SAN DIEGO 92104-2317
619-280-7224

SAN DIEGO CENTRAL OFFICE
7075 MISSION GORGE ROAD,
STE B
SAN DIEGO 92120-2454
619-265-8762/FAX 619-265-2954
www.aasandiego.org
sdaaco@aol.com

OFICINA CENTRAL HISPANA
383 VALENCIA STREET
SAN FRANCISCO 94103
415-554-8811
INTERCOUNTY FELLOWSHIP
OF A.A.
1821 SACRAMENTO STREET
SAN FRANCISCO 94109-3528
415-674-1821
www.aasf.org
aa@aasf.org

SANTA BARBARA CENTRAL
OFFICE
1213 STATE STREET, STE H
SANTA BARBARA 93101
805-962-3332
www.santabarbaraaa.com
sbaa@santabarbaraaa.com

SCV CENTRAL OFFICE OF A.A.
P.O. BOX 803063
SANTA CLARITA 91380-3063
661-250-9922
www.aascv.org
info@aascv.org

52nd DISTRICT ALCOHOLICS
ANONYMOUS
CENTRAL OFFICE
500 S. BROADWAY, STE 114
SANTA MARIA 93454
805-925-3782

OFICINA INTERGRUPAL
SURESTE DE VENTURA
949 ½ EAST MAIN STREET
SANTA PAULA 93060
805-525-6140

SONOMA COUNTY
INTERGROUP
750 MENDOCINO AVENUE #10
SANTA ROSA 95401-4822
707-546-2066/FAX 707-566-9677
707-544-1300
www.sonomacountyaa.org

SANTA CRUZ COUTY
INTERGROUP INC
5732 SOQUEL DRIVE
SOQUEL 95073-2811
831-475-5782
www.aasantacruz.org
info@aasantacruz.org

DELTA CENTRAL OFFICE
1525 N. ELDORADO #3
STOCKTON 95204
209-464-1509
209-943-1744
www.aadelta.org

A.A. SAN FERNANDO VALLEY
C.O.
7417 VAN NUYS BLVD, STE E
VAN NUYS 91405
818-988-3001
818-988-0342
www.sfvaa.org

N. SAN DIEGO CO. CENTRAL
OFFICE
604 E. VISTA WAY
VISTA 92084
760-758-2514
www.nosdco-aa.org
nosdcoaa@nosdco-aa.org

OFICINA INTERGRUPAL
HISPANA DE
985 S. SANTA FE, UNIT 9
VISTA 92083
760-758-6905

CONTRA COSTA SERVICE
CENTER
185 MAYHEW WAY
WALNUT CREEK 94596
925-939-5371
www.contracostaaa.org

OFICINA INTERGRUPAL
1150 MAIN STREET, STE 7B
WATSONVILLE 95076
831-768-9597
www.aacostacentral.com

OFICINA LATINA CENTRAL
DE AA
600 4TH STREET
WEST SACRAMENTO 96605
916-372-0343

COLORADO

BOULDER COUNTY CENTRAL
OFFICE
5375 WESTERN AVENUE, STE 7
BOULDER 80301
303-447-8201
www.bouldercountyaa.org

24 HOUR A.A. ANSWERING
SERVICE
BOULDER 80304
303-682-8032

COLORADO SPRINGS AREA
SVC. OFFICE
701 SOUTH CASCADE AVENUE,
STE B
COLORADO SPRINGS 80903
719-573-5020
www.coloradospringsaa.org
DENVER AREA CENTRAL
OFFICE
2785 NORTH SPEER BLVD, STE
224
DENVER 80211
303-322-4440
www.daccaa.org
denveraa@daccaa.org

OFICINA INTERGRUPAL
HISPANA DE
A.A. DE CO
2785 STEER BLVD, STE 116
DENVER 80211
303-433-2080

NORTHERN COLORADO
INTERGROUP, INC
155 NORTH COLLEGE AVENUE,
STE 221
FORT COLLINS 80524
970-224-3552
www.northcoloradoaa.org

CENTRAL OFFICE OF
WESTERN CO
1005 NORTH 12TH, STE 107
GRAND JUNCTION 81502
970-245-9649
www.aa-westerncolorado.org

ANSWERING SERVICE
PUTNAM 06260
888-268-2067

SOUTHWEST INTERGROUP
C/O CHRIST EPISCOPAL
CHURCH
2000 MAIN STREET
STRATFORD 06497

ANSWERING SERVICE
WESTPORT 06092
203-227-2496

24 HOUR ANSWERING
SERVICE
YUBA CITY 95992
530-673-9380

CENTRAL SERVICE OFFICE OF
SOUTH COLORADO
4035-A CLUB MANOR DRIVE
PUEBLO 81008
719-546-1173
www.southerncoloradoaa.org

CONNECTICUT

GREATER BRIDGEPORT ANSWERING
SERVICE
BRIDGEPORT 06606
203-333-5804

INTERGROUP ASSOC. OF FAIRFIELD
COUNTY
P.O. BOX 1605
DARIEN 06820
203-855-0075
877-855-0075

RELIABLE TELEPHONE
ANSWERING SERVICE
DERBY 06418
203-734-1621

ANSWERING SERVICE
GREENWICH 06836
203-869-5221

ANSWERING SERVICE
MIDDLETOWN 06457
800-530-9511

DERBY-NEW HAVEN ANSWERING
SERVICE
NEW HAVEN 06515
888-624-6063

NEW LONDON/NORWICH
ANSWERING SERVICE
NEW LONDON 06320
860-447-2190

ANSWERING SERVICE
NEW MILFORD 06460
860-354-9843

DELAWARE

CENTRAL DELAWARE
INTERGROUP
P.O. BOX 853
DOVER 19901
302-736-1567
www.cdiaa.org

SOUTHERN DELAWARE
INTERGROUP
P.O. BOX 248
OCEAN VIEW 19970
302-856-6452
www.sussexaa.org

NORTHERN DELEWARE
INTERGROUP
TROLLEY SQUARE, STE 21B
WILMINGTON 19806
302-655-5113
302-655-5999
www.ndiaa.org
office@ndiaa.org

SOUTH PALM BEACH COUNTY
INTERGROUP INC.
2905 S. FEDERAL HWY, STE C-16
DELRAY BEACH 33483
561-276-4581
www.aainpalmbeach.org
southcountyaa@bellsouth.net

ANSWERING SERVICE
DELTONA 32725
888-756-2930

BROWARD COUNTY A.A.
INTERGROUP
305 S. ANDREWS AVENUE,
ROOM 502
FORT LAUDERDALE 33301
954-462-0265
954-462-7202
www.aabroward.org
aainterg.@bellsouth.net

LEE COUNTY AREA
INTERGROUP
12734 KENWOOD LANE, STE 79
FORT MYERS 33907
239-275-5111
www.leecountyaa.org
lcai@leecountyaa.org

INTERGROUP COMM OF
DISTRICT 14
24 HOLLYWOOD BLVD S.W.,
STE 7
FORT WALTON BEACH 32548
850-244-2421
www.fwb-area-aa.org

NORTH CENTRAL FLORIDA
INTERGROUP
2632 N.W. 43RD STREET, ROOM
A-111
GAINESVILLE 32606
352-372-8091
www.ncfintergroup.com

INTERPROUPE FRANCAIS DE FLA
P.O. BOX 22-2562
HOLLYWOOD 33020
954-522-1838

PINELLAS CO INTERGROUP
INC
8340 ULMERTON ROAD, STE
220
AMERICAN BUSINESS CENTER
LARGO 33771
727-530-0415
www.aapinellas.org
central office@aapinellas.org

LAKE SUMTER INTERGROUP
2115-I CITRUS BLVD
LEESBURG 34748-3011
352-360-0960
www.lakesumterintergroup.com
lakesumter@aol.com

MID-KEYS INTERGROUP
P.O. BOX 1527
MARATHON 33050
305-743-3262
www.aafloridakeys.org

DISTRICT OF COLUMBIA

WASHINGTON AREA
INTERGROUP ASSN.
4530 CONNECTICUT AVE N.W.,
STE 111
WASHINGTON 20008
202-966-9115
202-966-9782
www.aa-dc.org
aa-dc@starpower.net

OFICINA INTERGRUPAL
HISPANA
DE WASHINGTON D.C.
1470 IRVING STREET N.W. 2ND
FLOOR
P.O. BOX 3313
WASHINGTON 20010
202-234-3719

FLORIDA

BREVARD INTERGROUP
720 E. NEW HAVEN AVENUE,
STE 3
MELBOURNE 32901-5474
321-724-2247
www.aaspacecoast.org
intergroup@aaspacecoast.org

OFICINA INTERGRUPAL
HISPANA DEL SUR
1770 W. FLAGER, STE 4
MIAMI 33135
305-642-2805

NAPLES AREA INTERGROUP
85 12 STREET SOUTH
NAPLES 34102
239-262-6535
www.naplesintergroup.org
naplesintergroup@yahoo.com

TRI-DISTRICT INTERGROUP
CENTRAL OFF.
3300 N. PACE BLVD, STE 322
PENSACOLA 32505-5149
850-433-4191
www.aapensacola.org
info@aapensacola.org

ST. LUCIE COUNTY
INTERGROUP ASSOC.
905 N.E. PRIMA VISTA BLVD,
STE D, 2 FL
PORT ST. LUCIE 34952
772-873-9299
www.aastlucieintergroup.com

CENTRAL OFFICE OF SARA-
MANA INC
1748 INDEPENDENCE BLVD,
STE B2
SARASOTA 34234
941-351-4818
www.aasrq.org
info@aasrq.org

HERNANDO COUNTY
INTERGROUP
6344 SHALIMAR AVENUE
SPRING HILL 34608
352-596-3704
www.aahernandocounty.com

INTERGROUP OF MARTIN
COUNTY
828 S.E. DIXIE HWY
STUART 34994
772-283-9337
www.martincountyaa.org
martincountyaa@juno.com

INTERGROUP 5 INC
1106-H THOMASVILLE ROAD
TALLAHASSEE 32303
850-224-1818
www.intergroup5.org

CENTRAL FLORIDA
INTERGROUP
SERVICE (ORLANDO AREA)
283 LIVE OAKS BLVD, BLDG 6
CASSELBERRY 32707
407-260-5822
407-260-5408
www.cflintgroup.org
cfi@embarq.com

MIAMI-DADE INTERGROUP
299 ALHAMBRA CIRCLE, STE
309
CORAL GABLES 33134
305-461-2425/FAX 305-461-2426
www.aamiamidade.org
aamiamidade@bellsouth.net

ANSWERING SERVICE
DELAND 32720
888-756-2930

NATURE COAST INTERGROUP
111 W. MAIN STREET, STE 308
INVERNESS 34450
352-344-0290
www.ncintergroup.com

NORTHEAST FLORIDA
INTERGROUP
3128 BEACH BLVD
JACKSONVILLE 32207
904-399-8535/FAX 904-399-8537
www.neflaa.org
neflintergroup@aol.com

OFICINA INTERGRUPAL
HISPANA
210 COMMERCE WAY
JUPITER 33468
561-748-7122

KEY WEST INTERGROUP
404 VIRGINIA
KEY WEST 33040
305-296-8654
www.aafloridakeys.org

OSCEOLA COUNTY
INTERGROUP
750 OFFICE PLAZA BLVD, STE
302 RM 2
KISSIMMEE 34744
407-870-8282
SPANISH HOTLINE/407-240-1181
www.osceolaintergroup.org

DISTRICT 16 HOTLINE
LAKE CITY 32055
800-505-0702
386-397-4272

HEARTLAND INTERGROUP
A.A. INC
1035 S. FLORID AVENUE, STE
180
863-688-0211
863-687-9275
www.heartlandintergroup.org

CENTRAL OFFICE OF WEST
PASCO
GREEN KEY PLAZA
6611 U.S. HWY 19, ROOM 505
NEW PORT RICHEY 34652
727-847-0777
www.wptsaa.org
news0777@yahoo.com

INTERGROUP SERVICE
COMM OF THE 5TH DIST INC.
12697 TAMIAMI TRAIL
NORTH PORT 34287
941-426-7655
941-426-7723
NORTH PORT 34287
www.district5.com
intergroupdist5@arq.net

INTERGROUP 17
3666 N.E. 25TH STREET, STE A
OCALA 33470
352-867-0660

ANSWERING SERVICE
ORANGE CITY 32763
888-756-2930

DISTRITO HISPANO 33 DEL
NORTE
P.O. BOX 592096
ORLANDO 32859
407-240-1181
www.aahispanos.org
webmaster@ahispanos.org

FLAGLER COUNTY DIST 22
INTERGROUP
P.O. BOX 352470
PALM COAST 32135
386-445-4357
www.thepromises.info

DISTRICT 15 INTERGROUP
P.O. BOX 1443
PANAMA CITY 32402
850-784-7431
www.panamacityaa.org

TRI-COUNTY CENTRAL
OFFICE, INC
8019 N. HIMES AVENUE, STE 104
TAMPA 33614
813-933-9722/FAX 813-936-0130
813-933-9123
www.aatampa-area.org
aainfo@aatampa-area.org

OFICINA INTERGRUAL DE
TAMPA-BAY
1936 W. DR. MARTIN LUTHER
KING, RM 203A
TAMPA 33607
813-870-0437

NO. MONROE COUNTY
CENTRAL OFFICE
P.O. BOX 841
TAVERNIER 33070
305-451-2314

INDIAN RIVER CENTRAL
OFFICE
1600 26TH STREET, STE 6
VERO BEACH 32960
772-562-1114
www.indianriveraa.org
info@indianriveraa.org

PALM BEACH COUNTY
INTERGROUP ASSOC.
1371 OKEECHOBEE ROAD
WEST PALM BEACH 33401
561-655-5700
www.aa-palmbeachcounty.org
pbciaa@bellsouth.net

GEORGIA

CENTRAL OFFICE
127 PEACHTREE STREET, STE
1310
ATLANTA 30303
404-525-3178
www.atlantaaa.org
atlantaaa@mindspring.com

12th DISTRICT CENTRAL
OFFICE
113 CAMILLA AVENUE-
MARTINEZ
AUGUSTA 30907-3406
606-860-8331
www.augustaaa.org
12thdistrictcentraloffice@comcast.net

GLYNN COUNTY INTERGROUP
P.O. BOX 397
BRUNSWICK 31521
912-265-0892
www.glynncountyaa.org

OFICINA INTERGRUPAL
HISPANA
3146 CHAMBLEE DUNWOODY
RD, STE 215
CHAMBLEE 30340
770-452-0059

DALTON INTERGROUP
P.O. BOX 486
DALTON 30722-0486

OFICINA INTERGRUPAL DE
HILTON HEAD
P.O. BOX 18305
GARDEN CITY 31418
843-338-6284

SAVANNAH INTERGROUP
ASSOCIATION
527 W. HWY 80, STE D2
GARDEN CITY 31308
912-965-0241
www.savannahaa.org

ATHENS AREA INTERGROUP
337 S. MILLEDGE AVENUE, STE
219
ATHENS 30605
706-543-0436
www.athensaa.com

GEORGIA SERVICE ASSEMBLY
145 FIRST STREET, LOWER
LEVEL
MACON 31201
478-745-2588
www.aageorgia.org

DISTRICT 07A 24 HOUR
ANSWERING SERVICE
MACON 31208
912-746-6652

DISTRICT 02A-B TIFTON-
VALDOSTA
TIFTON 31768
800-766-4653

HAWAII

EAST HAWAII INTERGROUP
485 KINOOLE STREET
HILO 96720-2958
808-961-6133

OAHU A.A. INTERGROUP OF
HAWAII
1400 KAPIOLANI BLVD, BLDG.
C-27
HONOLULU 96804
808-946-1438
www.oahucentraloffice.com

WEST HAWAII INTERGROUP
C/O KONA COAST CAB. 74-5583 PAWAI
PLACE, BAY 14
KAILUA-KONA 96740
808-329-1212
www.turquoise.net
whaa@turquoise.net

KAUAI INTERGROUP
P.O. BOX 3606
KAUAI
LIHUE 96766
808-245-6677

MAUI CENTRAL OFFICE
70 CENTRAL AVENUE #1
WAILUKU 96793
808-244-9673
www.aamaui.org
aamaui@maui.net

IDAHO

TREASURE VALLEY CENTRAL
OFFICE
1516 VISTA AVENUE
BOISE 83705
208-344-6611
tvico@qwest.net

CENTRAL OFFICE OF NORTH
IDAHO
118 N. 7TH STREET, STE B5
COEUR D'ALENE 83814-2759
208-667-4633

NORTH CENTRAL IDAHO
LEWISTON 83501
208-882-1597

DISTRICT 01 ANSWERING
SERVICE
POCATELLO 83204
208-235-2444

ILLINOIS

DISTRICT 18 ANSWERING
SERVICE
ALTON 62002
800-307-6600

DISTRICT 10 ANSWERING
SERVICE
ANTIOCH 60606
847-395-5988

DISTRICT 60, 62, 63, 64,
ANSWERING SVC
AURORA 60504
630-859-2444

DISTRICT 28 ANSWERING
SERVICE
BARRINGTON 60011
847-382-4455

DECATUR INTERGROUP
P.O. BOX 356
DECATUR 62525
217-422-3766

DISTRICT 73 ANSWERING
SERVICE
DIXON 61021
800-452-7990

DISTRICT 42 ANSWERING
SERVICE
DOWNERS GROVE 60515
630-887-8671

INTERGRUPAL NOROESTE
1530 WEATHER STORM
ELGIN 60123
847-695-9123

DISTRICT 41 ANSWERING
SERVICE
ELMHURST 60126
630-833-7897

DISTRICT 72 ANSWERING
SERVICE
FREEPORT 61032
800-452-7990

DISTRICT 91 CENTRAL OFFICE
P.O. BOX 1058
GALESBURG 61402-1058
309-343-1530

DISTRICT 40 ANSWERING
SERVICE
GLEN ELLYN 60138
630-653-6556

DISTRICT 51 ANSWERING
SERVICE
JOILET 60434
815-741-6637

DISTRICT 52 ANSWERING
SERVICE
KANKAKEE 60901
815-939-4996

DISTRICT 10 ANSWERING
SERVICE
LIBERTYVILLE 60048
847-362-1811

DISTRICT 12 HILLTOP
ANSWERING SVC
WAUKEGAN 60048
847-623-9660

DISTRICT 17 HELPLINE
WEST FRANKFORT 62896
800-307-6600

DISTRICT 23 ANSWERING
SERVICE
BARTLETT 60103
630-830-6091

BLOOMINGTON/NORMAL
ANSWERING SERVICE
BLOOMINGTON 61702-1384
309-828-7092

CARBONDALE HELPLINE
CARBONDALE 62901
800-307-6600
www.southernillinoisaa.org

DISTRICT 12 ANSWERING
SERVICE
CHAMPAIGN 61825-2413
217-373-4200

COMITE DE INTERGRUPOS
2814 ½ W. 59TH STREET
CHICAGO 60629
773-863-0172

OFICINA INTERGRUPAL DE
CHICAGO
2536 W. NORTH AVENUE
CHICAGO 60647
773-489-6438
aalatino@aol.com

CHICAGO AREA SERVICE
OFFICE
180 N. WABASH AVENUE, STE
305
CHICAGO 60601
312-346-1475/FAX 312-346-5477
312-346-8070
www.chicagoaa.org
caso@chicagoaa.org

DISTRICT 11 ANSWERING
SERVICE
CRYSTAL LAKE 60014
815-455-3311

DISTRICT 71 ANSWERING
SERVICE
DE KALB 60115
800-452-7990

ILLOWA INTERGROUP
1702 15 STREET PLACE
MOLINE 61265
309-764-1016
www.aaquadcities.com
Illowaintergroup@juno.com

DISTRICT 07 ANSWERING
SERVICE
MT. VERNON 62864
618-532-5007

DISTRICT 43 ANSWERING
SERVICE
NAPERVILLE 60565
630-355-2622

DISTRICT 21 ANSWERING
SERVICE
PALATINE 60067
847-359-3311

PEORIA AREA INTERGROUP
ASSN.
329 E. LAKE STREET
PEORIA 61614
309-687-1329
www.aapeoria.org

DISTRICT 80 ANSWERING
SERVICE
PRINCETON 61356
815-875-4279

ROCKFORD AREA
INTERGROUP
4040 CHARLES STREET, STE 210
ROCKFORD 61108
815-968-0333

SOUTHERN ILLINOIS
CENTRAL SERVICE OFFICE
409 BROADWAY UNIT C-1
SOUTH ROXANA 62087
618-251-4000

DISTRICT 61 ANSWERING
SERVICE
ST. CHARLES 60174
630-377-6610

INDIANA

MADISON COUNTY
INTERGROUP
P.O. BOX 326
ANDERSON 46015
765-644-3212

TRI-STATE INTERGROUP
BOX 583
ANGOLA 46703
866-608-3793
www.aaangola.org
tristate@aaangola.org

CENTRAL SERVICE OFFICE
949 A MIDDLEBURY STREET
ELKHART 46516
574-295-8188

SOUTHWESTERN INDIANA
CENTRAL
123 N.W. 4TH STREET, RM. 12,
COURT BLDG
EVANSVILLE 47708
812-464-2219/FAX 812-434-4870

FORT WAYNE AREA
INTERGROUP
2118 INWOOD DRIVE, STE 112
FORT WAYNE 46815
260-471-6262
www.aaftwayne.org

SOUTHEASTERN INDIANA
INTERGROUP
P.O. BOX 502
GREENSBURG 47240
812-663-0821
www.seig-aa.org

MICHIANA CENTRAL SERVICE
OFFICE
814 E. JEFFERSON BLVD.
SOUTH BEND 46617
574-234-7007/FAX 219-234-7043
www.michianasober.org
michianasober@galaxyinternet.net

WABASH VALLEY
INTERGROUP
P.O. BOX 8102
TERRE HAUTE 47808
812-460-4311
www.feverdream.com/aa.html

LAFAYETTE AREA DISTRICTS
49 & 51
WEST LAFAYETTE 47903
765-742-1666
www.aalafayette.org

CALUMENT AREA
INTERGROUP
7207 INDIANAPOLIA BLVD
HAMMOND 46324
219-844-6695
aahammond@sbcglobal.net

INDIANAPOLIS INTERGROUP
INC.
136 E. MARKET STREET, STE
1030
INDIANAPOLIS 46204
317-632-7864/FAX 317-632-2155
www.indyaa.org
intergroupmail@indyaa.org

OFICINA INTERGRUPAL
HISPANA
P.O. BOX 26330
INDIANAPOLIS 46226
317-631-5099

MARION AREA INTERGROUP
P.O. BOX 1401
MARION 46952
765-677-7535

MUNCIE TRI-DISTRICT 85, 87, 89,
INTERGROUP
P.O. BOX 2072
MUNCIE 74307
765-284-2515
www.aamuncie.org
info@aamuncie.org

ORIGINAL RECIPE
INTERGROUP
P.O. BOX 72
NEW PARIS 46553-0072

RICHMOND INDIANA ANSWERING
SERVICE
RICHMOND 47385
765-965-1800

DISTRICT 13 INTERGROUP
P.O. BOX 487
IOWA CITY 52244
319-338-9111

SIOUXLAND INTERGROUP
520 NEBRASKA STREET, STE 201
SIOUX CITY 51101
712-252-1333

WATERLOO/CEDAR FALLS
ANSWERING SERVICE
WATERLOO 50702
319-232-4117

IOWA

AMES INTERGROUP
P.O. BOX 1772
AMES 50010
515-232-8642
www.amesaa.org

24 HOUR ANSWERING
SERVICE
CEDAR RAPIDS 52213
319-365-5955

24 HOUR ANSWERING
SERVICE
DAVENPORT 52801
309-764-1016

CENTRAL OFFICE/
INTERGROUP
1620 PLEASANT STREET, ROOM 228
DES MOINES 50314
515-282-8550
www.aadesmoines.org
coffaa@aol.com

DUBUQUE AREA INTERGROUP
1593 MAIN
DUBUQUE 52001
319-557-9196

KANSAS

KANSAS AREA ASSEMBLY CENTRAL
OFFICE
P.O. BOX 1773
SALINA 67402
785-823-3058
www.kansas-aa-org

TOPEKA AREA ANSWERING
SERVICE
TOPEKA 66605
785-354-3888
www.aatopeka.org

UNITED SERVICE
INTERGROUP
P.O. BOX 702
ULYSSES 67880
316-356-3003

CENTRAL OFFICE
2812 E. ENGLISH
WICHITA 67211
316-684-3661
www.aawichita.org
info@aawichita.org

KENTUCKY

BOWLING GREEN CENTRAL
OFFICE
3255 GARRETT HOLLOW ROAD
BOWLING GREEN 42101
502-781-6454

NORTH KENTUCKY CENTRAL
OFFICE
1727-29 MADISON AVENUE
COVINGTON 41011
859-491-7181

WESTERN KENTUCKY
INFORMATION LINE
FREDONIA 42411
800-606-6047

BLUE GRASS INTERGROUP
1093 S. BROADWAY, STE 1110
LEXINGTON 40504-2677
859-225-1212
bluegrassintergroup@hotmail.com

WESTERN LOUISIANA
INTERGROUP
440 BYLES STREET
MANY 71449
318-256-3919

GREATER NEW ORLEANS AREA
CENTRAL OFFICE
638 PAPWORTH AVENUE, STE
101
METAIRIE 70005
505-838-3399
504-779-1178
www.aa-neworleans.org

GREATER LOUISVILLE
INTERGROUP INC
332 W. BROADWAY, ROOM 620
LOUISVILLE 40202
502-582-1849
www.louisvilleaa.org
glgi@bellsouth.net

A.A. CENTRAL OFFICE
1 HANNING LANE
OWENSBORO 42301
270-683-0371

LOUISIANA

BATON ROUGE CENTRAL
OFFICE
3955 GOVERNMENT STREET,
STE 5
BATON ROUGE 70806
225-388-0069
joyaa@juno.com

17TH DISTRICT INTERGROUP
P.O. BOX 211
HOUMA 70361-0211
800-285-3989

ACADIANA AREA CENTRAL
OFFICE
115 LEONIE STREET
LAFAYETTE 70506
337-991-0830

A.A. LOUSIANA DISTRICT 4
P.O. BOX 5063
MONROE 71211
800-371-4017
aaladistrict4online@hotmail.com

CENTRAL OFFICE
2800 YOUREE DRIVE #3620
SHREVEPORT 71104
318-865-2172
www.aacentraloffice.us
help@aacentraloffice.us

MAINE

CENTRAL SERVICE OFFICE
78 PORTLAND STREET
PORTLAND 04101
207-774-3034
207-774-4335
800-737-6237
www.aamaine.org
cso@aamaine.org

MARYLAND

NORTHEASTERN MARYLAND
INTERGROUP
28 CENTENNIAL LANE
ABERDEEN 21001
410-272-4150
www.nemdaa.org
nemdaa@verizon.net

LOWER SHORE INTERGROUP
P.O. BOX 2732
SALISBURY 21802-2732
410-543-2266
www.lsiaa.org

OFICINA INTERGRUPAL
HISPANA
P.O. BOX 7698
SILVER SPRING 20910
301-587-6191

ANNAPOLIS AREA
INTERGROUP INC.
P.O. BOX 2267
ANNAPOLIS 21404
410-268-5441
www.annapolisareaintergroup.org

BALTIMORE INTERGROUP
COUNCIL OF AA
8635 LOCH RAVEN BLVD, STE 4
BALTIMORE 21286
410-663-1922
www.baltimoreaa.org
aabalt@baltimoreaa.org

SOUTHERN MARYLAND
INTERGROUP
P.O. BOX 767
CHARLOTTE HALL 20622-0767
800-492-0209

WESTERN MARYLAND
INTERGROUP
P.O. BOX 323
CUMBERLAND 21502
301-722-6110
866-722-6110

MIDSHORE INTERGROUP
P.O. BOX 643
EASTON 21601
410-822-4226
www.midshoreintergroup.org
msig-aa@verizon.net

HAGERSTOWN AREA
INTERGROUP
P.O. BOX 1153
HAGERSTOWN 21741
301-733-1109
www.hagerstownaa.org

OCEAN CITY FELLOWSHIP
INTERGROUP
P.O. BOX 913
OCEAN CITY 21843
410-219-2117

MASSACHUSETTS

BOSTON CENTRAL SERVICE
12 CHANNEL STREET, STE 604
BOSTON 02210
617-426-9444
www.aaboston.org

OFICINA INTERGRUPAL
HISPANA DE
78 BLOOMINGDALE APT 2
CHELSEA 02150
617-889-4507

MARTHA'S VINEYARD
INTERGROUP
65 PEACE POINT WAY
EDGARTOWN 02539
508-627-7084
www.aaonmv.vinyard.net

WESTERN MASS INTERGROUP
OFFICE
474 PLEASANT STREET
HOLYOKE 01040
413-532-2111
www.westernmassaa.org

CAPE COD INTERGROUP
396 MAIN STREET
P.O. BOX 662
HYANNIS 02601
508-775-7060/FAX 508-775-5475
www.capecodaa.com
ccaa@interscape.com

LOWELL DISTRICT 21
ANSWERING SVC
LOWELL 01853
978-957-4690
www.aaemassd21.org

OFICINA INTERGRUPAL
HISPANA AA
1 MARKET STREET, STE 301
LYNN 01901
781-598-1032

NANTUCKET INTERGROUP
P.O. BOX 451
NANTUCKET 02554
508-228-2334

BERKSHIRE INTERGROUP
OFFICE
85 EAST STREET, ROOM 14-15
PITTSFIELD 01201
413-448-2382

WESTERN MASS DE HABLA
HISPANA
DE WESTERN
MASSACHUSETTS
SPRINGFIELD 01103
413-734-7500

WORCESTER AREA
INTERGROUP INC.
100 GROVE STREET, STE 314
WORCESTER 01605
508-752-9000
www.aaworcester.org
steps@aaworcester.org

MICHIGAN

LENAWEE INTERGROUP
P.O. BOX 332
ADRIAN 49221
517-265-3590
www.lenaweeaa.com

BAY COUNTY UNITY
INTERGROUP
P.O. BOX 471
BAY CITY 48707
989-894-1949

JACKSON AREA ANSWERING
SERVICE
JACKSON 49254
517-789-8883

KALAMOZOO AREA CENTRAL
OFFICE
933 S. BURDICK STREET
KALAMAZOO 49001
269-349-4410

LANSING CENTRAL OFFICE
1915 E. MICHIGAN AVENUE,
STE D
LANSING 48912
517-377-1444
www.aalansingmi.org
aalansingmi@sbcglobal.net

DISTRICT 18 ANSWERING
SERVICE
MARQUETTE 49855
906-249-4430

MIDLAND AREA UNITY
COUNCIL INT
P.O. BOX 523
MIDLAND 48640
989-695-2975
www.midlandaa.org

NEWAYGO COUNTY CENTRAL
OFFICE
P.O. BOX 900
NEWAYGO 49337
616-652-5574

DISTRICT 10 ANSWERING
SERVICE
OWOSSO 48429-1825
989-723-5711

A.A. OF OAKLAND COUNTY
168 UNIVERSITY DRIVE
PONTIAC 48342
248-332-3521
aa_oakland@sbcglobal.net

DISTRICT 16 ANSWERING
SERVICE
RIVERDALE 48877
800-821-3014

THUMB AREA UNITY COUNCIL
INTERGROUP
P.O. BOX 437
CASEVILLE 48725
989-550-4980
www.tauc.us
tauc@avci.net

MACOMB INTERGROUP
7308 STATE PARK
CENTER LINE 48015
586-756-8316
myrndd@yahoo.com

DETROIT & WAYNE COUNTY
OFFICE
4750 WOODWARD AVE, STE 407
DETROIT 48201
313-921-1778
313-921-1942

DISTRICT 10 INTERGROUP
5300 S. NEW LOTHROP ROAD
DURAND 48429-1825
989-288-5268
www.district10area32.org

A.A. OF GREATER DETROIT
380 HILTON ROAD, ROOM #1
FERNDALE 48220
248-541-6565

FLINT AREA UNITY COUNCIL 24
FLINT 48501
810-234-0815

DISTRICT 12 OF AREA 34 ANSWERING
SERVICE
GAYLORD 49735
866-336-9588

KENT COUNTY CENTRAL
OFFICE
GRAND RAPIDS 49505
616-913-9216
www.grandrapidsaa.org

SAGINAW VALLEY
ANSWERING SERVICE
SAGINAW 48608
989-776-1241

SOUTHWEST CENTRAL
INTERGROUP
P.O. BOX 7136
STURGIS 49091
616-467-1107

DISTRICT 11 CENTRAL OFFICE
124 NORTH DIVISION
TRAVERSE CITY 49684
231-946-8823

HURON VALLEY INTERGROUP
INC
31 SOUTH HURON STREET
YPSILANTI 48197
734-482-0707
734-482-5700
www.hvai.org
office@hvai.org

MINNESOTA

ANSWERING SERVICE
ALBERT LEA 56007-3703
507-373-7307

GREATER MINNEAPOLIS
INTERGROUP
7204 W. 27TH STREET, STE 113
ST. LOUIS PARK 55426-3112
952-922-0880/FAX 952-922-1061
www.aaminneapolis.org
info@aaminneapolis.org

ST. PAUL INTERGROUP
CENTRAL OFFICE
1600 UNIVERSITY AVENUE #407
ST. PAUL 55104
651-227-5502
www.aastpaul.org
lifeline@aastpaul.org

ANSWERING SERVICE
AUSTIN 55912
507-437-3797

TWIN PORTS AREA
INTERGROUP
331 E. 1ST STREET
DULUTH 55805
218-727-8117

INTERGROUP NORTHEAST
509 40TH AVENUE NE
MINNEAPOLIS 55421-3834
763-781-5102

ANSWERING SERVICE
OWATONNA 55060
507-451-2275

NORTH CENTRAL MISSISSIPPI 24-HR.
HOTLINE
OXFORD 38655
662-533-9102

DISTRICT 54 HOTLINE
SOUTH HAVEN 38632
662-280-3435

TUPELO CENTRAL OFFICE
1123 W. MAIN STREET
TUPELO 38803
662-844-0374

VICKSBURG ANSWERING
SERVICE
VICKSBURG 39180
601-636-1134

MISSOURI

DISTRICT 12 OFFICE 24 HR.
ANSWERING SERVICE
COLUMBIA 65205
573-442-4424
www.aa.columbia.missouri.org

NORTH ST. LOUIS COUNTY
INTERGROUP OFFICE
HAZELWOOD PLAZA
7246 N. LINDBERGH BLVD.
HAZELWOOD 63042
314-731-4854
www.ncoaa.org

JEFFERSON CITY ANSWERING
SERVICE
JEFFERSON CITY 65101
573-659-6670

KANSAS CITY AREA CENTRAL
OFFICE
200 EAST 18TH AVENUE
NORTH KANSAS CITY 64116
816-471-7229
www.kc-aa.org
centraloffice@kc-aa.org

MISSISSIPPI

SOUTH MISSISSIPPI
INTERGROUP
10536 AUTO MALL PARKWAY,
STE D1
D'LBEVILLE 39540
228-392-6662
smiggc@bellsouth.net

GREENVILLE ANSWERING
SERVICE
GREENVILLE 38756
601-332-5645

HUB CITY AREA INTERGROUP
715 ARLEDGE STREET
HATTIESBURG 39401
601-582-1475

MID MISSISSIPPI INTERGROUP
CTRL OFF.
4526 OFFICE PARK DRIVE, STE
3
JACKSON 39206
601-982-0081

LAUREL INTERGROUP
532 NORTH 6TH AVENUE
LAUREL 39440
601-426-0108

CENTRAL OFFICE
SPRINGFIELD 65807
417-823-7125

CENTRAL SERVICES OF A.A.
2683 S. BIG BEND BLVD., ROOM 4
ST. LOUIS 63143
314-647-3677
314-647-3683
www.aastl.org
alano@aastl.org

TRI COUNTY INTERGROUP
305 DEPOT
ST. PETERS 63376
314-946-1560

CENTRAL OFFICE OF S.W.
MISSOURI
102 A WEBB STREET
WEBB CITY 64870
417-673-8591

MONTANA

SOUTH CENTRAL MONTANA
INTERGROUP
P.O. BOX 21242
BILLINGS 59102
408-534-3076

A.A. 24 HOUR HOTLINE
DISTRICT 61
HELENA 59601
406-443-0438

DISTRICT 81 A.A.
MISSOULA 59881
406-543-0011

MISSION VALLEY
INTERGROUP
83 AVENUE W
POLSON 59860

VALLEY INTERGROUP
P.O. BOX 1935
WHITFISH 59937
406-257-7185

NORTHERN NEVADA
INTERGROUP
436 SO. ROCK BLVD
SPARKS 89431
775-355-1151
www.aanorthernnevada.org
officemanager@nnig.org

NEBRASKA

HASTINGS NEBRASKA
INTERGROUP
521 SOUTH STREET JOE
HASTINGS 68901
402-463-9024

LINCOLN CENTRAL OFFICE
2748 S. STREET, STE A.A.
LINCOLN 68503
402-438-5214

NORFOLK AREA INTERGROUP
303 MADISON AVENUE
NORFOLK 68701
402-371-9859
CENTRAL OFFICE
4901 DODGE STREET
OMAHA 68132
402-556-1880
800-833-0920
admin@aa1.omhcoxmail.com

NORTHEAST NEBRASKA ANSWERING
SERVICE
PLAINVIEW 68769
402-582-3944

NEVADA

OFICINA CENTRAL HISPANA
1115 CASINO CENTER, STE 10
BOX 179
LAS VEGAS 89104
702-387-8744

LAS VEGAS INTERGROUP
1431 E. CHARLESTON BLVD. #15
LAS VEGAS 89104-1734
702-598-1888
www.lvcentraloffice.org
lvcentraloffice@aol.com

INTERGROUP OF NORTHERN NEW
JERSEY
2400 MORRIS AVENUE
UNION 07083
908-687-8566
www.nnjaa.org
intergroup@nnjaa.org

NEW MEXICO

ANSWERING SERVICE
ALAMOGORDO & RUIDOSO
AREA
ALAMOGORDO 88310
505-430-9502

OFICINA INTERGRUPAL
HISPANA
2130 SAN MATEO BLVD NE, STE
B2
ALBUQUERQUE 87110
505-266-3688

CENTRAL OFFICE
ALBUQUERQUE INC.
1921 ALVARADO N.E.
ALBUQUERQUE 87110-5103

DISTRICT 4 ANSWERING
SERVICE
FAIRACRES 88033
505-527-1803

CENTRAL OFFICES OF SAN
JUAN
418 W. BROADWAY, STE J
FARMINGTON 87401
505-327-0731

ANSWERING SERVICE
FARMINGTON 88202
505-327-0731

ANSWERING SERVICE
HOBBS 88002
505-397-7009

ANSWERING SERVICE
LAS CRUCES 88002
505-527-1803

NEW HAMPSHIRE

NEW HAMPSHIRE AREA
SERVICE OFFICE
1330 HOOKSETT ROAD
HOOKSETT 03106
603-622-6967/FAX 603-624-9507
800-593-3330
www.nhaa.net
office@nhaa.mv.com

NEW JERSEY

OFICINA INTERGRUPAL
HISPANA N.J.
P.O. BOX 20354
NEWARK 07102
973-824-0555
www.alcoholicosanonimosnj.org

SOUTH JERSEY INTERGROUP
ASSOC.
5090 CENTRAL HWY, STE 3
PENNSAUKEN 08109
856-486-4446
www.aasj.org
sjintergroup@verizon.net

CAPE ATLANTIC INTERGROUP
P.O. BOX 905
PLEASANTVILLE 08232
609-641-8855
www.capeatlanticintergroup.org
caig@capeatlanticintergroup.org

CENTRAL JERSEY
INTERGROUP
P.O. BOX 4096
TRENTON 08610
609-298-7795
609-298-7785
www.centraljerseyintergroup.org

ANSWERING SERVICE
ROSWELL 88202
505-623-0166

CENTRAL OFFICE OF SANTA
FE/INTERGROUP
1942 ½ CERILLOS ROAD
SANTA FE 87505
505-982-8932

ANSWERING SERVICE
TAOS 87571
505-758-3318

ANSWERING SERIVCE
SILVER CITY 88062
505-388-1802

NEW YORK

CAPITAL DISTRICT CENTRAL
OFFICE
575 BROADWAY, STE 128-130
ALBANY 12204-2804
www.albanynyaa.org

OFICINA DE INTERGRUPO DE
SUFFOLK
1572 5TH AVENUE
BAYSHORE 11706
516-435-2863

TRIPLE CITIES INTERGROUP
P.O. BOX 2103
BINGHAMTON 13902-2103
607-722-5983

BROOKLYN INTERGROUP
1425 KINGS HWY
BROOKLYN 11229
718-339-4777
www.users.vei.net/bklyn-aa
bklyn-aa@vei.net

INTERGRUPO DEL AREA DE
BROOKLYN
74 EAST 17TH ST 2DO PISO
BROOKLYN 11226
718-462-9449

HISPANO INTERGROUP
NASSAU
8 SMITH STREET
FREEPORT 11520
516-223-9590

FINGER LAKES AREA
ANSWERING SVC
GENEVA 14456
315-789-5955

CEN SVC INTERGROUP OF
ORANGE COUNT
P.O. BOX 636
GOSHEN 10924
845-534-8525

BATH AREA INTERGROUP
P.O. BOX 722
HAMMONDSPORT 14840-0722
607-868-4164

CORTLAND HOMER
INTERGROUP
P.O. BOX 44
HOMER 13077
607-753-1344

COLUMBIA COUNTY
ANSWERING SERVICE
HUDSON 12534-9999
518-625-2002

ITHACA INTERGROUP
BOX 43
ITHACA 14851
607-273-1541

ULSTER COUNTY ANSWERING
SVCS GRP
KINGSTON 12401
845-331-6360

24 HOUR ANSWERING
SERVICE
LAKEWOOD 14750-0203
716-488-2233

SUFFOLK INTERGROUP
ASSOCIATION
P.O. BOX 659
PATCHOGUE 11772
631-654-1150
www.suffolkny-aa.org

ANSWERING SVC OF ST.
LAWRENCE COUNTY
POTSDAM 13676
315-268-0120

DUTCHESS CO. DIST. 11
CENTRAL OFFICE
P.O. BOX 3547
POUGHKEEPSIE 12603
845-452-1111
www.ny-aa.org/dutchess

DISTRICT 13 ANSWERING
SERVICE
QUEENSBURY 12804
518-793-1113

ROCHESTER AREA
INTERGROUP INC
10 MANHATTAN SQUARE
DRIVE, STE D
ROCHESTER 14607
585-232-6720/FAX 585-454-3949
www.rochester-ny-aa.org
raacog@frontiernet.net

OFICINA INTERGRUPAL
HISPANA DE
27-23 ALANTIC AVE
BROOKLYN 11207
718-348-0387

BUFFALO CENTRAL OFFICE
681 SENECA STREET, LOWER
BUFFALO 14210
716-853-0388/FAX 853-0389
www.ny-aa.org
buffaloaa@hotmail.com

GREENE COUNTY
ANSWERING SERVICE
CATSKILL 12414-9999
518-625-2002

CORNING INTERGROUP
P.O. BOX 244
CORNING 14830
607-962-8161

CORNING ANSWERING
SERVICE
CORNING 14830
877-501-1249

SYRACUSE SERVICE CENTER
INTERGROUP
100 E. MANLIUS STREET
EAST SYRACUSE 13057
315-463-5011

ELMIRA INTERGROUP
P.O. BOX 14
ELMIRA 14902
607-737-6733

QUEENS INTERGROUP OF A.A.
105-29B METROPOLITAN
AVENUE
FOREST HILLS 11375-9088
718-520-5021
www.queensaa.org

SULLIVAN COUNTY
INTERGROUP ASSOC.
P.O. BOX 283
LIBERTY 12754
845-295-1010

INTERGROUP ASSOCIATION
307 SEVENTH AVENUE, 2ND
FLOOR
NEW YORK 10001
212-647-1680
212-647-1649
www.nyintergroup.org
generalinformation@nyintergroup.org

OFICINA CENTRAL HISPANA
DE A.A.
2334 1ST AVENUE
NEW YORK 10035-3606
212-348-2644/FAX 212-348-2689

NIAGARA INTERGROUP
P.O. BOX 2841
NIAGARA FALLS 14302
716-285-5319
niagaraintergroup.tripod.com/id4.html
naigcountyaa@yahoo.com

OLD FORGE 24 HOUR ANSWERING
SERVICE
OLD FORGE 13420
315-369-2281

NY-PENN INTERGROUP
P.O. BOX 421
OLEAN 14760
716-782-2444
716-372-4800

CITY OF ONEIDA 24 HR. ANSWERING
SERVICE
ONEIDA 13421
315-533-1227

TIOGA COUNTY INTERGROUP
P.O. BOX 322
OWEGO 13827

GENESEE WYOMING
INTERGROUP
P.O. BOX 683
STAFFORD 14143
877-522-0446
UTICA 24 HR DISTRICT 9 ANSWERING
SERVICE
UTICA 13505
315-732-6880

JEFFERSON COUNTY
INTERGROUP
44 PUBLIC SQUARE, ROOM 20
WATERTOWN 13601
315-788-2280
www.aajci.org

NASSAU INTERGROUP
361 HEMSTEAD TURNPIKE
WEST HEMPSTEAD 11552
516-292-3040
www.nassauny-aa.org
intergroup@nassauny-aa.org

ROCKLAND COUNTY
INTERGROUP
P.O. BOX 706
WEST NYACK 10994
845-352-1112
www.rocklandnyaa.org

ROME 24 HOUR ANSWERING
SERVICE
DISTRICT 12
ROME 13440
315-210-6644

DISTRICT 5 CENTRAL OFFICE
P.O. BOX 111
SARATOGA SPRINGS 12866

SARATOGA 24 HOUR
ANSWERING SERVICE
SARATOGA SPRINGS 12866
518-587-0407

NORTH CAROLINA

BOONE INTERGROUP
P.O. BOX 3513
BOONE 28607
828-264-0208
828-264-1212
www.booneaa.org

ANSWERING SERVICE
BURLINGTON 27616-1438
336-228-7611

OFICINA INTERGRUPAL
CENTRO ESTE DE NC
705 A ROSEMARY STREET
CARRBORO 27510
919-929-9010

METROLINA INTERGROUP
1427 SOUTH BLVD, STE 106
CHARLOTTE 28203
704-377-0244
www.charlotteaa.org
information@charlotteaa.org

OFICINA INTERGROUP
HISPANA DEL AREA D
P.O. BOX 790121
CHARLOTTE 28212
704-537-7999

DURHAM COUNTY
ANSWERING SERVICE
DURHAM COUNTY 27705
919-286-9499
ALBEMARLE AREA
INTERGROUP
P.O. BOX 2673
ELIZABETH CITY 27906
252-338-1849
800-350-2538

CAPE FEAR INTERGROUP
310 GREEN STREET, STE 202 B
FAYETTEVILLE 28301

DISTRICT 93 INTERGROUP COVERING
OUTER BANKS
P.O. BOX 2841
KITTY HAWK 27949
252-449-8133
www.aaobx.org

CARTERET COUNTY
ANSWERING SERVICE
MOREHEAD 28557
252-726-8540

MACON COUNTY ANSWERING
SERVICE
OTTO 28763-0212
828-349-4357

TRI-COUNTRY INTERGROUP
3948 BROWNING PLACE #205
RALEIGH 27609
919-783-8214
919-783-6144
www.nctriaa.org

SANDHILLS INTERGROUP
P.O. BOX 2513
SOUTHERN PINES 28388
800-496-1742

IREDELL INTERGROUP
432 WEST BELL STREET
STATESVILLE 28677
704-878-6404

WILMINGTON INTERGROUP
ASSOCIATION
5001 WRIGHTSVILLE AVENUE
WILMINGTON 28403
910-794-1840
www.wilmingtonaa.org
ig2@earthlink.net

CENTRAL OFFICE WINSTON-
SALEM
1020 BROOKSTOWN AVENUE
#10
WINSTON-SALEM 27101
336-725-6031
www.wsaa.org

ASHEBORO INTERGROUP
707 WILLOW CREEK COURT
ASHEBORO 27203

N.C. MOUNTAIN CENTRAL
OFFICE
206 PARK PLACE OFFICE
70 WOODFIN PLACE
ASHEVILLE 28801
828-254-8539
800-524-0465
www.ashevilleaa.org
ncmco@bellsouth.net

WESTERN PIEDMONT INTERGROUP
ASSOC. INC.
625 EAST 2ND AVENUE, STE 8
GASTONIA 28054
704-865-1561
www.wpintergroup.org

DISTRICT 33 ANSWERING
SERVICE-
ALAMANCE, CASWELL
GRAHAM 27253
866-640-0180
www.aanc33.org

DISTRICT 33 ANSWERING
SERVICE
GRAHAM 27253
866-640-0180

INTERGROUP COUNCIL OF
A.A.
4125-C WALKER AVENUE, STE 2
GREENSBORO 27407
336-275-7910
www.aagreensboronc.com
info@www.aagreensboronc.com

PITT COUNTY INTERGROUP
P.O. BOX 20342
GREENVILLE 27858-0342
252-758-4357

HIGH POINT INTERGROUP
1222 EASTCHESTER DRIVE,
STE 101
HIGH POINT 27265
336-885-8520

TRI-COUNTY CENTRAL
OFFICE
612 NEWBRIDGE STREET
JACKSONVILLE 28540
910-455-3666
www.aajacksonvillenc.org

NORTH DAKOTA

FARGO-MOORHEAD
INTERGROUP
P.O. BOX 3121
FARGO 58108-3121
701-235-7335

OHIO

AKRON INTERGROUP
COUNCIL
775 N. MAIN
AKRON 44310
330-253-8181
www.akronaa.org
info@akronaa.org

ASHTABULA AREA
INTERGROUP
529 WEST PROSPECT STE #100
ASHTABULA 44004
440-992-8383

CANTON AREA INTERGROUP
COUNCIL
4125 HILLS & DALES ROAD
N.W., STE 400B
CANTON 44708-1676
330-491-1989
www.cantonaa.org

CINCINNATI INTERGROUP
OFFICE
INTERGROUP
3040 MADISON ROAD, ROOM
202
CINCINNATI 45209
513-351-0422
www.aacincinnati.org
cso@aacincinnati.org

CLEVELAND DISTRICT
OFFICE
1701 EAST 12 STREET
RESERVE SQUARE - LOWER
COMMONS
CLEVELAND 44114
216-241-7387
www.aacleveland.com
info@aacleveland.com

DISTRICT 11 ANSWERING
SERVICE
MIDDLETON 45042
513-423-0102

DISTRICT 4 INTERGROUP/
CENTRAL OFFICE
C/O ST. PAUL'S CHURCH
100 EAST HIGH STREET
MT. VERNON 43050

740-393-2439

A.A. INTERGROUP OFFICE
438 MT. VERNON ROAD
NEWARK 43055
614-345-5227

NORTH CENTRAL OHIO AREA
INTERGROUP
3416 COLUMBUS AVENUE
P.O. BOX 338
SANDUSKY 44871-0338

NW OHIO & SE MICHIGAN
CENTRAL OFFICE
2747 GLENDALE AVENUE
TOLEDO 43614
419-380-9862
419-380-9978
www.toledoaa.com
toledoaa@accesstoledo.com

YOUNGSTOWN AREA A.A.
INTERGROUP
4445 MAHONING AVENUE
YOUNGSTOWN 44515
330-270-3000
www.aayaig.org

CENTRAL OHIO FELLOWSHIP
INTERGROUP
1561 OLD LEONARD AVENUE
COLUMBUS 43219-2580
614-253-8501
614-253-5444
www.aacentralohio.org

CENTRAL OFFICE OF DAYTON,
INC
120 W. 2ND STREET, STE 211
HULMAN BLG
DAYTON 45402
937-222-2211
937-299-7587

LANCASTER AREA
INTERGROUP
111 W. WHEELING STREET, STE
206
LANCASTER 43130
740-653-4869

WEST CENTRAL OHIO
INTERGROUP
618 N. MAIN STREET
LIMA 45802
419-229-7484

LORAIN COUNTY CENTRAL
OFFICE
577 BROADWAY
LORAIN 44052
440-246-1800

RICHLAND COUNTY A.A.
INFORMATION
P.O. BOX 5231
MANSFIELD 44901
419-522-4800

MARION AREA FELLOWSHIP
INTERGROUP
197 E. CENTER STREET
MARION 43302
740-387-5546

OKLAHOMA

INTERGROUP SERVICE OFFICE
INC.
2701 NORTH PORTLAND, STE E
OKLAHOMA CITY 73107
405-949-0910/FAX 405-942-8377
405-524-1100
www.okcintergroup.org
admin@okcintergroup.org

NORTHEAST CENTRAL
SERVICE OFFICE
4853 S. SHERIDAN ROAD, STE
612
TULSA 74145-5720
www.aaneok.org
necs@aaneok.com

OREGON
OFICINA INTERGRUPAL
HISPANA
18926 S.W. SHAW STREET, STE A
BEAVERTON 97007
503-848-0102

EMERALD VALLEY
INTERGROUP
1259 WILLAMETTE STREET
EUGENE 97401-3509
541-342-4113
www.eviaa.org
eviaa@efn.org

CENTRAL OFFICE OF
SOUTHERN OREGON
432 N.W. 6TH STREET, ROOM 202
GRANTS PASS 97526
541-474-0782

KLAMATH/LAKE INTERGROUP
1229 MAIN STREET
KLAMATH FALLS 97601
541-883-4970

YAMHILL COUNTY
INTERGROUP
1275 N.W. ADAMS STREET,
ROOM C
JONESTONE CENTER
McMINNVILLE 97128
503-474-3028

A.A. JACKSON COUNTY
CENTRAL OFFICE
110 EAST. 6TH STREET, STE A
MEDFORD 97501
541-732-1850

PORTLAND AREA
INTERGROUP
1212 S.E. DIVISION STREET
PORTLAND 97202
503-223-8569
www.portland-aa.org
1212@portland-aa-org

OFICINA INTERGRUPAL
HISPANA
914 N.E. 28TH AVENUE
PORTLAND 97232-2461
503-234-0848

CENTRAL OREGON
INTERGROUP
754 S.W. 11TH STREET
REDMOND 97756
541-923-8199
541-548-0440
www.coigaa.org
coigoffice@coigaa.org

WILLAMETTE VALLEY
INTERGROUP, INC.
687 COTTAGE STREET N.E.
SALEM 97301-2412
503-399-0599
www.aa-salem.com
centraloffice@aa-salem.com

OFICINA INTERGRUPAL HISPANA
DE SALEM
3545 PORTLAND ROAD N.E.,
STE 230
SALEM 97303
503-363-4882

PENNSYLVANIA

DISTRICT 17 GEN SERVICE
COMM
ANSWERING SERVICE
ALTOONA 16401
814-946-9002

A.B.E. INTERGROUP
2285 SCHOENERSVILLE ROAD,
STE 208
BETHLEHEM 18017-7450
610-882-0558
www.aalv.org
contact@aalv.org

LAUREL HIGHLANDS
INTERGROUP
604 OAK STREET
JOHNSTOWN 15902
814-535-6863
814-533-5907

JOHNSTOWN AREA
ANSWERING SERVICE
JOHNSTOWN 15907
814-533-5907

TRI-COUNTY OFFICE
46 FRALEY STREET
KANE 16735
814-837-9495
814-730-6739
help.line@verizon.net

LANCASTER A.A. CENTRAL
SERVICE OFFICE, INC
1116 MANHEIM PIKE A
LANCASTER 17601-3159
717-394-3238

LEBANON AREA INTERGROUP
353 NORTH 10TH STREET
LEBANON 17042
717-270-4989

LEHIGHTON ANSWERING
SERVICES
LEHIGHTON 18235
800-640-7545

LEWISBURG ANSWERING
SERVICES
LEWISBURG 17837
570-286-7436

LEWISTOWN ANSWERING
SERVICES
LEWISTOWN 17044
717-242-1517

BUTLER VICINITY
ANSWERING SERVICE
LYNDORA 16045
800-434-7985

NORTHEASTERN
PENNSYLVANIA
INTERGROUP - PENN PARK
BLDG
48 SOUTH MAIN STREET, STE
206
PITTSTON 18640
570-654-0488

SCHUYLKIL VALLEY ANSWERING
SERVICE
POTTSTOWN 19464
610-323-3450

POTTSVILLE ANSWERING
SERVICE
POTTSVILLE 17901
570-628-4550

READING-BERKS
INTERGROUP
P.O. BOX 184
READING 19607
610-373-6500
www.readingberksintergroup.org

A.A. UPPER BUCKS COUNTY
SELLERSVILLE 18960
215-721-3656

A.A. TELE ANSWERING
SERVICE COMM
SHARON 16146
724-342-0162

CENTRAL ANSWERING
SERVICE
STATE COLLEGE 16804
814-237-3757

ANSWERING SERVICE
STROUDSBURG 18360
570-424-8532

SUNBURY ANSWERING
SERVICE
SUNBURY 17801
570-286-7436

24 HOUR ANSWERING
SERVICE
BLOOMSBURG 17815
570-387-4940

CUMBERLAND VALLEY
INTERGROUP
P.O. BOX 1453
CARLISLE 17013
888-930-4589

DISTRICT 62 ANSWERING
SERVICE
DINGMANS FERRY 18328
570-296-5344

DUBOIS ANSWERING SERVICE
DUBOIS 15801
800-400-2300

ERIE AREA ANSWERING
SERVICE
ERIE 16501
814-452-2675

FREELAND ANSWERING
SERVICES
FREELAND 18224
570-454-3173

DISTRICT 23 WESTMORELAND
COUNTY
ANSWERING SERVICE
GREENSBURG 15601
724-836-1404

HANOVER INTERGROUP
P.O. BOX 101
HANOVER 17331
717-633-2661
www.hanoverintergroup.org

HARRISBURG INTERGROUP
1251 S. 19TH STREET, STE C
HARRISBURG 17104
717-234-5390
www.aaharrisburg.org
aa@harrisburg.org

INDIANA AREA ANSWERING
SERVICE
INDIANA 15701
724-349-4061

BUTLER COUNTY SOUTH
ANSWERING SVC.
MARS 15086
724-935-7238

MEADVILLE AREA
ANSWERING SERVICE
MEADVILLE 16335
814-337-4019

MID-MON VALLEY
ANSWERING SERVICE
MONESSON 15062
724-489-0740

DISTRICT 61 ANSWERING
SERVICE
NEW CASTLE 16108
724-658-0585

OIL CITY ANSWERING
SERVICE
OIL CITY 16301
800-227-2421

INTERGRUPAL HISPANA DE PA
3565 NORTH 7TH STREET
PHILADELPHIA 19140-4401
215-229-3800

SOUTH EASTERN PENNA
INTERGROUP ASSOC.
444 N. 3RD STREET, STE 3E
PHILADELPHIA 19123-4179
215-923-7900
www.sepennaa.org
manager@sepennaa.org

PITTSBURG AREA CENTRAL
OFFICE
401 WOOD STREET, STE 906
ARROT BUILDING
PITTSBURG 15222
412-471-7472/FAX 412-471-7476
www.pghaa.org
formgr@pghaa.org

TAMAQUA ANSWERING
SERVICE
TAMAQUA 18252
800-640-7545

WARREN ANSWERING
SERVICE
WARREN 16365
814-726-2345

24 HOUR ANSWERING
SERVICE
WASHINGTON 15301
724-225-4188

ANSWERING SERVICE
WILKES-BARRE 18703
570-829-0007

WILLIAMSPORT ANSWERING
SERVICE
WILLIAMSPORT 17701
570-327-2860

YORK AREA INTERGROUP
P.O. BOX 1085
YORK 17405
717-854-4617
www.york-pa-aa.org

PUERTO RICO

A.A. OFICINA DEL AREA DE
PUERTO RICO
CALLE 1 A-4 ALTOS, STE 5
URB. CONDADO MODERNO
CAGUAS 00725
787-704-1634

RHODE ISLAND

RHODE ISLAND CENTRAL
SERVICE OFFICE
410 N. BROADWAY
EAST PROVIDENCE 02914
401-438-8860
www.rhodeisland-aa.org

OFICINA INTERGRUPAL
HISPANA
P.O. BOX 73042
PROVIDENCE 02907
401-621-9698

PRIMERA OFICINA
INTERGRUPAL
HISPANA DE SOUTH CAROL
P.O. BOX 70
RIDGELAND 29936
843-726-5401

SOUTHERN R I INTERGROUP
2845 POST ROAD, ROOM 112
WARWICK 02886
401-739-8777

DISTRICT 01 INTERGROUP
SERVICE
P.O. BOX 124
WOONSOCKET 02895-0780

SOUTH CAROLINA

LOWCOUNTRY INTERGROUP
PMB 105
20 TOWNE DRIVE
BLUFFTON 29910
888-534-0192
www.area62.org/intergroup/lowcount.
htm
1cig@area62.org

GREATER COLUMBIA
INTERGROUP
P.O. BOX 50484
COLUMBIA 29250
803-254-5301
www.area62.org/intergroup/columbia
gcig@area62.org

GREENVILLE INTERGROUP
101 WILSHIRE DRIVE
GREENVILLE 29609
864-250-2461
www.area62.org/intergroup/greenville
greenvillei@yahoo.com

GRAND STRAND INTERGROUP
P.O. BOX 2553
MYRTLE BEACH 29578
843-445-7119
www.area62.org/intergroups.htm
gsig@area62.org

TRI-COUNTY INTERGROUP
3005 W. MONTAGUE AVENUE,
OFFICE D
NORTH CHARLESTON 29418
843-554-2998
tcig@area62.org

MIDDLE TENNESSEE
CENTRAL OFFICE
176 THOMPSON LANE, STE G-1
NASHVILLE 37211
615-831-1050/FAX 615-834-5982
800-559-2252
mtcoaa@aol.com

OFICINA CENTRAL DE
INTERGRUPOS
HISPANA DE NASHVILLE
2803 A NOLENSVILLE PIKE
NASHVILLE 37211
615-582-2677

SOUTH DAKOTA

SIOUX FALLS AREA
INTERGROUP
P.O. BOX 182
SIOUX FALLS 57101
605-339-4357
www.siouxfallssaa.org
info@siouxfallssaa.org

TENNESSEE

CHATTANOOGA AREA
CENTRAL OFFICE
5932 PINE GROVE TRAIL, STE
104
CHATTANOOGA 37421
423-499-6003
chattaca@aol.com

JACKSON/WEST TENNESSEE
INTERGROUP
2053A HOLLYWOOD DRIVE
JACKSON 38305
877-426-8330

EAST TENNESSEE
INTERGROUP
1409 MAGNOLIA AVENUE, STE
3
KNOXVILLE 37917
865-522-9667
865-974-9888
www.korrnet.org/etaa

1835 UNION AVENUE, STE 302
MEMPHIS 38104
901-726-6750/FAX 901-726-6790
www.memphis-aa.org
memphisarea@bellsouth.net

TEXAS

24 HOUR ANSWERING
SERVICE
ABILENE 79604
915-673-2711

DISTRICT 111 24 HR ANSWERING
SERVICE
AMARILLO 79102
806-373-4600

HILL COUNTRY INTERGROUP
1825 FORTVIEW ROAD, STE 104
AUSTIN 78704
512-444-0071/FAX 512-444-7586
www.austinaa.org
austinaa@austin.rr.com

OFICINA INTERGRUPAL
HISPANA A.A.
P.O. BOX 144942
AUSTIN 78714
512-832-6767

NINTH DISTRICT
INTERGROUP
6640 EASTEX FREEWAY, STE
149/A
BEAUMONT 77708
www.aadistrict90.org
intergroup9@aol.com

CENTRAL OFFICE OF FORT
WORTH
316 BAILEY AVENUE, #100
FORT WORTH 76107
817-332-3533
www.fortworthaa.org
office@fortworthaa.org

OFICINA INTERGRUPAL
HISPANA DE
502 W. CENTRAL STREET
FORT WORTH 76016
817-694-0841

INTERGRUPAL HISPANA
8880 BRAESMONT
HOUSTON 77096

INTERGROUP ASSOCIATION
INC.
4140 DIRECTORS ROW, STE D & E
HOUSTON 77092
713-686-6300
www.aahouston.org
houintergroup@sbcglobal.net

OFICINA INTERGRUPAL HISPANA DE
HOUSTON
480 W. 34TH STREET, STE C-5
HOUSTON 77092
713-683-9277

A.A. CENTRAL OFFICE
DISTRICT
P.O. BOX 3975
McALLEN 78502
956-686-8381

INTERGRUPAL DEL VALLE DE RIO
GRANDE
711 W. HIGHWAY 83 #5
PHARR 78566-4643
956-638-6346

CENTRAL SERVICE OFFICE
8804 TRADEWAY
SAN ANTONIO 78217
210-828-6235/FAX 210-822-4491
www.aasanantonio.org
csosa@stic.net

INTERGROUP CENTRAL
OFFICE
3318 DOUGLAS AVENUE
EL PASO 79903
915-562-4081

DISTRICT 12 ANSWERING
SERVICE
FREDERICKSBURG 78624
888-816-8800

OFICINA INTERGRUPAL
HISPANA
3814 S. FLORES STREET, STE A2
SAN ANTONIO 78214-1063
210-533-9770

CENTRAL SERVICE OFFICE
401 EAST FRONT STREET, #145
TYLER 75702-8250
903-597-1796
www.tyler.aa.org
admin@tyler-aa.org

CENTRAL TEXAS
INTERGROUP
3201 FRANKLIN, STE 9
WACO 76710
254-754-3336

UTAH

CACHE VALLEY INTERGROUP
OF A.A.
P.O. BOX 3587
LOGAN 84323-3587
435-755-7772

CENTRAL OFFICE OF
NORTHERN UTAH
3480 WASHINGTON BLVD, STE
107-A
801-393-4728
www.utahaa.org
aaogden@qwest.net

UTAH VALLEY CENTRAL
OFFICE
420 N. 200 W #6
PROVO 84601
801-375-8620
www.utahvalleyaa.org
utahvalleyaa@mcleodusa.net

CENTRAL OFFICE OF SALT
LAKE CITY INC
80 WEST LOUISE AVENUE
SALT LAKE CITY 84115
801-484-7871
www.saltlakeaa.org

ST. ALBANS ANSWERING
SERVICE
ST. ALBANS 05478
802-524-5444

ANSWERING SERVICE
WHITE RIVER 05641
802-295-7611

DIXIE CENTRAL OFFICE
165 NORTH 100 EAST STE #6
ST. GEORGE 84770
www.dcoaa.org

VERMONT

ANSWERING SERVICE
BARRE 05641
802-229-5100

ANSWERING SERVICE
BENNINGTON 05641
802-447-1285

ANSWERING SERVICE
BRATTLEBORO 05641
802-257-5801

ANSWERING SERVICE
BURLINGTON 05401
802-860-8382

ANSWERING SERVICE
DORSET 05641
802-447-1285

ANSWERING SERVICE
MANCHESTER 05641
802-477-1285

ANSWERING SERVICE
MIDDLEBURY 05401
802-388-9284

ANSWERING SERVICE
MONTPELIER 05641
802-229-5100

ANSWERING SERVICE
RUTLAND 05641
802-775-0402

ANSWERING SERVICE
SPRINGFIELD 05641
802-885-8281

VIRGINIA

OFICINA INTERGRUPAL
HISPANA
8143 RICHMOND HWY
ALEXANDRIA 22309
703-360-5447

JEFFERSON DISTRICT
INTERGROUP
P.O. BOX 6911
CHARLOTTESVILLE 22906
434-293-6565
www.avenue.org/aa

ANSWERING SERVICE
DANVILLE 24541
434-799-4111

NORTHERN VIRGINIA
INTERGROUP
8501 LEE HIGHWAY
FAIRFAX 22031
703-876-6166
www.nvintergroup.org
info@nvintergroup.org

12th STEP INTERGROUP
P.O. BOX 777
HARRISONBURG 22801
540-434-8870

DISTRICT 16 INTERGROUP
P.O. BOX 1294
HOPEWELL 23860
804-452-1959
www.vasouthcentralaa.org

NORTH PIEDMONT CENTRAL
OFFICE
245 ALLEGHANY AVENUE #6
LYNCHBURG 24501
434-847-4733
www.aacentralva.org

N.W. WA-WHATCOM CTY
DISTRICT 11
ANSWERING SERVICE
BELLINGHAM 98225
360-734-1688

S.E. WASHINGTON 24 HOUR
ANSWERING SERVICE
CLARKSTON 99403
509-758-2821

OFICINA INTERGRUPAL DEL
NORTE
CENTRAL DE WASHINGTON
44 ROCK ISLAND ROAD #3
EAST WENATCHEE 98802
509-881-2001

EVERETT CENTRAL OFFICE
3231 RUCKER AVENUE, STE A
EVERETT 98201
425-252-2525

GREATER TRI-CITY CENTRAL
OFFICE
P.O. BOX 6918
KENNEWICK 99336
509-735-4086
www.district4area92aa.org

SNO-KING INTERGROUP
P.O. BOX 30
MOUNTLAKE TERRACE 98243
425-672-0987
snokingintergroup@hotmail.com

DISTRICT 22 ANSWERING
SERVICE
PORT ANGELES 98362
360-452-4212
www.nopaa.com

GREATER SEATTLE
INTERGROUP
5507 6 AVENUE SOUTH
206-587-2838
www.seattleaa.org

VIRGINIA EASTERN SHORE
INTERGROUP
P.O. BOX 405
PUNGOTEAGUE 23422

RICHMOND INTERGROUP INC.
3600 W. BROAD STREET, STE 684
RICHMOND 23230-4916
804-355-1212
www.aarichmond.org
office@aarichmond.org

ROANOKE VALLEY
INTERGROUP
3451 BRANDON AVENUE S.W.,
ROOM 2
ROANOKE 24018
540-343-6857
www.aaroanoke.org

VALLEY INTERGROUP
P.O. BOX 113
STAUNTON 24402-0113

TIDEWATER INTERGROUP
4968 EUCLID ROAD, STE C-1
VIRGINIA BEACH 23462
757-490-3980
www.tidewaterintergroup.org

WILLIAMSBURG AREA
INTERGROUP
P.O. BOX 1525
WILLIAMSBURG 23185
757-253-1234

BLUE RIDGE AREA
INTERGROUP
P.O. BOX 593
WINCHESTER 22601
540-667-0322

WASHINGTON

EASTSIDE INTERGROUP
1299 156 AVENUE N.E., STE 160
BELLEVUE 98007-7564
425-454-9192
www.eastsideintergroup.org

OFICINA INTERGRUPAL
HISPANA DE
12003 DESMOINES MEMORIAL
DRIVE
SEATTLE 98168
206-433-3435

SPOKANE CENTRAL OFFICE
1614 W. RIVERSIDE LI-55
SPOKANE 99201-1206
509-624-1442
netperspectives.com/central office/
centraloffice@netperspectives.com

CENTRAL SERVICES OFFICE
3640 S. CEDAR, STE S
TACOMA 98409
253-474-8897
www.piercecountyaa.org

SOUTH SOUND SERVICE
CENTER
344 CLEVELAND AVENUE S.E.,
STE K
TUMWATER 98512
360-352-7344
www.aadistrict8.org

VANCOUVER AREA
INTERGROUP
2203 FAIRMOUNT AVENUE, STE
A
VANCOUVER 98661
360-694-3870
www.vanintgrp.com
vancaa@vanintgrp.com

OFICINA INTERGRUPAL
WENATCHEE
1128 WEDGEWOOD AVENUE
WENATCHEE 98801
509-662-8249

CENTRAL WASHINGTON CENTRAL
OFFICE
616 RIVER ROAD
YAKIMA 98907
509-453-7680
cwcorule62@nwinfo.net

WEST VIRGINIA

WEST VIRGINIA STATE
ANSWERING SVC
CHARLESTON 25301
800-333-5051

GREATER KANAWHA VALLEY
24 HOUR ANSWERING
SERVICE
CHARLESTON 35201
304-342-4315

MORGANTOWN TELEPHONE
ANSWERING SERVICE
MORGANTOWN 26505
304-291-7918

DISTRICT 3 INTERGROUP
P.O. BOX 695
MT. HOPE 25880-0695

TRI-STATE INTERGROUP
FELLOWSHIP INC
3310 MAIN STREET
WEIRTON 26062
304-748-8006
304-748-8002

WISCONSIN

**ANSWERING SERVICE
APPLETON 54915
920-731-4331**

**HEART OF THE NORTH
INTERGROUP
BOX 83
BARRONETT 54813
715-822-8988**

**WINNEBAGO LAND CENTRAL
OFFICE
280 N. MAIN STREET
FOND DU LAC 54935
920-922-7512**

**LA CROSSE AREA
INTERGROUP
BOX 1212
LA CROSSE 54602
608-784-7560**

**DISTRICT 02 INTERGROUP
P.O. BOX 7312
SHERIDAN 82801
307-672-6257**

MADISON AREA INTERGROUP
CENTRAL OFFICE
6033 MONONA DRIVE, STE 204
MADISON 53716
608-222-8989
www.aamadisonwi.org
maico@tds.net

FOX VALLEY CENTRAL
OFFICE OF AA
324 NICOLET BLVD.
MENASHA 54952
920-720-0522

OFICINA INTEGRUPAL
1663 SOUTH 6TH STREET
MILWAUKEE 53204
414-384-4813

RACINE AREA CENTRAL
OFFICE
3701 DURAND AVENUE, STE 225
LOWER LEVEL
RACINE 53405-4458
262-554-6611
262-554-7788
www.racinecentraloffice.com

MILWAUKEE CENTRAL
OFFICE
7429 WEST GREENFIELD
AVENUE
WEST ALLIS 53214
414-771-9119
www.aamilwaukee.com

WYOMING

DISTRICT 06 ANSWERING
SERVICE
CASPER 82601
307-266-9578

DISTRICT 12 ANSWERING
SERVICE
CHEYENNE 82007
307-632-7706

DISTRICT 10 ANSWERING
SERVICE
LARAMIE 82070
307-745-3322

HIV/AIDS REFERENCES

Across the Nation	
AIDS Action	http://aidsaction.org
Gay & Lesbian Victory Fund and Leadership Institute	http://www.victoryfund.org
Gay Men's Health Crisis	http://www.gmhc.org
National Association of People with AIDS	http://www.napwa.org
Project Inform	http://projectinform.org
ACLU Lesbian & Gay Rights	http://www.aclu.org/LesbianGay-Rights
Gay & Lesbians Alliance Against Defamation	http://www.glaad.org
Human Rights Campaign	http://www.hrc.org
Lesbian/Gay Rights Lobby of Texas	http://www.lgrl.org/home
National Gay and Lesbian Task Force National Health Facts by State	http://www.thetaskforce.org http://www.statehealthfacts.org/
National Latina/o GLBT Organization	http://www.llego.org
University of California San Francisco School of Medicine	http://hivinsite.ucsf.edu
Assistance Programs	
NeedyMeds, Inc.	http://needymeds.com
Partnership for Prescription Assistance	http://pparx.org
Family Issues	
Family Pride Coalition	http://www.familypride.org/index.php
Parents, Families and Friends of Lesbians and Gays	http://www.pflag.org

Fitness & Health

AIDS Meds.com	http://AIDSmeds.com
American Council of Exercise	http://www.acefitness.org
American Diabetes Association	http://diabetes.org
American Heart Association (healthy recipes)	http://www.deliciousdecisions.org
American Heart Association	http://americanheart.org
Scripps Research Institute	http://fightaidsathome.scripps.edu
Yahoo! Health	http://health.yahoo.com/center/fitness/index

General Information

AIDS Education Global Information System	http://www.aegis.com
About.com	http://aids.about.com
Aware Talk Radio	http://awaretalkradio.org
CDC National Prevention Information Network (NPIN)	http://cdcnpin.org
Centers for Disease Control	http://www.cdc.gov
HIV & Hepatitis .com	http://hivandhepatitis.com
John Hopkins	http://hopkins-aids.edu
Medicinenet.com	http://www.medicinenet.com
Tarrant County Public Health	http://www.tarrantcounty.com/eHealth
The Body	http://thebody.com/index.shtml
The Well Project	http://www.thewellproject.org
U.S. Dept. Health & Human Services	http://www.aidsinfo.nih.gov
U.S. Food & Drug Administration	http://www.fda.gov/oashi/aids/hiv.html

Medications	
Each drug company has a link for their medications. You may either visit the company website, or visit	http://www.aidsmeds.com
Testing	
National HIV Testing Resources	http://www.hivtest.org
Texas	
AIDS Interfaith Network	http://aidsinterfaithnetwork.org
AIDS Resources of Rural Texas	http://aidsresources.com
Collin County Area Gay Outings	http://www.ccago.com
Dallas Voice	http://www.dallasvoice.com
Vaccine & Clinical Trials	
HIV Vaccine Trials Network	http://www.hvtn.org
National Institute of Health (NI-AID)	http://vrc.nih.gov/VRC
U.S. National Institutes of Health	http://www.clinicaltrials.gov
World issues	
Asian Pacific AIDS Intervention	http://apaitonline.org
AVERT	http://www.avert.org
International AIDS Economic Network	http://www.iaen.org
International AIDS Vaccine Initiative	http://www.iavi.org
Joint United Nations Programmed on HIV/AIDS	http://www.unaids.org

ABOUT THE AUTHOR

Cynthia Banks is the owner and director of The Little Teapot Daycare, in Fort Worth, Texas, is President of Banks Entertainment, a Concert, Tour Booking and Management Company, an Accreditation Validator for the National Association of Family Childcare and a board member of Agape Kids, an organization that supports the needs and concerns of children of battered women. One of the most rewarding organizations that Cynthia has the privilege of being a part of is the Stop Six Aids Leadership Project. S.S.A.L.P. was conceived out of the concern for the growing number of AIDS/HIV infected African Americans in the community.

Cynthia is also the author of *Prayers of the Innocent*, a true story of fraud and exploitation. The crimes occurred at historically black colleges in the South. The story follows a young college student who unwittingly is caught-up in bank fraud that leads to racketeering, sexual exploitation and theft. *Prayers of the Innocent* is a story of fear, compassion and a need to protect. Banks is working on her third book, *Broken Trust*, another true story of corruption in a county governmental office in Florida. The story follows Charles, one of Miami-Dade County Water and Sewer Department's most trusted employees for over sixteen years. Unbeknownst to the company, Charles found a way to embezzle over 4 million dollars over a 3 year span. Broken Trust is a story that proves that things and people are not always as they seem.

Public speaking is no stranger to Cynthia Banks. She has spoken at the United Negro College Fund conference, and has been interview by several radio stations. She has had several book signings in Public Libraries, schools, colleges, churches and expos. Banks has also appeared on CCTV Channel 31 in Fort Worth, Texas and WCTV in Tallahassee, Florida.

CPSIA information can be obtained at www.ICGtesting.com
Printed in the USA
BVOW02*0547090316

439647BV00001B/23/P